Diamond Jim Brady

Diamond Jim Brady

Prince of the Gilded Age

H. Paul Jeffers

John Wiley & Sons, Inc.

New York • Chichester • Weinheim • Brisbane • Singapore • Toronto

This book is printed on acid-free paper. ∞

Copyright © 2001 by H. Paul Jeffers. All rights reserved

Published by John Wiley & Sons, Inc.
Published simultaneously in Canada

This publication is designed to provide accurate and authoritative information in regard to the subject matter covered. It is sold with the understanding that the publisher is not engaged in rendering professional services. If professional advice or other expert assistance is required, the services of a competent professional person should be sought.

Library of Congress Cataloging-in-Publication Data

Jeffers, H. Paul (Harry Paul), 1934–
    Diamond Jim Brady : prince of the Gilded Age / H. Paul Jeffers.
       p. cm.
    Includes bibliographical references and index.
    ISBN 0-471-39102-6 (cloth : alk. paper)
    1. Brady, James Buchanan, 1856–1917. 2. Businessmen—New York (State)—New York—Biography. 3. Millionaires—New York (State)—New York—Biography. 4. New York (N.Y.)—Social life and customs—19th century. 5. New York (N.Y.)—Biography. I. Title.

CT275.B5943 J44 2001
974.7′1′041092—dc21
[B]   2001026768

Printed in the United States of America

10 9 8 7 6 5 4 3 2 1

To Dr. Hossain Awini

"God, Nell, ain't it grand!"
    —Diamond Jim Brady to Lillian Russell

Contents

❦❦❧❧

Introduction

Table for One, Dinner for Twenty-five

❧❧❧

W HEN DIAMOND JIM BRADY'S weighty coffin was carried in a misty rain into St. Agnes's Roman Catholic
Church on Forty-third Street in the shadow of New York City's
Grand Central Terminal on April 16, 1917, the flamboyant fat
man who'd made millions from railroads was rendered final
homage by actresses and actors, newspapermen, laborers, cops,
lawyers, and so many notables of café society, show business,
and American commerce that police reserves were called out to
control the throng.

Even in death in a city crammed with the rich and famous,
everyone wanted to be near Diamond Jim. When he lived they
copied what he wore, dined where he dined, and ate what he
ate. Those trying to keep up included Pearl Jim Murray, a
Montana miner who kept pockets filled with hundreds of thousands of dollars' worth of loose pearls, the "Pittsburgh Millionaires" who had gotten rich when Andrew Carnegie sold his
steel business to J. P. Morgan, and the patrons of a Broadway
restaurant described by its proprietor as "a cathedral of froth,
national museum of habits, bourse of gossip, the clearing house
of rumors, and the supreme court of triviality, where the who's
who went to learn the what's what."

"He was an odd character," observed restaurateur George
Rector. "His name was derived from his jewelry, and when

1

Diamond Jim had all his illumination in place, he looked like an excursion steamer at twilight. He had powerful diamonds in his shirt front that cast beams strong enough to sunburn an unwary pedestrian. He had diamonds in his cuffs and in suspender buttons fore and aft. He wore diamonds on his fingers and there was a rumor that he had diamond bridge work."

When Rector once chided Jim for this excessive display of gems, Jim replied, "Them as has 'em wears 'em."

Six months after Jim's funeral, the Columbia Trust Company of New York put up for unrestricted public auction at the Madison Square galleries of the American Art Association "costly furnishings and embellishments" accumulated by the most astonishing and engaging personality of that time. The illustrated catalog listed thousands of items in 1,748 groupings of ivories, bronzes, marbles, porcelains, "bijouterie," armor, prints, textiles, silver and plated ware, china, glassware, linen and cushions, furniture, billiard and other sporting games and sporting pictures, Oriental carpets, Japanese and Austrian objêts d'art, and miniatures of the world's most famous actresses. Not on the selling block was more than $2 million worth of adornments that had been the basis of the era's most famous nickname. Had Diamond Jim's gem-encrusted pins been offered for bidding at one item a day, the sale would have taken a month. The jewels had been the emblem of a singular individual who fashioned himself into the brash symbol of plush years that historians named the Gilded Age. In the words of one student of the era, Jim was a walking jewelry store, always surrounded by the most beautiful women on earth.

He was also the unquestioned biggest eater. A typical lunch consisted of two lobsters, deviled crabs, clams, oysters, and beef. He finished with several whole pies. This lasted him until dinner at four-thirty. That meal began with a couple of dozen oysters, six crabs, and bowls of green turtle soup. The main course was likely to be two whole ducks, six or seven lobsters,

The famous Brady belly in profile in a picture taken at
a racetrack. On such outings he limited his display of
diamonds on the advice of police, who feared he might
be an easy target for pickpockets.

a sirloin steak, two servings of terrapin, and a variety of vegetables. Desserts were pastries and perhaps a five-pound box of
candy. Because Jim did not partake of alcohol, all this was
washed down with carafe after carafe of orange juice. When he
sat down for a meal he tucked his napkin into his shirt collar
because one placed on his knee would have been useless under
his big belly. He stationed his chair so that there were four

inches between the edge of the table and his stomach. Eating ended when the gap had been closed.

"How he ate!" George Rector recalled. "He loved to be surrounded by handsome men and beautiful women at the table, and it was no unusual thing for us to lay covers for eight or ten guests of Mr. Brady. If they all kept their appointments, fine! If but two or three were able to be present, fine! And if nobody showed up but Diamond Jim, fine! Mr. Brady proceeded gravely to eat the ten dinners himself."

Rector once pronounced Jim "the best twenty-five customers I ever had."

No one had been Jim's eating companion more frequently than the area's most famous actress. Known to one and all as the American Beauty, Lillian Russell had been so lavishly showered with jewelry by Jim that a latter-day writer called them a duet in diamonds. Author John Burke wrote, "Fleshly arm in arm, plump shoulder to shoulder, they toddled together into the social history of their time."

During the presidencies of Grover Cleveland, Benjamin Harrison, William McKinley, and Theodore Roosevelt, Diamond Jim had been a portly prince. He sat ringside for boxing bouts featuring his friend John L. Sullivan. He found himself in the inner circle of the horsey set at Saratoga Springs. He was a big player on Wall Street and in the boardrooms of the country's railroad tycoons. He'd hobnobbed with everyone in the Gay Nineties, from robber barons to chorus girls, and picked up the tab. The first automobile to scare the horses on the streets of 1890s New York had been his. He attended theatrical first nights of Weber and Fields, Oscar Hammerstein, and Florenz Ziegfeld. Before and after each of these shows he was a regular at Rector's, Tony Pastor's, Delmonico's, and all the "lobster palaces" of Manhattan.

Lucius Beebe, the chronicler and arbiter of good food and where it could be found in New York, observed, "The lobster-palace set entered into the historic record. Assured of a fragrant immortality in the folklore of the land, they radiated good times and good humor and they spent money, always the ultimate American attribute of status, like crazy."

In that splashy period of carefree abundance, conspicuous consumption, ragtime music, and millionaire stage-door Johnnies showering Floradora Girls and lovelies from Flo Ziegfeld's bevy of chorus beauties with flowers, furs, and gems, no one sparkled more than Diamond Jim.

When he passed away in 1917, so did his era.

1

Make Them *Like* You

❦❧❦

I N THE MIND OF Daniel Brady in the summer of 1856, the
most important things in life were the customers who
bought beer at three cents a stein in his waterfront saloon on
the corner of Cedar and West streets on New York's Lower
West Side, the Roman Catholic Church, and the Democratic
Party. Consequently, when Dan's second son was born on the
twelfth of August, the beer flowed freely. Presently the parish
priest was informed that the boy he would be called on to bap-
tize had been named after the Democratic nominee for president of the United States.

If the father of the newborn had his way, James Buchanan
Brady and his older brother (their father's namesake) would
follow him in the saloon business. The first years of Jim's life,
therefore, were filled with the voices of hardworking, hard-
drinking, mostly Irish longshoremen and teamsters who lived
nearby. They earned their wages from the ships whose masts
resembled a leaf-bare forest on the edge of the Hudson River
that reached from the tip of Manhattan north to the human
wasteland of spirit-crushing tenements called Hell's Kitchen.

A dozen years before Jim was born, England's most famous
author, Charles Dickens, had toured the New York waterfront
and found the bowsprits of hundreds of ships stretching across
the waterside streets and almost thrusting themselves into the

7

windows of adjacent buildings. These "noble American vessels," he wrote, "have brought hither the foreigners who abound in all the streets." So many immigrants had come to New York in the two decades before Jim Brady's birth that the city's population had nearly quadrupled. Most of the newcomers were Irish. Almost all settled in lower Manhattan.

The section in which Jim Brady was born was described by the pre–Civil War Irish writer Fitz-James O'Brien as a "melancholy, mysterious and dreary place." The men who patronized Dan Brady's saloon talked wistfully of their green homeland, the famine that had driven most of them out, and their work. The politics of city and country was discussed primarily in terms of the unjust distribution of wealth between haves and have-nots. In the opinion of Dan Brady and his customers, only the Democratic Party and its New York branch, Tammany Hall, could remedy this imbalance.

How much of this was understood at the time by young Jim Brady isn't known, but at some point in his growing-up as he helped himself to free food that his father made available to his drinking patrons, he made two decisions. He chose not to emulate what many Americans saw as the inborn trait and flaw of the Irish; he would not take up drinking. He also decided that if the world was arranged according to haves and have-nots, he would do all he could to be counted among the former. How far up the economic ladder an Irish lad with a healthy appetite for food but no taste for drink might ascend remained to be seen.

As much as he loved his father, Jim saw that being a saloon keeper was not the route to riches. Perhaps it was because he was a saloon keeper's son and had witnessed the effects of strong drink that he chose to eschew it for his entire life.

That he would not go into the saloon business was reinforced after his father died in 1863 and his widow took up with and then married a man named John Lucas.

Lacking Dan Brady's flair and exhibiting no interest in continuing Dan's policy of mixing beer with politics, Lucas changed the tenor of the saloon from what had been a neighborhood "watering hole" to a place for roistering sailors. They soon flocked to the bar in such numbers that it became in the lingo of seamen a "flag house," meaning a "sailors-only saloon."

To make matters worse, John Lucas demonstrated no aversion to accepting money from shipowners to lace steins of beer with knockout drops. When the unwitting sailors woke up, they found that they'd been shanghaied.

This sin was compounded in the minds of eleven-year-old Jim and his thirteen-year-old brother, Dan, by Lucas's demand that the boys quit school and work in the saloon.

Dan's answer was to run away from home and take a job as a bellboy at the St. James Hotel. Opened in 1863 at Broadway and Twenty-sixth Street, it overlooked Madison Square and was by 1867 one of the most popular hostelries in a post–Civil War city that was increasingly prosperous and rapidly spreading northward.

Admiring brother Dan in his smart uniform and hearing his tales of the "swells" who patronized the St. James, Jim noted that his brother's pockets jangled with gratuities for his services. He envied Dan's rubbing elbows, if only as a servant, with the upper classes of the city and with the nattily dressed men from elsewhere who earned their livelihoods as salesmen. But to a writer named Mary Eliza Tucker, these free-spending men who treated prospective clients to lavish dinners in the grandest restaurants on Broadway and along Fourteenth Street embodied her title character of *Lewis Bridge, a Broadway Idyll*. Published in the year Dan got the job at the St. James, it disdained such men in verse:

> *Each eager face in passing seems to say—*
> *"Chasing a dollar, comrades, clear the way!"*

Jim Brady preferred the contrary viewpoint of another writer of a best-seller of the day. In *Ragged Dick,* Horatio Alger's main character exemplified the American ideal of pursuing success and the benefits of the riches that came with it, not the least of which was plenty of food.

Three months after young Dan Brady found employment at the St. James, he informed Jim that the hotel had need of another bellboy. The next morning Jim appeared in the manager's office. Whether he was asked his age isn't known. He was eleven, but because of his size, he looked fifteen. Perhaps because the manager knew of his experience as a helper in the family's saloon from brother Dan, he was put to work in the hotel's bar. If business was brisk, he helped served drinks. In slacker periods he filled the duties of bellboy and messenger. He found the latter more satisfying because the men who sent him on errands provided generous gratuities. Most weeks afforded the genial, roly-poly, blue-eyed Irish youth more in tips than he found in his pay packet. This largesse allowed him to spend his day off—Sunday—in pursuit of his favorite repasts in East River fish markets of Catherine Slip between Cherry and South streets. High on his list of favorite places was the eel market, where eels were sold by the foot or the pound by vendors with street carts or in hole-in-the-wall eateries known as eel shops. When Jim had his fill of eel, he ventured to South Street in search of oysters at a penny each. Zestfully downing them by the two bits' worth, he watched the hustle and bustle of wharves crowded with stately vessels under sail and less graceful but speedier ones powered by steam.

IN 1863, as Dan Brady Sr. was being mourned by the "dock wollopers" who had been his customers, a man whose steamboats provided them employment decided to go into the railroading business. For sixty-nine-year-old Cornelius Vanderbilt this was a dramatic change of heart. Only six years earlier, when asked to invest in the New York & Harlem line, the man whose shipping empire earned him millions and the nickname "Commodore" had replied, "Bring me a steamboat and I can do something, but I won't have anything to do with your damn railroads."

Vanderbilt's abrupt switch in outlook had resulted from his realization that the future of the United States after the Civil War would lie in settling a western frontier that stretched far out of reach of ships. Determined to profit by the "westward-ho" fervor that swept the nation, and to play a leading role in connecting the East with the West by steel rails, he bought three railways in four years. He started with the once-scorned New York & Harlem. He acquired control of its rival Hudson River Railroad the next year and the New York Central in 1866. These enterprises were consolidated by legislative action in 1869 into the New York Central and Hudson River Railroad. In subsequent years this emerging empire would include lines to connect Vanderbilt's New York system with those serving Buffalo and Chicago and points between. While assembling a national railroad network controlled from New York City, the Commodore turned his attention to building a suitable headquarters in the form of a "grand central depot." He chose an uptown area that many saw as too far away. Vanderbilt envisioned the area becoming the locus of a northward-moving city squeezed between rivers. The site for the jewel of Vanderbilt's railway domain was smack in the center of Manhattan at Forty-second Street and Fourth Avenue.

The Commodore also bought surrounding land between Madison and Lexington avenues and from Forty-second to Forty-eighth streets. Ground was broken for the depot in May of 1869, with construction completed in 1871.

The result was the largest train shed in the world, standing 600 feet long, 200 feet wide, and 100 feet high. Beneath an arching roof supported by thirty semicircular trusses ran twelve tracks. At night its platforms were illuminated by twelve enormous chandeliers whose gas lamps were ignited automatically by an electric spark.

The Forty-second and Lexington facades were red pressed brick with window frames of cast iron that were painted white to simulate the look of marble. Five towers rising above Forty-second Street were topped by mansard roofs. Hailing the terminal as "the largest railway and passenger caravansary in the world," the *New York Herald* extolled it as a "ferruginous palace." The depot provided operating space for Vanderbilt's railroads and another line, the New Haven. Each had its own waiting and baggage rooms.

For the day-to-day running of the new depot and the trains that flowed out from it, Vanderbilt assembled a cadre of superintendents and foremen. Among them was a native of Connecticut by the name of John M. Toucey. A precursor of many thousands of men who in the decades ahead would work in the city but live in its suburbs, Toucey frequently found himself having to stay in town overnight. On those occasions, especially during the building of the Grand Central Depot, he checked into the St. James Hotel.

An amiable man, Toucey prided himself on being "self-made" and wholly in tune with the gospel of success preached in the popular Horatio Alger books that followed *Ragged Dick*. He also had a keen eye for spotting young men with potential for making successes of themselves if someone was willing to give them a start.

In the year Grand Central opened, Toucey thought he'd found such a youth in one of the hotel bellboys. Ample in size, apple-cheeked, and an energetic worker, fifteen-year-old Jim Brady seemed to Toucey to be just the kind of young man who could start at the bottom of the ladder and work his way up, perhaps to the top.

In the railroading business, the bottom-rung job for such a fellow was derisively known as baggage smasher. If Jim was interested in giving up bellhopping, Toucey proposed, why not come to work for the New York Central Railroad by starting in the baggage room at the new Grand Central terminal? If he did, and if he went to night school to catch up on his education, and if he applied himself to the work at hand, there was no saying what the job might lead to.

There were two reasons not to take up Toucey's offer. Being a baggage smasher would mean no tips and so would pay him much less. And the Grand Central baggage room didn't have a bar loaded with plates and bowls of free food. Yet what future was there in the hotel business for someone who'd dropped out of school and was both Catholic and Irish?

Weighing on the side of accepting Toucey's job offer with its promise of advancement in status and salary was a change in the situation of Jim's mother. Because of the saloon's decline, John Lucas had abandoned both the business and his wife. As a result, she had sold the saloon and opened a small hotel and a kind of employment agency for Irish girls who left Erin in hope of becoming household servants in New York. Because this enterprise brought the still-married Mrs. Lucas less income than had the saloon, she expected her two sons to assist her and to help meet the needs of their ten-year-old sister. (When she was born in 1861, Jim was five. At the time he left home for the job at the St. James, the girl was six.)

In Horatio Alger stories a young man's life took a dramatic turn for the better because of a twist of fate in the form of a benefactor. Alger fashioned such events into moral lessons. Playwrights spun them into dramas. Comedians twisted them to get laughs. Biographers marked them by exclaiming "Here! After this moment everything would change."

For Jim Brady it happened in 1871 in the offer from John Toucey.

❦❦❦

WHEN JIM reported for work, Commodore Vanderbilt's colossal terminal was handling an average of 130 train movements a day. Their arrivals and departures were controlled by a dispatcher in a cabin high on the north wall of the train shed. At the heart of this complex venture was an elaborate system of electric bell signals to guide the actions of train crews, gatemen, and the baggage handlers waiting on the platforms. The passengers who stepped from these trains had come from distant places known to the burly young baggage smasher only by names—Albany, Troy, Buffalo, Erie, Chicago. Almost all who waited for their luggage to be taken off the trains were well-dressed men sporting gold rings and cuff links and ties with diamond studs. Jim could tell from snatches of overheard conversation that they were important. Many were salesmen. All headed from Grand Central Depot to the finest hotels in the city. He recognized some—and they remembered him—from his four years at the St. James. More than a few teased him by noticing that he appeared to have added a few pounds around his midsection. All wished him well.

In keeping with his vow to improve his education, Jim enrolled in Paine's Business College for night courses in bookkeeping and chirography (penmanship). Soon the crude, schoolboyish signature "Jim Brady" became a flourished "James Buchanan Brady."

After Jim had spent eighteen months at Paine's, Toucey rewarded his diligence with a new position and a boost in salary, to $3 a week. The new job was ticket agent and baggage master at the New York Central's new station many miles north of Forty-second Street at Spuyten Duyvil. The name, given to a creek in the area by the Dutch, meant "in spite of the devil." The creek divided the island of Manhattan from the Bronx. That gap had been closed in 1693 by the building of the King's Bridge. To connect the New York Central and Hudson River rail line on the shore of the river to Grand Central in the middle of Manhattan, Commodore Vanderbilt spent $1 million to lay seven miles of tracks along the creek and the Harlem River. To reach his new post, Jim had to get up at five in the morning and take a special train from Grand Central that carried the railroad's employees to the outlying points of Fordham, Highbridge, Morris Dock, Kingsbridge, Marble Hill, Fort George, and Spuyten Duyvil.

In Commodore Vanderbilt's grand railroad network, Spuyten Duyvil was a "flag stop," which meant that a train halted there only when Jim signaled that he'd sold a ticket. This also meant that there were few bags to be handled. In the long intervals between passengers, Jim kept busy by learning telegraphy. This bit of enterprise did not go unnoticed by his patron.

It was during Jim's two years at Spuyten Duyvil that he engaged in what he later called "the only dishonest thing in my life." One Sunday morning as he tallied the previous day's sales, he found to his horror that he was ninety-five cents short. It was money he would have to make up out of his own pocket—almost a third of his weekly salary. While he pondered this calamity, he looked up and found at the ticket window five men carrying brass horns. They were part of a German band that had been hired to entertain at a picnic. None of the musicians spoke English, but their leader managed to communicate that they wanted round-trip tickets to their destination. Jim sold them one-ways and pocketed the difference.

"When the leader of the band came back the next day, he was hopping mad, but I made believe I couldn't understand him," Jim recalled. "After a while he got tired of shouting and went away. That night I took the money that was left over from the tickets, had a fine dinner at Smith and McNell's, and went to the theater afterwards."

Fortunately, this act of fraud against passengers and embezzlement of New York Central funds did not reach the ears of a man who had also worked his way up in the ranks of the firm.

John Toucey was now ensconced in an office of the railroad's headquarters in Grand Central Depot as general manager. No employee did more to further the fortunes of the New York Central system than he. Under his leadership, the system would be one of the first to adopt the air brake, the automatic coupler, an interlocking switching system, and the vestibule car. His sensitivity in dealing with the labor force kept a large majority of New York Central employees on the job during a strike in 1877.

In his rise to the top Toucey brought his protégé with him. In 1874, after nearly two years at Spuyten Duyvil, Jim was given a clerkship in Toucey's office at Grand Central. Expected to continue improving his education, Jim again enrolled at Paine's. The reward from his benefactor was promotion to chief clerk at $50 a month.

Toucey also listened to Jim's pleas on behalf of his unemployed brother. Dan was given a job in the same office.

Earning a handsome salary, Jim was a twenty-one-year-old bachelor in a city overflowing with ways to spend money. A portion of Jim's went for a new wardrobe of Prince Albert coats, fine shirts and trousers, elegant cravats, a shiny black stovepipe hat, and shoes from Manhattan's finest makers on Canal Street. But most of his wages were spent on sumptuous daily dinners, meals on Saturday night before and after the theater, and lavish leisurely lunches on Sundays. These were almost always in the company of a boyhood friend, Jules Weiss, who would take up the trade of tailoring and find his best customer in Diamond Jim Brady.

As chief clerk, Jim found himself immersed in all aspects of railroad management, from the cost of repairing a locomotive and the operation of air brakes, to the intricacies of corporate maneuvering in the increasingly fierce competition among railroads in a westward-moving nation that had validated Commodore Vanderbilt's foresight by falling in love with trains and becoming dependent on them.

After having created one of the great networks of steel rails in less than a decade, Cornelius Vanderbilt died on January 4, 1877. At the age of eighty-three, he was America's richest man.

The Commodore had not approved of most forms of charity and, with the exception of Vanderbilt University, he made few contributions. One newspaper took the opportunity provided by his passing to decry "that a free government professedly founded on the equal rights of man can make it possible for one man to accumulate so much of what other people earned."

A few years earlier, when Vanderbilt was forging his railway empire by scooping up roads such as the Erie, Mark Twain had bitterly called his methods "lawless violations of commercial honor." In an "Open Letter to Com. Vanderbilt," the country's most popular author wrote, "The immoral practices, in so prominent a place as you occupy, are a damning example of the rising commercial generation—more a damning thing to the whole nation. Go now, and do something that isn't shameful, do go and do something worthy of a man possessed of seventy millions—a man whose most trifling act is remembered and imitated all over the country. You must certainly feel a vague desire to do some splendid deed in the interest of commercial probity or human charity, or of manly honor and dignity."

The Commodore left the bulk of his $70 million estate to his oldest son, William Henry. With it went control of the New York Central system. He took over at a time when other lines were cutting wages. Central brakemen were earning an average $2.15 for a trip of 150 miles. To remain competitive with his rivals, William ordered the rate cut to $1.90. A conductor's hourly wage of $2.87 was slashed to $2.60. Rail workers went on strike everywhere. Summering at the United States Hotel in Saratoga Springs, William said the strikers belonged to "the Communistic classes" and were "manifesting a disposition to pillage and destroy private property." He told a reporter for the *New York Times* that there was little difference between him and his workers. "Although I may have my millions and they have the rewards of their daily toil," he said, "still we are about equal in the end."

The railroads prevailed in the strike in which a hundred men were killed and five times as many were injured, but its legacy was the ultimate formation of railroad workers' unions and even more violent clashes in the 1880s.

Although the strike had not affected James Buchanan Brady's pay and terms of employment, something his brother did had disastrous consequences. Exactly what sin he committed is not known because Jim never spoke of it. The result was Dan's immediate dismissal. Then, for what John Toucey said was "the sake of discipline and morale," Jim was also fired. However, sacking him was not as easy as dismissing Dan. As chief clerk, Jim knew as much about the New York Central as Toucey. In an atmosphere of public bitterness toward railroads because of the strike, along with a general feeling that railroads were run by crooks, cutting Jim Brady loose carried with it the danger of him retaliating by revealing company secrets to the press or the state legislature, and possibly both. An even more worrying possibility was that Jim would be hired by one of the New York Central's competitors. With these concerns in mind, and feeling sympathetic toward his protégé, whose only crime was having Dan as a brother, Toucey turned to a friend who was a partner in the railway supply firm of Manning, Maxwell and Moore.

At the moment that Jim was being let go, Charles A. Moore was looking for a salesman to handle a new item in the firm's line of equipment. It was a patented handsaw that could cut steel rails to size at the point where track was being laid. The tool saved time, labor, and, most important, money.

Moore asked Toucey what Jim Brady knew about selling railroad equipment.

Toucey replied, "Nothing. The only things he's ever sold were tickets."

But the lad knew a great deal about almost every phase of railroading. He was shrewd, honest, and loyal. He'd worked hard, studied to get ahead, and proven himself worthy in all he was called on to do. And he was not a drinker.

Moore interviewed Jim for more than an hour. He certainly was no beauty, and his girth attested to an appetite that if it had been for drink would certainly have resulted in him being a drunkard. His speech left a lot to be desired, but the men to whom he'd be selling saws were not exactly expert users of the language, either. He dressed well, which was important in a salesman. No one wanted to buy from someone who did not look prosperous. Questions posed to him about the railroad business confirmed that he knew his stuff. And he was definitely not lacking in self-assurance. With that confidence, combined with a smile and a shoeshine and a few lessons in the tricks of the trade, Moore decided, James Buchanan Brady might sell quite a lot of handsaws.

His advice to Jim was taken from the gospel of the traveling salesman but amended to the business of railroad building. "Get to know the important men in every line," he advised. "Find out which ones are doing the buying and if you can, find out which ones will be buying in the years to come. Make them your friends, make them understand that you are the man who will serve them. Make them trust you, make them respect you, and most important of all, make them *like* you."

When Jim began this job in 1879, there were 93,000 miles of railroad in a country that was looking westward. Fervor to lay new miles of roadway swept the nation. "The clamor for the Iron Horse and its glittering land of tracks was presently to assume the proportions of an uproar," wrote historian Parker Morrell of the period. "Nothing could stop it, nothing could lessen its din. In a single decade the people of the United States were to build as many miles of new railroads as the people of the three leading countries of Europe had constructed in the previous fifty years." Ten years after Jim Brady became a railroad equipment salesman, there would be more than 160,000 miles of track.

In preparing to venture forth on behalf of Manning, Maxwell and Moore, Jim reflected on the demeanor and style of dress of the hundreds of successful salesmen he'd observed during his years at the St. James and as a baggage smasher and ticket agent for the New York Central. They had told him, "If you're going to make money, you've got to look like money."

As the salesman shared this maxim of his trade, Jim's attention was diverted by the glint of the man's large diamond ring. He expressed admiration for it.

"In the selling game you've got to have at least one," said the salesman. "Nothing says money more than a display of diamonds. When you check into a hotel, a sparkler can mean all the difference between a very nice room and one the size of a broom closet. For some reason, nothing impresses a hotel room clerk more than a diamond ring. The same is true for the head waiters in the good restaurants."

During the two years Jim had been John Toucey's chief clerk, he'd saved $200. Ninety of it was now spent for a one-carat diamond ring. The rest was apportioned for three suits made by Jules Weiss, other wardrobe items befitting a successful-looking salesman, and a suitcase built to withstand the most savage baggage smasher.

With a bundle of order books in his bag, the portly, well-turned-out, diamond-sporting twenty-three-year-old who had never ventured farther than Spuyten Duyvil boarded a New York Central train and headed for the vast expanse of America that awaited him beyond the Allegheny Mountains. In doing so, he was one of an army of men flooding "Out West" to drum up business and add to the lexicon of American commerce the term "drummer." They went on behalf of the makers of everything required to build and to populate the only nation in the world whose bounding oceans were now linked by trains.

In 1870, one year after a golden spike had been driven into a tie at Promontory Point in Utah to complete a transcontinental railroad and only forty-four years after the Granite Railway Company of Boston built and operated the first railway in the United States, a train had carried passengers from Boston to San Francisco. Nine years later, a railroad was transporting a chubby fellow carrying in his wallet the business cards of the company of Manning, Maxwell and Moore embossed with "James Buchanan Brady, Sales Representative."

Wherever trains took him, Jim presented the cards and himself to superintendents, master mechanics, section foremen, road gang bosses, station masters, train crews, roundhouse workers, conductors, and anyone else connected with railroading.

Charles Moore's mandate to him was to sell saws and to make friends. Because the saws were so obviously time, labor, and money savers, they practically sold themselves. Jim did so much business that at the end of each day's work he suffered from writer's cramp. When orders were completed and mailed back to New York each evening, he left his hotel room to carry out his second task. Having sealed every sale with a handshake and an invitation to the buyer to join him for dinner, he was rarely without companionship for the meal. If during the day he'd dealt with several officials of a railroad, he invited them all to dinner or to a private party in his room, which was invariably the hotel's best. But it was not simply because he picked up the check that his customers joined him at the table. They found Jim Brady to be a charming fellow who knew and understood railroading and spoke their language. Most of them discovered that after dinner he was also a boon companion at the card table.

The costs of these entertainments were charged to Jim's expense account. Toward the end of his first year on the road, Henry S. Manning looked it over and was so alarmed that he called Charles Moore into his office. "If your young favorite is going to spend all our money entertaining men just so he can sell them that damn little handsaw," he said, "we'll be bankrupt in no time at all."

Manning proposed that Brady handle the firm's entire line of equipment.

"Brady's doing very well as it is," said Moore. "We'll let him alone a while longer, and when we do start him selling the whole line, I'll wager that he proves to be our best man."

The expense reports that arrived each week contained more than a tally of the sums Jim had spent in the cause of selling handsaws. Written in the hand that had been trained in chirography at Paine's came detailed reports covering the past, present, and future needs of whichever rail system Jim had visited that week. Decades before American industries and stock market analysts routinely researched, studied, and documented the condition of companies, James Buchanan Brady was doing just that for his employer. He was also building a foundation for a career that fifty years hence would earn Diamond Jim Brady the accolade of *Fortune* magazine as "the greatest capital goods salesman of them all."

When Charles Moore decided in the fall of 1881 that Jim was ready to expand his mandate to include the entire Manning, Maxwell and Moore line of equipment, he offered Jim both a salary and a commission on each sale. Jim replied, "I ain't interested in sellin' goods for you on a salary. The only way I want to work is on a straight commission basis. I got an idea that we'll both make more money that way."

His only other condition was that his expense account be unlimited.

On the road again with authority to sell everything in the firm's catalog from the saws to freight and passenger cars, he set his sights on being the most successful—and richest—man in the game of selling railway equipment. He would do so by combining his knowledge of the business with princely courting and entertainment of customers and the plain old Irish charm known in his father's homeland as blarney.

Not all his customers were quite so easily won over, however.

Soon after being given the entire Manning, Maxwell and Moore line, he called at the Philadelphia office of the president of the Reading Railroad. Jim's research had shown that the company was badly in need of new freight cars. Notorious for being ill-tempered, George Baer despised salesmen and refused to see him. Irked by this lack of common courtesy, Jim returned the next day and was again ignored. He was there for a third day and a fourth.

When Baer arrived on the fifth day, he glared at Jim for a moment and demanded, "Why are you still here?"

"I've been waiting to tell you, sir," said Jim quietly, "that you can go straight to hell."

Baer blinked with astonishment, then barked a laugh. "All right, young man," he said as he took Jim's arm. "I'll see you."

An hour later, Jim left the office with a contract tucked in the pocket of his Prince Albert coat for freight cars to the tune of $5 million.

Jim celebrated the coup by purchasing a ring, a pair of cuff links, and a stick pin, each set with a sparkling emblem of the incarnation of the commercialization that went hand in hand with industrialization.

Half a century after Jim Brady became a traveling salesman, Iowa-born writer/composer Meredith Willson caught the essence of such men in his Broadway musical *The Music Man*. Its main character was a purveyor of band instruments and uniforms, "Professor" Harold Hill. In the opening number a group of drummers on a Rock Island line train chugging its way crossing Iowa sang, "You gotta know the territory."

In an era before mass communication and selling products by advertising that reached millions, products of manufacturers had to be sold person to person. Salesman to shop owner. Door-to-door drummer to "the lady of the house." One on one with whoever did the buying of equipment for a railroad. For a traveling salesman aboard the trains in the hinterlands, diamonds were a signboard. They testified to the pedigree not only of whatever he was peddling but of his own. Whether you were selling a handsaw for trimming rails or $5 million in freight cars, you first had to sell yourself. To do that you had to be more than a name on a business card. In order to get past a receptionist in an outer office you had to look important, and nothing was so potent in making that point, Jim had been advised, than the flash of a diamond ring.

If one diamond had the desired effect, Jim reasoned, what result might several achieve? If he were to become the most successful salesman possible, he first had to look the part. He would have to be perceived as more than just another drummer with another order book to fill. If flash counted, he'd outflash everyone.

If picking up the dinner check would land him a deal, the repast would be one that the guest would never forget. And neither would the man who had bought it be forgotten. If being a great salesman required being *liked,* as Charles Moore had counseled, James Buchanan Brady would be the best-liked railroad equipment salesman ever to get off a train. If sporting diamonds assured that once he'd been met, he would be remembered, then he would appear to be encrusted with them.

While on the road, Jim found other salesmen to be a source for gems. He garnered many by winning them at cards and dice. Some stones had been hocked by long-gone drummers. If Jim spotted a ring in a pawn shop with a gem that he wanted, he asked the pawnbroker to remove it from its mounting. The pawnbroker kept the gold. If a ring contained other gems, they also were left to the broker. Jim desired only diamonds. Sometimes the stones were only half a carat. Large or small, he carried them away in a pocket of his wallet. In later years as his wealth increased, he toted them around in a miner's belt and delightedly spread them out by the handful before the astonished eyes of customers and other salesmen. Should someone doubt that they were genuine, he scratched "James Buchanan Brady" on a pane of glass.

He became so identified with the stones that in 1884 "Markie" Mayer, a top salesman of cotton for the firm of H. B. Claflin & Company, walked into the barroom of Cincinnati's Burnet House hotel and coined the most colorful and indelible nickname in American history. Looking around the room, he asked, "Has anyone here seen Diamond Jim?"

2

The American Beauty

❧❦❧

WITH A TROVE of diamonds attesting to the triumphs of a selling tour in the West, Jim Brady returned to New York in the fall of 1881 determined to celebrate his success by setting out "to paint the town red."

A few years earlier, when he'd more than made up a cash-drawer shortage by bilking the members of a German band who thought they were getting round-trip tickets, he had used the surplus to buy a fine dinner and take in a show at an establishment known as a concert saloon. The antecedents of twentieth-century dinner theaters and patterned on the English music hall, they offered drinks, food, and entertainment by bands, piano players, dancers, and singers.

In 1881 in Manhattan there were upward of eighty of them. One observer, Junius Henry Browne, noted that the clientele of these places were "the laborer and the mechanic, the salesman and the accountant, the bank-clerk and merchant." Their chief attraction was "pretty waiter girls." As Michael and Ariane Batterberry wrote in *On the Town in New York,* their work consisted of "raising their hemlines, lowering their bodices, and shaking the bells on their kid boots" while offering "sweet companionship and a welcome respite from workaday care" for the businessman, "succor by the glass" for the traveler, and for "the lonely and bleak of heart, an occasional dance or whatever else they cared to work out between themselves after hours."

A few of the larger concert saloons offered auditoriums for theatrical presentations. It was to one of these that Jim had repaired to spend the ill-gotten gains of his ticket swindle. At Prince Street and Broadway, Niblo's Garden had been operating since before the Civil War. Its attraction for Jim on that evening was a dramatization of Dickens's *The Old Curiosity Shop* with the parts of Little Nell and the Marchioness being played by the famed actress Lotta Crabtree.

Attractive, graceful, and saucy, she'd first appeared in the piece at Wallack's Theater in 1868. Although critics scoffed, the public fell in love with her, allowing her to make a career of touring in the play and eventually to retire the richest actress in the country. Jim was so smitten by Lotta's charms that he went back to Niblo's night after night to gaze adoringly at her from the cheaper seats in the balcony and dream of a future when he would be rich enough to afford a seat front row center.

A few blocks uptown from Niblo's Garden was Harry Hill's. It was a combination bar, theater, and restaurant cobbled together in an irregular cluster of two-story buildings owned by show business, museum, and circus impresario P. T. Barnum. The precursor of Madison Square Garden, Harry Hill's was described in Ed Van Every's *Sins of New York* as "the sporting centre of the United States" in which every important boxing match was held, with Hill refereeing. It was in Harry Hill's that a fighter who'd come down from Boston became famous for a second-round knockout of the "unbeatable" Steve Taylor and in the next year beat Paddy Ryan for the heavyweight championship.

Jim Brady had met John L. Sullivan at Harry Hill's the year before the Taylor bout and had impressed "the Boston Strong Boy" by keeping up with him drink after drink. Amazed at Jim's capacity, John L. slapped Jim on the back and blared, "By God, Sir, you're a man! I'm proud to call you my friend."

Sullivan assumed Jim was quaffing Pilsner. It was ginger ale.

One of the most popular New York restaurants of the Gay Nineties was Harry Hill's Concert Saloon on Houston Street, where Diamond Jim Brady met and became a close friend of boxer John L. Sullivan.

While Jim broke Irish tradition by shunning alcohol, he had not strayed from his father when it came to politics. Just before he went on the road for Manning, Maxwell and Moore in 1881 he became a member of the Tammany Society. Named after a legendary Indian chief, it had been formed a month after the inauguration of President George Washington and had evolved into the controlling machine of the New York Democratic Party. To be an Irishman in New York was to be a Tammany man. In 1881 its headquarters was at Third Avenue and Fourteenth Street.

Also located in the building was a recently opened establishment of a showman named Tony Pastor. Born in New York in 1834, he had launched his career when he was ten years old, singing and playing a tambourine as a blackface minstrel at P. T. Barnum's museum. In the 1860s Tony was a saloon singer and songwriter. One of his most popular ditties, "The Upper and Lower Ten Thousand," dealt with social and economic inequities:

The Upper Ten Thousand in mansions reside,
With fronts of brown stone, and with stoops high and wide
While the Lower Ten Thousand in poverty deep,
In cellars and garrets, are huddled like sheep.
The Upper Ten Thousand have turkey and wine,
On turtle and ven'son and pastry they dine.
While the Lower Ten Thousand, whose meals are so small,
They've often to go without dinner at all.

Ironically, the composer/lyricist of this protest against the class system would become the most famous host and entertainer of the rich of his day. Recognizing that his future did not lie only in singing and songwriting, he went into the business of staging shows at 201 Bowery. In his Bowery Opera House, he promised a "great family resort" and a "Temple of Amusement where heads of families can bring their Ladies and children." Calling these presentations "variety shows," Pastor appeared in them himself and wrote much of the musical material. He also edited the content of other acts to make it accord with his policy of attracting more than the traditional male saloon crowd.

"If women could be induced to attend," he explained, "patronage should be materially extended." A writer for the *New York Herald* described patrons of Tony Pastor's Opera House wanting shows that were hearty, genial, racy, and, above all, varied. "They require something congenial to their own natures, which love mirth in its broadest phases and passion delineated by its strongest dramatic agencies," the article continued. "The patrons of Bowery amusements have little time for sentiment, but just enough time for fun and that relief from the exacting obligations from everyday life like that [offered at] Tony Pastor's. Variety, above all this, is a necessity with this class. They must have histrionic art and music and the ballet combined, in order to spend an evening profitably, for they have neither the leisure nor means to enjoy them in any other way."

When Pastor shifted location to Broadway in 1875, his shows retained their character. One day's bill offered "Miss Kathy O'Neil, the champion lady jig dancer"; Ferguson and Mack, "original and eccentric Irish comedians"; and "French twin sisters in splendid execution of jig, clog and reel dancing." Such offerings continued at Pastor's Broadway address for six years.

Moving into the Tammany building in October 1881, he advertised his "Casino Theater" as one in which good acts could be enjoyed by a wide audience in a setting free from smoking, drinking, and carousing. The new address put Tony Pastor's in the very heart of the Union Square theater district known as the Rialto. It was also convenient to Fourteenth Street, Broadway, and Fifth Avenue department stores.

A Pastor newspaper advertisement exclaimed, "How convenient to horse cars and elevated railroad stations!"

Pastor arrived on Fourteenth Street with a reputation for having changed what had been the male-dominated concert saloon with its dubious reputation into a place where a decent man could bring wife and family. His theater presented various kinds of performers in a wholesome atmosphere. The name that would soon be given these shows was taken from a French term, *voix de ville* ("voice of the city"). The American word was "vaudeville."

New Yorkers flocked to the new program every week, with matinees on Tuesday and Friday, at fifty cents admission. The material Pastor wrote and performed centered on subjects he defined as "the fads and the ultra-fashions of both men and women" and themes such as "a man's best girl, the old man's boot, the mother-in-law, a scolding wife" and other domestic topics. Plucking stories from the day's news as themes for his songs, he established the pattern of the topical monologues of a century hence, late-night television shows on which Jack Parr, Johnny Carson, Jay Leno, and David Letterman squeezed laughs from current events.

"I believe not only in the power of the public press, but in its utility," Pastor said. "It is the most valuable agent the vocalist has ever had for securing subjects for popular songs. The comic vocalist must be quick to perceive the topic or phrase of human life which is liable to interest the amusement-going public."

The devout son of Italian Catholics, Tony would not allow off-color humor on his stage. He pledged to women that an evening spent at Tony Pastor's would be as moral an experience as a prayer meeting, but a lot more fun. Customers also got their money's worth. A show never ran less than three hours. For the women the bill offered refined tenor soloists, side-splitting comics, and graceful tap dancers. Men were able to ogle pretty girls by the score. But in all Tony Pastor shows the unquestioned star was Pastor himself. Immaculate in white tie and tails, he skipped from the wings, bowing and smiling and carrying a trademark collapsible silk opera hat. Short, round, and pudgy, he moved center stage, snapped open the hat, cocked it to one side of his head, and launched into the first of what would be five or six numbers written by himself.

Another component of his shows was new faces. Fifty years before radio introduced the American audience to Major Bowes's *Amateur Hour,* which featured fresh talent, including ventriloquists, and tap dancers whose talents the radio audience could only imagine, Tony Pastor prided himself on presenting promising neophyte performers. He called them "Pastor's Boys and Girls" and presented as many as ten or fifteen per show. The dancing duo Ray Bailey and Dave Genaro were the first hoofers to do the cakewalk on any stage. "Little Elsie, the Child Wonder," grew up to be Elsie Janis and pioneer a tradition of stars entertaining troops by going to the front in France in World War I. Tony's stage also featured "The Four Cohans." Of the Irish song-and-dance quartet, the youngest, Georgie, would adopt Tony's trick for getting an ovation from the crowd by singing at least one patriotic number accompanied by vigorous waving of the Stars and Stripes.

At the dawn of the 1880s there was no better way to launch a show business career than by being introduced by Tony Pastor. One historian of such debuts wrote, "Gently leading the bewildered—and sometimes palsied—tyro out onto the stage by one shaking hand he would pause for a moment, smile benignly to the audience, say a few words of introduction and then, with an explosive pop of his opera hat, get the audience into a properly receptive mood."

On the evening of November 22, 1880, Tony had led onto the stage a nervous, beautiful, slim, nineteen-year-old blonde with an hourglass figure wearing a white voile dress with silver spangles shimmering in the limelight.

"Ladies and gentlemen—friends and customers," said Tony, "tonight I have a most unusual treat in store for you. At great personal trouble and expense I have brought here for your admiration and entertainment the beautiful English Ballad Singer. Ladies and gentlemen, I give you a vision of loveliness and a voice of gold—Miss Lillian Russell."

EXCEPT FOR the beauty and the voice, Tony's introduction was a lie. The stunning girl was not English. The only trouble and expense for Tony was bringing her to Fourteenth Street from Brooklyn. But the truth about her would have made no difference to the audience. In the lingo of Vaudeville, the English Ballad Singer "wowed 'em."

Her true name was Helen Louise Leonard. Born in Clinton, Iowa, in 1861, the fifth child of newspaper publisher Charles E. Leonard and the former Cynthia Rowald Van Name, a feminist and author, Helen grew up being called Nell. When she was four years old, the family moved to Chicago. She was educated in the Convent of the Sacred Heart and the Park Institute. In 1878 her mother found promise in Nell's voice. She left Charles

Lillian Russell considered this photo portrait of her in her twenties "my favorite profile."

and took Nell to New York City to study singing under Leopold Damrosch. Transfixed by the qualities of the beautiful eighteen-year-old's soprano voice, the maestro envisioned an operatic career.

Of course, that would require years of training.

Impatient and impetuous, Nell declared she was more interested in light and comic opera and auditioned for a role in a production of Gilbert and Sullivan's *Pinafore* that was to be staged by theatrical manager Edward R. Rice. Hired for the chorus, she made her debut at the Boston Museum on November 15, 1878. Almost immediately, she found herself being courted by the orchestra conductor, Harry Braham. They married a few months later, and within a year Helen had given birth to a boy. When she resumed her role in *Pinafore,* the child was put in the care of a nurse. Young and inexperienced, she accidentally stuck the child's stomach with a diaper pin and the infant died in convulsions. Braham blamed the death on Helen, accusing her of putting her career ahead of the baby. The couple separated.

Not long after this tragic series of events, Helen attended a dinner party at the home of a friend and was asked to sing. Among the guests was Tony Pastor. When he offered her $75 a week to perform at his theater, Helen said she could not accept because her mother would not approve of her daughter singing in an "unrefined" music hall.

Pastor replied, "We'll give you a new name and not tell her until we see how it goes."

A list of names provided by Pastor included Lillian Russell. Helen chose it, she said, because "I loved all the l's in it."

EXACTLY WHEN Jim Brady first saw Lillian Russell and fell under her spell is not known. He had been going to concert saloons and attending the theater whenever he found himself with a little extra money from his job at the St. James Hotel. He was able to go more often while running the station at Spuyten Duyvil and as chief clerk at Grand Central Depot. But because he was on the road on behalf of Manning, Maxwell and Moore, he had not been able to enjoy as many evenings on the town as he would have liked. It may have been during his return to the city in March 1881 that he donned his evening wear and adorned it with newly acquired diamonds to take in the new show at Tony Pastor's, an *opera bouffe* called *Olivette*.

Playing the title role and costumed as a cabin boy, Lillian sang "In the North Sea Lived a Whale." At the end of each verse she danced a hornpipe. A notice in the *Dramatic Mirror* raved, "If the young lady does not allow adulation to conquer her ambition and elevate her too high in her own esteem, she will become a bright and shining light on the lyric stage."

In Jim's opinion, she already outshone Lotta Crabtree and every other stage beauty he'd seen. However, he was not the only man who felt that way. During a very short apprenticeship in the theater, Lillian had learned to expect to be courted by stage-door Johnnies, some of whom were millionaires and many of whom were young and handsome. Yet when she was introduced to Jim, there was something about the fat and plain-looking Irishman who eschewed Pilsner for ginger ale that caught her fancy. He seemed perfectly content to be in her presence and want nothing more than to have her keep him company at supper.

When she accepted, Jim discovered that she had no trouble keeping up with him. While course after course was served, they reached an unspoken understanding that what they were in the process of forging was not a romance but friendship.

Through this association a new world was opened. It was made for Jim and he for it. It was tawdry, vulgar, blatant, gay, pretentious, and reckless. It put both hands in his wallet and he surrendered with a happy smile. He was a realist. Being neither a handsome youth nor possessing one of the town's prestigious names, he was grateful to be included on any terms among what he considered "the elect."

3

Mr. First Nighter

❧❦❧

SOON AFTER Diamond Jim met Lillian Russell, they learned
that Tony Pastor was farming her out for a tour with a
comic named Willie Edouin and a company of players to perform *Fun in a Photograph Gallery* and *Babes in the Woods*. The ultimate destination was San Francisco.

As she pondered making a transcontinental train trip that
was generally undertaken with presentiments of wild adventure, the expert on railroads named Jim Brady assured her that
she would find the experience not only comfortable but more
luxurious than a millionaire's mansion thanks to the "Palace
Car" that had been invented by a man named George Pullman.

Success in the building-construction business in Chicago
had left Pullman financially well off in a booming city determined to become the mecca of the country's expanding railroad network. As long-distance travel brought with it a need
for sleeping cars, Pullman tinkered with several design ideas.
He was not alone in the quest. (The story of efforts of several
designers to build and put a sleeper into service is told in detail
in several histories of American railroading.) What others in
the competition did not have was Pullman's luck. On a visit to
Chicago in early 1865 Mary Lincoln, the wife of the president
of the United States, became so enchanted with the car's beautiful appointments that a few months later, when the funeral train

36

Diamond Jim Brady earned his millions by selling equipment to America's expanding railroad industry, symbolized by the luxurious Pullman "palace cars" and opulent dining rooms.

carrying the body of her assassinated husband stopped at Chicago on its way to the Lincoln burial place in Springfield, Illinois, Mrs. Lincoln requested that Pullman's car, *Pioneer,* be attached to the train for her use. Pullman's reputation as sleeping-car builder was later enhanced when President Ulysses S. Grant rode the *Pioneer* from Detroit to his old home in Galena, Illinois. Pullman soon started building other kinds of luxurious cars that transformed trains into hotels on rails.

Wrote one historian of these luxuries on wheels and rails, "Their seats were likened to Roman couches. They were soft and extravagantly upholstered in velvet, with gilded braid and tassels dangling from every available inch of surface. Even the floors had a voluptuous texture. Thick pile carpeting, embellished with floral designs in all the primary colors, was spread on the floor. Everything was ornate and refined. In such surroundings one was almost willing to suffocate with the dust that constantly swept in from the cinder roadbed."

Lillian made good use of the time she spent in such railroad cars on her way across the country mastering the skills of pinochle and poker. This dexterity would serve to strengthen the bond of friendship between her and Jim.

While she ventured west of her Iowa birthplace for the first time, Jim Brady was also on the road selling Manning, Maxwell and Moore equipment and employing his own considerable talents at the card table to win other salesmen's diamonds.

Determined to make himself the top salesman in America, he spent nine months of each year making the rounds and forging friendships with executives and with the men in the field. He could feel just as at home and welcome in the noise and grime of a roundhouse or helping to pump a handcar out to a storage shed with a foreman in overalls as he was seated opposite a president or purchasing officer in fine suits in plush offices. He saw selling as a continuing process. When he left an office he did so with an invitation extended to whomever he had visited, whether they had given him an order or not. "If you're ever in New York City, look me up," he said, "and I'll show you the town."

Those who took him up on the offer found it an unforgettable experience. The Diamond Jim Brady treatment consisted of champagne and cigars in his hotel suite and dinner in one of the best restaurants, then out to a show or other diversion. But of all entertainments of the evening, none proved more remarkable to the recipients of Jim's hospitality than observing the spectacle of him eating.

Before or after a meal a Brady guest was treated to Tony Pastor's or another of the many concert saloons. If a guest's timing were right he might find himself being introduced to John L. Sullivan at Harry Hill's, still one of Jim Brady's favorite haunts. Considering himself a poet, Harry posted signboards bearing his rhymes. One read:

> *Punches and juleps, cobblers and smashes,*
> *To make the tongue waggle with its merry flashes.*

"Mr. Hill himself is a man of about fifty years of age, small, stocky and muscular, a complete type of the pugilist," wrote a patron. "He keeps the peace of his own concern, and he does not hesitate to knock any man down, or throw him out the door, if he breaks the rules of the establishment. He is at the bar; in the hall, at the stage, where the low comedies and broad farces are played. With burly face and stocky form, he can be seen in all parts of the hall, shouting out, 'Order! Order! Less noise there!'"

Should an out-of-towner yearn for excitement elsewhere, there were plenty of options in the form of gambling and other kinds of "houses" in a section called Satan's Circus and also known as the Tenderloin.

Stretching along Fourteenth Street from Union Square westward to Sixth Avenue and as far uptown as Thirty-fourth Street, it was given its name by a police captain, Alexander Williams.

Another popular Gay Nineties' restaurant was Satan's Circus in the infamous "Tenderloin" section where Diamond Jim often entertained out-of-town customers.

Nicknamed "Clubber" because of his adept subduing of crooks, he coined a maxim that is still taught in law schools and in police academies: "There is more law at the end of a policeman's nightstick than in any ruling of the United States Supreme Court."

When informed that he was being moved out of a rough, low-graft East Side area known as the Gas House District to a section of gambling dens and houses of prostitution, and that he was being elevated in rank to inspector and thereby eligible for a financial windfall in bribes, he remarked, "I've been living on chuck steak and now I'm moving up to the tenderloin."

The establishments that paid Williams and his superiors in the police department could easily afford it. They were by no means cheap brothels, saloons, dance halls, and gaming rooms. Among them was the classy whorehouse of the "French Madame," Mrs. Matilda Hermann. She was obese and so tough that she did not need to hire a bouncer. Other resorts were the Oriental White Elephant with stained-glass windows, pictures of pachyderms on the walls, and a bowling alley; the Strand; Idlewile; Cremorne; Egyptian Hall; Sailor's Hall; Buckingham Palace; Star and Garter; Tom Gould's; and The Haymarket dance hall, which maintained such flamboyant standards that Diamond Jim felt no qualms about introducing it to his guests.

If one of Jim's out-of-town visitors preferred the theater, there were several on the Rialto. The newest of them opened in August 1881 as Theatre Comique. Located at 728 Broadway, it was an older house that had been refurbished by the producing team of Ned Harrigan and Tony Hart. A newspaper thought its "extravagant bronze and bric-a-brac style much too gaudy."

Their new show, *The Major,* drew a warmer notice. A reviewer wrote, "Nothing could exceed in heartiness and friendliness the fashion which Mr. Harrigan and other favorites of the familiar company were received, and several of the noisily hailed comedians were forced to acknowledge the public welcome in a few informal words."

Other offerings of the 1881–1882 season were *Le Voyage en Suisse,* a French musical in which the stars were a family of five acrobats; *Mme. Favart,* another French work that recounted an imaginary romance of a real eighteenth-century prima donna; and *Michael Strogoff,* an epic at the Booth on the subject of Napoleon's siege of Moscow. This spectacle included elaborate sets and waterfalls, which the *Times* derided as "ridiculous competition with nature."

But the theatrical evening that set Jim Brady's heart fluttering with excitement opened at the Bijou on October 29. Produced by John A. McCaull, *The Snake Charmer* (also known as *The Mogul*) was about a ruler who fell in love with the snake charmer. Named D'Jemma, she was played by none other than Lillian Russell, just back from a triumph in San Francisco.

She'd left the booming, pleasure-loving city of steep hills having become the toast of the town. Each night after her performance she had been whisked to the Poodle Dog, Maison

Riche, and Maison Doree for champagne, caviar, and more lasting tributes to her talent and beauty in the shape of gold, pearls, rubies, sapphires, and diamonds. One admirer who could not escort her to dinner because his ship was sailing had tossed a bouquet of roses over the footlights. Nestled among the petals were a diamond ring and a note. "Tomorrow I leave for Russia and will never see you again," wrote Lieutenant Commander Anatol Royal Ivanovsky of the *Moskva*. "Believe me, Madame, a Russian bear can be pleased with great talent."

Although she was nervous about her Broadway debut, Lillian's performance as the snake charmer drew this bouquet from the *Dramatic Mirror:* "A year ago we noticed this little lady at Tony Pastor's; now she is a bright particular star of *opera bouffe*. There is nothing to compare with her in this country."

Each week a hamper of fruit or huge bouquet of flowers was delivered to her dressing room anonymously. Then came two sealskin coats, one for Lillian and one for her mother. Soon she had accumulated a ruby and diamond bracelet, a pair of ruby earrings, a ruby ring, and a pearl and diamond chain. According to her autobiography, she finally met the man who had showered her with the gifts. A wizened figure of indeterminate age, he introduced himself at a dinner party as Jack Duncan. He invited her to join him in viewing paintings at the Metropolitan Museum of Art the next day.

Among the Old Masters, he said to her, "I sent you the jewelry because I know you are as good as you are beautiful. You should have the things you want without temptation. I shall never speak to you again. So this is goodbye."

Although Lillian never saw him again, she remembered him in her memoirs. "There is much reward," she wrote, "for unselfish love."

Musing on the episode in *Duet in Diamonds,* John Burke wrote, "Her benefactor needn't have worried about Lillian being tempted by a yearning for material things. For her temptation would always assume an emotional rather than a material guise. The incident, however, illuminated one of the more striking facets of her public personality. The prismatic quality of stage lighting somehow transformed her into something as fragile as a porcelain figure. This brought out the protective instinct of the males in the audience."

That certainly was true of Jim Brady. By electing not to try to be her lover, he was close to her for nearly forty years. The arrangement was a good bargain for both. She was a trusted and loyal friend in whom he found a door to a world that had always fascinated him.

WHEN JIM WAS fourteen years old, he saw Edwin Booth mount the stage of a theater he owned and named for himself at Twenty-third Street and Sixth Avenue. The play was *Othello*. Many years later a reporter asked if Jim had enjoyed it. "Concerning William Shakespeare," Jim said with a booming belly laugh, "one always says the acting was fine. And so it was."

When Jim began going to the theater, his tickets were not obtained at the box office. He bought a pass for ten cents from shopkeepers who were given two a week for allowing playbills to be displayed in their windows. More often than not when he took his seat he found himself behind a woman in a hat. Because the prevailing fashion in millinery dictated voluminous lace, feathers, and birds, his view of the stage was obscured so frequently that he vowed that when the day arrived that he could afford to pay the box office price, his seat would be front row.

He vowed, "I'll be damned if I'm gonna pay my money to sit and look at a lot of stuffed birds and laces."

Thanks to railroads and a talent for wooing and winning customers, when Lillian Russell returned from the West he was front and center to applaud her performance as a snake charmer even more warmly than he'd hailed Lotta Crabtree.

Because he was able to afford the best seats in the house, he'd gotten to know a man who had built up one of the greatest repertory companies in the history of the American stage. Owner of the Broadway Theater near Thirtieth Street, Augustin Daly employed such famous performers as Agnes Ethel, Clara Morris, Blanche Bates, Mary Mannering, and Ada Rehan.

In the year John Toucey hired Jim to be a baggage smasher, Miss Rehan had been in a play about railroads titled *Across the Continent*. When *Under the Gaslight* was staged in 1867, Jim was twelve and working for his stepfather in the saloon that still called itself Dan Brady's. Had Jim attended the melodrama, he would have seen in the third act a railroad track across the stage and behind it a switch shack. Tied up on the tracks lay the hero. Standing over him, the villain in a silk hat looked at a pocket watch in the moonlight and ominously informed the breathless audience, "The *Lake Shore Express* is due on the hour."

Billboards for the play depicted this climactic moment with a gigantic locomotive bearing down on the hapless hero. No doubt wondering how this scene could be reproduced on a stage as the moon dimmed behind a cloud and the villain crouched in bushes to observe the result of his dastardly handiwork, the audience heard the distant wail of a train whistle. A moment later it was closer. Then a shaft of light cut through the dark—the locomotive's headlamp. The beam caught the figure of the heroine as she dashed from the wings, raced to the shack, and threw the switch to divert the oncoming train to another track. Only the front of the locomotive was seen, but it was enough to create a sensation and sell a lot of tickets.

Jim Brady preferred plays with such strong and simple themes. Typical was *The County Fair* in which the widow Bedott befriended an indigent jockey. When the jockey discerned makings of a racer in one of her horses, he trained it and then rode it to victory to pay off the mortgage on the widow's farm. The race was simulated on stage with real horses on treadmills.

When Edwin Booth had strutted the stage in *Othello,* Jim, in the cheap seats, had worn his only suit. Occupying a front-row seat to cheer the Broadway debut of Lillian Russell in the fall of 1880, he was dressed to the nines, aglitter with diamonds, and the rival of everyone in a fashionable footlight fraternity whose membership boasted Civil War general William Tecumseh Sherman. The pacesetter of these elegantly bedecked men whom the lower classes (and Jim's brother Dan) called "swells" was a leader of café society, E. (Evander) Berry Wall.

So resplendently clothed was he that newspaper writer Blakely Hall crowned him "King of the Dudes." The title had been prompted by a display of fincry exhibited at the Grand Union Hotel in Saratoga Springs at the height of the summer racing season. Thin, smallish, with a long, drooping mustache with the ends curled up, Wall had always been meticulously attired, but on that August day he'd appeared in a new outfit every eighteen minutes. News of this amazing display went out over telegraph lines to the New York newspapers. The stories made Berry an instant celebrity.

The royal title bestowed by Blakely Hall was immediately challenged by a writer for a competing paper. He dubbed fashion-plate–actor Robert "Handsome Bob" Hilliard the "champion dude." The rivalry between him and Berry continued unabated until March 12, 1888, when New York was hit by the greatest blizzard in its history and all transportation was paralyzed. Hilliard proved himself equal to the occasion by arriving at the Hoffman House Hotel in patent leather boots that reached all the way to his hips. Not only had the actor been prepared for a storm that caught everyone by surprise, he'd met and vanquished it in high style. Legend has it that Berry was so disconsolate that he retired to Monte Carlo, leaving the crown to Hilliard and spending his remaining years looking moodily at the Mediterranean Sea and brooding on the lack of boots suitable for a dude in a blizzard.

Lavish and outrageous clothing was sported in the 1880s and 1890s by "fashion plates" called "dudes." *Left*: The acknowledged "King of the Dudes" was Evander "Berry" Wall, shown "taking the air on the Avenue" in this photograph in the *New York American*. *Right*: The "dude style" even reached to Syracuse, New York, as shown in an advertisement for A. W. Palmer, a clothier in that city.

In the autumn of 1880 one of these well-turned-out men was the twenty-two-year-old scion of one of the city's most prominent families. Having graduated from Harvard that June, he was running for election to the New York Legislature on the Republican ticket. When he won and arrived in Albany to assume his seat in January 1881, he typified the style of dress of men his age. His appearance was remembered and recorded for posterity in 1922 in a newspaper article by John Walsh. He wrote, "He had on a cutaway coat with one button at the top, and the ends of his tails almost reached the tops of his shoes.

He carried a gold-headed cane in one hand, a silk hat in the other, and he walked in the bent-over fashion that was the style of the young men of his day. His trousers were as tight as a tailor could make them, and had a bell-shaped bottom to cover his shoes."

Walsh asked another legislator, "Who's the dude?"

The reply was "That's Theodore Roosevelt."

One observer saw the clothing of the dudes as the manifestation of their overdeveloped exhibitionist complexes. They were men of their time and founding fathers of fortunes forged from steel and railroads and other industries of an ever-expanding country that they believed had a manifest destiny to fill the continent and take its place as a power on the world stage. In *The Age of the Moguls* Stewart Hall Holbrook wrote, "These were tough-minded fellows, who fought their way encased in rhinoceros hides. The men were as magnificent in their practical wars as they were in their dude clothes, trying to eat with a fork, wondering how best to approach a chaise longue. They were a motley crew, yet taken together they fashioned a savage and gaudy age as distinctly purple as that of Imperial Rome, and infinitely more entertaining."

Recognized as "men about town," they adorned all the best restaurants and never missed the occasions that each autumn signaled the start of the city's social calendar—opening nights of the new theater season. While Jim Brady could not yet compete with most of these men in terms of money and there was no way to outshine them sartorially (formal duds were formal duds, after all), he was certain no one could outdo him in jewelry. Arriving at a theater with a front-row-center ticket in hand, he sported huge diamond studs in his shirtfront whose glitter attracted not a few admiring glances from the ladies and the envy of dudes.

Diamond Jim also went one better than young Theodore Roosevelt. TR's walking stick when he appeared in the New York Assembly had a plain gold head. The one Jim carried to the opening nights of the theatrical season was embedded with a three-carat diamond.

LIKE EVERYONE ELSE in New York's overlapping circles of theater, commerce, and wealth, Jim and Lillian were agog in the new year over the arrival in the harbor of the steamship *Arizona*. Aboard when she docked on January 2, 1882, was the most talked about figure on both sides of the Atlantic. Irish playwright, chief promulgator of the "Aesthetic Movement," and famed for his wit, Oscar Wilde immediately demonstrated it and gave everyone a belly laugh when he told a customs official, "The only thing I have to declare is my genius."

This bon mot was giddily reported along with his retort to a fellow voyager's question about their crossing. "I am not exactly pleased with the Atlantic," Oscar had said. "It is not as majestic as I expected."

Although none of the newspapermen described Wilde as a majestic figure, the adjective would not have been wrong. Well over six feet in height, he was taller than any of the scribes, broad-shouldered with long arms and hands, with what one newsman called "a large white face." One finger bore a great seal ring with a Greek classic profile. The same hand held a cigarette that he did not smoke. A *New York Tribune* reporter expected the voice to be effeminate. He found it to be "burly." Another observed that the poet spoke "in hexameters." A third was interested in the visitor's views on beauty. Pointing to a grain elevator on the New Jersey shoreline, he asked, "Could that have aesthetic value?"

Wilde replied, "It's a wide field which has no limit."

Not since Charles Dickens had visited the city before the Civil War had a literary visitor arrived from England with such a stir. Everyone wanted to meet him. If that was not possible, it was sufficient to be in the same room with him. His purpose was to promote his new play *Vera* and travel the country giving lectures on "modern life in its romantic aspects."

After completing his tour, he boasted to his friend the American painter James Whistler, "I have civilized America."

Of Oscar's odyssey his biographer Richard Ellmann wrote, "The whole tour was an achievement of courage and grace, along with ineptitude and self-advertisement. Wilde succeeded in naturalizing the word 'aesthetic,' even if Americans dropped the initial *a*. However effeminate his doctrines were thought to be, they constituted the most determined and sustained attack upon materialistic vulgarity that America had seen."

"The God of this century is wealth," he said. "To succeed you must have wealth. At all costs one must have wealth."

ONE OF THE PLACES Wilde visited in New York City was Harry Hill's. What he thought of the saloon and whether he encountered Diamond Jim Brady and his diamonds went unrecorded. Because Wilde remained in New York for two and a half months after he stopped lecturing, it's likely that the proponent of the Aesthetic Movement and the exponent of diamonds as the measure of success crossed paths in the lobbies of theaters or glimpsed one another across a restaurant. It is safe to state that in Oscar's transcontinental journeys, he benefited from Diamond Jim's effectiveness in selling railroad equipment, which afforded Wilde a comfortable journey.

His purpose in delaying his return to England was to be on hand to welcome a friend and actress/singer who was also coming to make money performing on a national tour—Lillie Langtry. Known in Britain as the Jersey Lily because she was born on the island of Jersey, she was a "professional beauty" who although married to Edward Langtry was reputed to have been the lover of the Prince of Wales and others. She'd taken to the stage at Oscar's urging. When a reporter asked if he had "discovered" her, Oscar replied, "I would rather have discovered Mrs. Langtry than have discovered America."

Greeting her carrying an armful of lilies when her ship arrived on October 22, 1882, Oscar gave new meaning to "dude" style. Noted the reporter from the *New York Times,* "He was dressed as probably no grown man in the world was ever dressed before. His hat was of brown cloth not less than six inches high; his coat was of black velvet; his overcoat was of green cloth, heavily trimmed with fur; his trousers matched his hat; his tie was gaudy."

A week after setting foot in New York, Mrs. Langtry was to open as Hester Grazebrook in Tom Taylor's *An Unequal Match* at the Park Theater. Unfortunately, a fire swept through the theater on the day of the opening, forcing the play to debut at Wallack's Theater the next week. She received rave reviews, including one by Oscar. The gist of the notices was that America had been graced with a singer and actress to rival the "American beauty" named Lillian Russell.

Five days before Mrs. Langtry came to New York, Lillian had opened at the Bijou in John McCaull's production of *The Sorcerer.* An early work by Gilbert and Sullivan, the operetta was little known in America and had been eagerly awaited by the press, the public, and Lillian's biggest admirer in both enthusiasm and avoirdupois, Diamond Jim Brady.

As Aline, a sweet and beautiful maiden who drinks a powerful aphrodisiac brew, she was in one critic's opinion "a revelation." Never had she sung better or looked more radiant or "acted with more charm and sincerity."

Everyone who saw the production predicted it would have a long run, and indeed it did, staying on the boards into the spring. But for two weeks in November, audiences were shocked and disappointed to learn that Lillian would not be appearing. When McCaull was told by Lillian's mother that his star was ill, he sensed a case of "artistic temperament" and acute desire for more money. The *New York Dramatic Mirror* attributed Lillian's suffering to "contract morbus."

Infuriated by this aspersion on her daughter, Mrs. Leonard shot off a missive averring her daughter's ill health. "It is not unusual for singers to be troubled with bronchial infection," wrote the outraged parent, "and Miss Russell is subject to trouble of this kind in damp, unwholesome weather. She has never shirked her duty, but on the contrary appeared in her role even when she could not do justice to herself in singing. After her first attack, she returned to work much too soon, which was the occasion of her present illness. I am happy to state she is mending, and we hope will soon be able to assume her duties."

A worried Jim Brady sent bouquets of flowers sprinkled with diamond trinkets. When he learned in the spring that she would resume her role for the final week of the show, he was greatly relieved.

With *The Sorcerer* closed and herself fully recovered, Lillian immediately took her talents to the stage of impresario Rudolph Anderson's new theater. Located "way uptown" at Broadway and Thirty-ninth, the Casino was hailed as the most gorgeous showplace in town. The production was Offenbach's *Princess of Trebizonde*. Lillian was paid an unprecedented $300 a week. The orchestra leader was handsome, dashing Edward Solomon, and Lillian was head over heels in love with him.

Of this turn of events she wrote in her memoirs, "After my long illness the first one to come to see me was Edward Solomon. While I was convalescing, he would sit at the piano and play for me. He had the peculiar gift of expressing in a melody the serious and romantic as well as the ludicrous incidents happening in a room where many people were congregated. While various individuals were talking and laughing he would quietly play a bit of music which accented their peculiarities and appealed to my sense of humor. Naturally, when I was quite well again, I fell in love."

And why not? She was young and healthy again, it was springtime, and a divorce she'd sought from Harry Braham, with whom she hadn't lived for years, would soon become a reality.

The Casino engagement was a happy one. Between working again and being in love, she found herself in a pleasant whirl. Furthermore, other managers were deluging her with contracts. Each carried the inducement of more money. Lillian blithely signed all of them.

While Diamond Jim was delighted that Lillian was enjoying personal and professional happiness, he and everyone else in New York who admired her were soon shocked to learn that she and Solomon had secretly sailed to England. She did so to accept a lucrative engagement in London. Because her departure broke several American contracts, an outraged *Music and Drama* exclaimed, "Our community is to be congratulated upon her breach of contracts. The stage is burdened by far too many Lillian Russells, who usurp places of better artists and more estimable women. It is to be sincerely hoped that she will achieve so great a success [in London] that she may never deem it advisable to afflict us with her presence again."

The publication attributed Lillian's successes to notoriety rather than artistry. "What little public distinction she has achieved," it sniped, "has been as a worshiped idol of the dudes."

As Lillian sailed to England with her new love, the fat, bejeweled salesman who thought of himself as her best friend was close to realizing his ambition to become one of those "young men about town." His promotion to full salesman for Manning, Maxwell and Moore with an unlimited expense account had boosted his earnings more than sufficiently to indulge in all the expensive frivolities. Evermore a commanding figure on opening nights, he found himself making the acquaintance of theater managers, actors, actresses such as Mary Anderson (a singer who was invariably described by reviewers as "glorious" and "Our Mary"), and other "first nighters" with reputations as dudes.

A recognized pacesetter among the men who showed up for the openings was Freddie Gebhard. Possessor of a considerable private fortune, he admired both Jim Brady's flair for self-advertisement in the form of diamonds and his capacity for having a good time. Consequently, Jim found himself invited to Freddie's frequent supper parties. It was at one of them that Jim was introduced to Mrs. Langtry. As with everyone who met Diamond Jim Brady, the Jersey Lily was immediately charmed by his counterpoint of amusing rough-hewn speech that attested to a lowly start in life and his polished manners, impeccable attire, and dazzling display of diamonds. Like Lillian Russell, Mrs. Langtry learned that in return for a breathtaking gift of a ring, a brooch, or a bracelet he wished nothing in return but the pleasure of her company at dinner or supper.

The visiting beauty discovered another benefit of being considered a friend by Diamond Jim Brady. When the time came for her to leave New York on a national tour, Freddie Gebhard asked Jim to make the travel arrangements. The result was a luxurious private train.

Being a salesman whom the bosses at Manning, Maxwell and Moore wisely left to set his own travel schedule, Jim was able to arrange his trips to suit his purposes. This meant arranging to be in New York, or nearby, in order to attend each opening night of the theatrical season. He was not interested in seeing a show after its debut. A large part of the fun of going to the theater was being known as a first nighter.

The impressive commissions that bankrolled his evening attire and the diamonds that adorned it also fueled a zest for wagering in the gambling palaces of the Tenderloin. On most opening nights he was likely to be found at roulette or baccarat tables at Joe Hall's gaming emporium at 818 Broadway. But even more attractive in the plush establishment was the bill of fare in the dining room. Like the casinos of Las Vegas, Atlantic

City, and other gaming spas of America in the twentieth century, Joe Hall provided meals at the expense of the house, inviting patrons to help themselves to "all you can eat."

Partaking of the lavish menu in 1883, twenty-seven-year-old James Buchanan Brady ate and pondered how far he had come from the free hard-boiled eggs of his father's bar, eels by the foot or the pound of Catherine Slip, and penny apiece South Street oysters, and that along the way he'd picked up a satisfying nickname. The second son of Dan Brady who'd cooled off in summers by plunging off a wharf into the Hudson River was now the Diamond Jim Brady who could afford to escape the stifling heat of July and August in New York City for Long Island and the best suite of the Manhattan Beach Hotel. In the cool shade of the canopy of its vast veranda or having a mid-morning splash in the surf of the Atlantic Ocean, he was, Parker Morrell wittily noted in a 1934 biography, "one of the larger landmarks."

When Jim grew tired of swimming, he waddled back to the terrace knowing that waiters had laid out for him a huge platter of iced oysters on the half shell. This repast was a mere snack in a daily regimen of eating that began with a "light" breakfast of beefsteak, chops, eggs, flapjacks, fried potatoes, hominy, corn bread, and a pitcher of milk.

Lunch at eleven-thirty was more oysters, clams, deviled crab, a broiled lobster or two, a steak, salad, and two kinds of pie. This was generally followed by a box of chocolate.

Not the least of the hotel's attractions was a fifteen-course "shore" dinner. The music of Gilmore's Band was accompanied by the crunch and crackle of lobster claws being opened, most of the noise emanating from Mr. Brady's table. Along with the lobster came a huge serving of green turtle soup, broiled fresh shad, Long Island's famous canvasback duck, a choice of other fowl, terrapin, and fresh asparagus. Dessert was likely to be vanilla mousse, fruits, nuts, bonbons, and chocolate mints.

In the mid-1880s with money rolling in, counted among the first-nighter dudes, and a bachelor in a city alive with lovely women even without the presence of the American Beauty, Diamond Jim found life a banquet in every way.

4

"Nell, I'm Rich!"

❧❦❧

I N AUGUST 1884 when the Democratic Party nominated Governor Grover Cleveland of New York to be its candidate for president of the United States, Diamond Jim Brady was of two minds about the nominee who, if elected in November, would be the first Democrat to occupy the White House since Jim's namesake surrendered the executive mansion to Abraham Lincoln in 1861. When President James Buchanan left office after one term, Jim had been seven years old. Now he was thirty and a loyalist in the ranks of Tammany. The New York City Democrats had fought the Cleveland nomination tooth and nail because the governor's program of reforms struck at the very heart of Tammany's power. Yet Jim found much to like about the bachelor candidate who was even fatter than himself, who spoke his mind in blunt language, and who had a reputation for devouring enormous meals.

As the campaign began against Republican candidate James G. Blaine, Jim learned that when Cleveland was a lawyer, district attorney, and then mayor of Buffalo, he was known both as a man about town and a ladies' man. The evidence of the latter came during the campaign with the revelation that Grover had fathered a boy whose mother he refused to marry. Republicans came up with a campaign taunt in the form of a poem in which the "out-of-wedlock" child asked his mother,

56

"Ma, ma, where's my pa?" The reply was "Gone to the White House, ha, ha, ha."

When Cleveland admitted parentage, Jim admired his courage and demonstrated it by adding his vote to a majority of Americans who dismissed the scandal and voted Cleveland in.

A great deal of opposition to Cleveland came from men with whom Diamond Jim Brady did business. Railroads had benefited from two decades of Republican governments that encouraged railway expansion through vast land grants for rights-of-way from which many of those in government profited. Between 1862 and 1871 the federal government and the states had handed over to railroad promoters more than 300,000 square miles of public lands. In addition to this territory, larger than some European countries, the government had furnished loans and outright grants to back railway ventures. Much of this largesse was obtained by such tycoons as Leland Stanford, Collis P. Huntington, Russell Sage, and Jay Gould through bribery of congressmen and state legislators.

During the presidential campaign of 1884 an issue was made of Blaine's involvement in passage of legislation affecting the Little Rock & Fort Smith Railroad. Blaine had been Speaker of the House of Representatives. The outcome of the action of Congress had been a windfall for the railroad. When it became known that the measure passed after Blaine had bought LR&FSR bonds and Blaine was caught in a lie about the timing of the legislation, gleeful Democrats went around campaigning for Cleveland with doggerel of their own:

Blaine, Blaine, James G. Blaine,
The continental liar from the state of Maine.

With Cleveland elected, railroad tycoons dreaded an attack on their stubborn retention of lands that they had never earned. Most of the grants contained clauses providing for reversions of the properties if the railroads failed to carry out their obligations. When Cleveland came into office, the area subject to forfeiture equaled the combined territories of New York, New Jersey, Pennsylvania, Delaware, Maryland, and Virginia. The tycoons also worried that the new president and his administration would take the side of farmers and others in the West who saw the railroads as greedy bullies in grabbing land and in the setting of rates for the shipment of goods.

Nothing evidenced the power of the railroads more than an action they took a year before Cleveland's election. On Sunday, November 18, 1883, the railroads of America imposed the "General Time Convention." Entirely for the convenience of railroads and with authorization from no governments, the agreement created four time zones: Eastern, Central, Mountain, and Pacific. Based on the 75th, 90th, 105th, and 120th meridians west of Greenwich, England, they were approximately on the longitudes of Philadelphia, Memphis, Denver, and Fresno.

"The sun is no longer boss of the people," declared an irate editorial writer for the Indianapolis *Sentinel* and on behalf of a nation on whom the system had been imperially imposed. The editor continued, "People—55,000,000 of them—must eat, sleep and work as well as travel by railroad time. It is a revolt, a rebellion. The sun will be requested to rise and set by railroad time. The planets must, in the future, make their circuits by such timetables as railroad magnates arrange. People will have to marry by railroad time, and die by railroad time. We presume the sun, moon, and stars will make an attempt to ignore the orders of the Railroad Convention, but they, too, will have to give in at last."

While Americans adopted railroad time with little difficulty or discomfort, it would take Congress considerably longer to get in step. (The Standard Time Act, which essentially ratified railroad time, would not become law until March 19, 1918.)

Meanwhile, coordination of time made Jim's life on the road easier. He could now rely on the clocks at his destination being in tune with those by which he had set his diamond-studded pocket watch at his point of departure. Men he dealt with could count on seeing him on a reliable schedule. They also knew that when he arrived he would be well informed regarding their needs. And they could look forward to enjoying the full Brady treatment even if they didn't buy every item he proposed from his catalog.

On April 17, 1885, Jim made certain he was back in New York to fill a front-row seat of the Casino Theater for the opening of *Polly, the Pet of the Regiment*. It marked the triumphal return to the American stage of Lillian Russell.

In private life she was now Mrs. Edward "Teddy" Solomon and the mother of a daughter, Dorothy. With the transgression of having skipped out on contracts forgiven by producers, the press, and the public, she found herself again the beneficiary of Diamond Jim Brady's attention in the form of lavish gifts. *Polly* was given fifty-five performances.

On March 16, 1886, Diamond Jim Brady was front and center at the Union Square to see Lillian as *Pepita, or the Girl with the Glass Eyes*. She is the daughter of the eccentric Professor Pongo, a maker of automatons. When a mechanical prima donna breaks down before the start of an opera, Pepita takes its place. In one scene in the production Lillian astonished everyone in the audience by playing a violin. The show's music was composed by her husband.

Pepita ran until May 22. Soon after it closed, Teddy surprised Lillian by announcing that he had to go back to England on business. Lillian learned the reason for the trip through the front pages of newspapers. They headlined that at the moment Teddy set foot on English soil he had been arrested on a charge of bigamy.

Unknown to Lillian when she wed him, Solomon already had a wife. He and Jane Isaac had been married for several years.

The sensation dominated the news for nine days. Shocked and humiliated, Lillian issued a statement in which she said she would seek annulment of her marriage, then went into seclusion, even refusing to see Jim. As far as he and her countless admirers among theatergoers were concerned, she needn't have withdrawn. To them and in fact she was "the wronged woman" and still "the American Beauty" whom they loved to see dividing her time between the theater and cafés where she made glorious entrances.

Needing money and wanting to work again, Lillian resumed her career by appearing on the West Coast in the role of Phyliss in *Iolanthe*. With public interest in the unpleasantness with Teddy Solomon fading, she returned to New York for a long run in *The Queen's Mate*. In one scene she appeared in a costume with tights.

When the show's producer, James Duff, told her that when he took the production out of town he expected her to wear the tights again, she refused. Infuriated, Duff took her to court, claiming breech of contract. The judge ruled for Lillian.

Her legal victory was saluted by an unknown newspaper poet:

> *There was a young lady named Russell*
> *Who wouldn't wear tights 'neath her bustle,*
> >   *Cause it gave her a cold*
> >   *Where it cannot be told*
> *And she and Jim Duff had a tussle.*
>
> *Then, Jimmy, the young man, he sued her,*
> *Rather tough for a person who'd wooed her.*
> >   *But you can't quite explain*
> >   *The regrets in the brain*
> *Of a man who finds out he don't suit her.*
>
> *The judge was a sort of Golightly,*
> *And treated the latter politely;*
> >   *Made a speech against tights*
> >   *And gave Russell her rights*
> *While Jimmy went home very quietly.*

Lillian immediately signed a contract with a new theater manager for one year at a salary of $20,000. Now she was working for Rudolph Aronson, the slim and dapper manager of the Casino Theater. On Broadway at Thirty-ninth Street opposite the new Metropolitan Opera House, the Casino was to New York of the 1880s what the Radio City Music Hall would be for two-thirds of the next century and into the twenty-first.

Forty years before the Rockettes enchanted New Yorkers with their high kicks, "Casino Girls" were doing so for audiences of dudes, stage-door Johnnies, and the city's foremost lechers who hoped to lure the leggy beauties around the corner to the bar and perhaps up to a room of the Normandic Hotel.

"All turned out well and good indeed—far better, in fact, than Aronson had dared hope," noted Parker Morrell in Lillian's biography. "Lillian soon became the reigning queen of comic opera, and the Casino her castle. Courtiers danced attendance on her, and the world of affairs and fashion sought her favor. New York took Lillian to its generous heart and she reveled in the adulation. Forgotten were the vicissitudes of London and the sad disenchantment following the discovery that she had been wedded but no wife. Now an all-pervading love for mankind in general and no man in particular became a delectable and welcome respite."

The one man she permitted in her life presented no danger of another disastrous romantic entanglement. As always, Jim Brady sought from her only unfettered companionship as they indulged in uncomplicated pleasures of being seen, admired, and envied in the lobster palaces.

Everyone recognized her and felt that they knew—and were entitled to know—everything about her. As to the fat man at her side who devoured gargantuan dinners, dressed like a dude, and flaunted a dazzling display of diamonds, few people knew how he'd gotten all that wealth.

❦

HAVING TURNED THIRTY in 1886, James Buchanan Brady had much for which to be grateful and about which he could congratulate himself. He'd been blessed with two benefactors in the persons of John Toucey and Charles Moore. They'd given him jobs, but his success in them was entirely his own doing. Money rolling in from commissions allowed him to provide financially for his mother and sister and to give himself a comfortable, well-ordered life. The namesake of a president and a loyal follower of Tammany Hall had proven himself to be a skillful salesman in a country with seemingly boundless space in which to build railroads to serve an expanding and prosperous economy.

As standardization of time had simplified rail travel, a decision by the federal government in 1886 affected Jim's work as purveyor of railroad equipment and passenger and freight cars. The government action dealt with discrepancies in the gauges of some of the railways with which he did business. Gauge is the distance between the rails. Since the invention of the railroad in England, the gauge had been the same as the space between the chariot wheels of the Roman Empire—four and one-half feet. British wagons and carts had followed the tradition since Caesar's army gave up trying to subdue Britannia. When iron rails were laid, the spacing was set to the same gauge. Because the first locomotives in the United States had been built in Britain, American rails had to be laid to fit their wheels. But as manufacture of trains became a domestic industry, other gauges were introduced. With so many railroads blooming in the 1860s, President Lincoln's administration proposed a width of five feet. The recommendation was ignored. By the time the country was forced into setting its clocks according to the dictate of railroads, tracks on which the trains ran were a welter of odd gauges. When standardization was decreed in 1886, the width remained the distance between the wheels of chariots and carts of Caesar's cohorts.

This decision did not require narrower tracks to be ripped up and replaced. It did require all new lines to run on standard-gauge tracks, however. While conforming the rail widths was important to railroad firms, the distance between the wheels on the left side of a passenger car and those on the right was immaterial to the growing number of people who took trains. Their chief concerns were having comfortable journeys in safety.

For all trains in 1886 the possibility of an accident and how smoothly passengers rode depended in large measure on undercarriages of cars, which held the wheels, and huge springs, which acted as shock absorbers. They were (and are) called trucks. If something went wrong with a truck on a freight or passenger car, the result was at the very least a derailment of that car, forcing the train to a halt, and at worst a crash. Hardly any passenger who boarded a train in 1886 could not recall ghastly accidents. Most were the result of one train running into another, but derailments caused by a truck parting ways with a rail were common. And an undercarriage of a car breaking off entirely was not unheard of.

This happened because all freight and passenger trucks were made of thick wooden beams and wrought iron bolted together with wrought-iron bolts. Should a bolt snap or a beam splinter, the apparatus could fly to pieces. But even if the trucks held together, the rides they provided were always bumpy. Because of the bulk of the combined wood and iron, the trucks also added a great deal of weight to the cars being pulled by the locomotives. The heavier the load, the more coal was needed to fuel them. In the increasingly feverish competitive atmosphere of railroading, anything that could reduce operating costs would put the line that introduced it at a distinct advantage.

Confident that he held the answer to the problems presented by the American trucks, a short, chubby English railroad man arrived in New York from Britain in the summer of 1888. His name was Sampson Fox. President and chief owner of a forging company in Leeds, England, he'd come to sell the firm's main product—a railway truck made from pressed steel that was strong but light and had been standard equipment on England's railways for years.

Ensconced in the Albemarle Hotel, Fox set out to gather orders from American railroads for the truck that bore his name. He quickly ran into resistance. A few nationalistic executives rebuffed him simply because he was English. Some believed that an all-steel truck would prove impractical. They thought it would be too light to carry American freight cars, which were heavier than those in England. There was also the problem of varying gauges. While the gauge had been standardized, many rail lines still operated with different ones. After two months on the road in an effort to sell steel trucks, Fox returned to New York without a sale.

Dismayed and dejected, he paid a call on the firm of Manning, Maxwell and Moore. In a conversation with the latter partner he was advised to have a chat with a man whom Moore said knew more about American railroads than anybody. While Manning, Maxwell and Moore were not interested in representing the Fox truck, said Charles Moore, the firm would have no objection if its best salesman took on the product as a sideline.

That evening at the Albemarle Hotel over an enormous dinner, Jim Brady listened to Fox extol the virtues of the pressed steel truck and grew increasingly enthusiastic. When Diamond Jim's turn to speak came, he opined that the only way to convert American railroads to the truck was by showing them its obvious advantages. This meant conducting demonstrations. To do that a quantity of the trucks would have to be manufactured in the United States and fitted to enough American cars to make up a train for test runs.

If Fox would supply the financing to build or acquire a forging plant to press the trucks, Jim proposed, he would arrange the demonstrations and then act as Fox's sales representative. For this service he would receive a one-third commission on the sale of every Fox truck in the United States and Canada.

Fox had done everything he could think of to sell his truck and failed. If the diamonds on the fingers and shirtfront of the man seated across the dining table were a measure of Mr. Brady's successes as a salesman, there was probably more to gain than to lose in accepting his proposal. If it worked, Brady deserved to profit handsomely.

Four weeks later a tall, soft-spoken, young Welshman named Clem Hackney was met at a pier by the most outrageous figure ever to extend him a hand in greeting. That the diamond-sporting fat American meant business was immediately demonstrated when Jim rushed Hackney through customs and to a meal of gargantuan proportions at the opulent Astor House hotel.

As the men had lunch Jim advised Hackney that he had rented a blacksmith shop in the city of Joliet, Illinois. It was ideal for making Fox trucks, close to several steel mills, and near the railroading center of Chicago. The shop had been equipped with all the necessary tools and equipment from the stocks of the firm of Manning, Maxwell and Moore (all subject to the usual Brady commission). After a good night's rest in an Astor House bed, Jim continued, Hackney would board a train for Joliet to take charge of the manufacture of the Fox trucks.

A month later Hackney had the plant running. Two weeks after that, working alone, he'd produced enough trucks to convert ten freight cars.

During those six weeks, Diamond Jim tried to generate interest in the Fox truck on the part of the superintendent of motive power for his former employer, the New York Central. (In one of those coincidences that speckle the pages of history, the superintendent's name was James Buchanan.) Undaunted by Buchanan's refusal to sign up the Central immediately, Jim threatened to make a deal with the line's chief competitor, the Pennsylvania Railroad.

Buchanan wavered.

Recognizing an opening, Diamond Jim said, "Be a sport. Take a chance. Run a test load. It won't cost you a cent. I'll pay all the costs of the test myself."

It was a daring move, for Jim had no authority from Fox to make such an offer. It worked. Buchanan agreed to test Fox trucks on a New York Central train of ten fully loaded freight cars on a run from New York to Albany and back. The test went flawlessly. Buchanan agreed to conversion of all Central freight cars as rapidly as Jim could deliver them, with passenger cars to follow.

With the New York Central on board, Jim had no difficulty in getting a contract for Fox trucks signed by George B. Roberts, president of the Pennsy. Roberts trumped his rival in New York by giving Diamond Jim an order for enough trucks to equip 250 new cars.

When word spread that the country's two biggest railroads were converting to the Fox truck, other companies quickly fell into line. Jim was writing orders by the hundreds per week at a commission to him of fifty dollars per truck. As he did so, he remained loyal to Charles Moore by continuing to represent his firm's line of equipment.

As Jim raked in commissions from both Manning, Maxwell and Moore and Fox's Leeds Company, he found himself venturing into new territory.

BECAUSE OF Diamond Jim Brady's prowess as salesman, Clem Hackney's blacksmith shop in Joliet was swamped with so many orders that more space was needed. A company with one small building expanded during the next two years to three huge steel and brick factories that covered two and a half acres. Hackney was now in charge of a large cadre of experts in pressed steel whom the Leeds Company transferred to Illinois. The most significant of these men to take up residence in America in the cause of the Fox truck was a young draftsman, F. H. Rapley. In very short order he designed and supervised the building and the installation of hydraulic and compressed-air equipment to turn out finished truck parts. This machinery and refinements in the design of the trucks lowered manufacturing costs from $120 per truck to a mere $15.

Another element in cost saving was the plant's proximity to steel mills, which sold their materials to the Fox truck operation at bargain prices. Unfortunately, at the time that Rapley was bringing down the per-item cost of Fox trucks, another industrialist who had come to America from the British Isles was busy manipulating the price of steel. His name was Andrew Carnegie and in furtherance of his aims he gobbled up the steel mills that had afforded Fox a bargain in raw steel. Faced with the loss of a price advantage, Jim Brady decided the only way out of the predicament was for Fox to acquire its own source of steel. Never a man to pose only a theoretical solution to a dilemma, he had a plan. It involved buying an almost abandoned plant of the Carbon Steel Company of Pittsburgh.

Adapting his talent for selling railroad equipment to pushing an idea, he sat at the bar of the Hoffman House Hotel in New York with a pair of Wall Streeters with an appetite for getting into the steel business. Armed with Hackney's calculations concerning the advantages of Fox's ownership of its source of steel, Jim persuaded Munson Raymond and Frank Robinson to buy the Pittsburgh plant. They and he would incorporate it in New Jersey with a capital stock issue of $1 million. Sales of shares would present no problem, Jim pointed out, once investors were informed that the entire output of the plant's open hearths would be bought to make Fox trucks.

Almost as soon as the Pittsburgh steel plant was running at full speed, Jim saw that its output exceeded the amount needed for the Joliet truck plant. Consequently, Sampson Fox was asked to provide funds to build a second factory for trucks in Pittsburgh. When the amount of steel flowing from open hearths still exceeded the need, Jim proposed that the surplus be sold to two makers of locomotive fireboxes and boilers. Deals he closed with the American Locomotive Works and the Babcock and Wilcox Company included, of course, a handsome commission for the man who brokered the pacts.

With breathtaking speed Diamond Jim had become in less than two years a powerful and important figure not only in railroads but in steel. As a result, he was infinitely wealthier than the second son of saloon keeper Dan Brady had ever dreamed possible.

"Darling Nell," Diamond Jim declared to the American Beauty during a pause between courses one evening at dinner, "I'm rich. It's time I had some real fun."

5

Ain't It Grand?

❦❧❦

WHEN NEW YORKERS flocked into City Hall Park or thronged saloons and restaurants on the night of December 31, 1889, to bid farewell to the 1880s, no one forecast that the dawning decade would be known as the Gay Nineties. Such categorizations are made reflectively. Few, if any, of the New Year's Eve participants could have paused in their celebrations to note that the great railroad expansion era was at its end, a virgin continent with an incalculable wealth of natural resources was being wastefully exploited, and swaggering, blustering men with new fortunes were determined to flaunt suddenly gilded lives.

None of those men was more eager to do so than Jim Brady. On January 1, 1890, he had almost $100,000 in three banks. Other men had millions, but thanks to the commissions from the Fox Solid Pressed Steel Company, the value of his shares in the Carbon Steel Company, and his continuing relationship with Manning, Maxwell and Moore, Jim could count on his coffers being swelled further. This liquidity was sweetened by the unlimited expense accounts that enabled him to pursue whatever whim struck his fancy in fostering his business interests and promoting himself.

The second son of a waterfront saloon keeper with ambition, skill, charm, and "luck of the Irish" had made a great deal of money. More important, he'd invented a character known as Diamond Jim. He had done so because it was good business. The diamonds opened doors to offices of men with power to purchase his goods. Now he breezed through those portals on the strength of his name alone. Being Diamond Jim Brady provided an excellent living. Whatever he wanted to do, he did. Whatever he wanted to buy was bought.

If flash mattered, he could outglitter everyone. In *looking* rich, no one would eclipse him. Prince Albert coats and beautiful black cutaways donned during working hours were made of the finest bolts of cloth that Jules Weiss could find. Silk toppers were imported from London. New York's most famous haberdasher, Mark Herald, tailored eighteen-and-a-half-inch-neck silk shirts and trousers with ever-expanding waist measurements by the dozen. Underwear was Paris made. For such a huge figure of a man of average height, shiny, buttoned shoes crafted by the best boot makers on Canal Street were surprisingly diminutive: eight and a half.

Bedecked with his hallmark diamonds, Jim set out on a blustery February 1890 evening for a front-row seat in Rudolph Aronson's Casino. The show was a revival of an old French operetta, *The Grand Duchess,* by Henri Meilhac and Ludovic Halevy, with music by Offenbach. Starring in the title role was Lillian Russell.

Keenly aware that the audience had not bought tickets for a time-worn and tawdry story of a duchess who fell in love with a lowly army recruit and lost him because he had pledged his heart to a peasant girl, Aronson gave Lillian a splendid grand entrance. Swathed in ermine, she entered in a sleigh in a blinding paper snowstorm.

The effect was marvelous, but the American Beauty upstaged it.

"Everybody looked forward to something astonishing in the way of scenic effects," said the reviewer from the *Dramatic Mirror,* "but very few persons, if any, expected Lillian Russell to burst forth as a right down regular royal queen of the operatic stage. The fair Lillian has evidently been studying the noble art of song with energetic determination to outdo herself."

The gossipy paper *Town Topics* bubbled with praise. "If Lillian Russell does not cease to take on new phases of beauty every month or so," it exclaimed, "there will be no reason why the flowers of spring should bloom, for the resplendent lady will crowd the neighborhood with all the tint and tenderness that can be safely withstood."

Lillian's triumph as the Grand Duchess made more than theatrical history. Because her performance coincided with perfection of the long-distance telephone, she retired to her dressing room on May 8 after the first act to sing into Alexander Graham Bell's device. On the receiving end in Washington, D.C., was a group of distinguished Americans, including former President Grover Cleveland. (Defeated for reelection by Republican Benjamin Harrison, who had lost the popular vote but won in the Electoral College in 1888, Cleveland would return to the presidency in 1893, making him the country's only chief executive to serve two nonconsecutive terms.) In reporting Lillian's long-distance performance, the *New York World* noted that her voice would soon be preserved for posterity by another recent invention. Thomas A. Edison, the paper noted, "is to visit Miss Russell at her flat to bottle up her voice in a phonograph. This has been a pet idea of Prof. Edison's for a long time. He will send her a piece of her preserved voice in the shape of a roll of foil."

An observer of Lillian as the Grand Duchess when she took the show on the road to New Haven was the future author of one of the longest-running Broadway plays and a hit movie with William Powell, *Life With Father*. In a future article for the *Saturday Evening Post,* Clarence Day described seeing *The Grand Duchess* with friends. Because they did not have the price of tickets, they'd wangled themselves into the theater and on stage as extras. They were to be French and Russian soldiers (*muzhiks*). Day recalled, "There was nothing wraithlike about Lillian Russell; she was a voluptuous beauty, and there was plenty of her to see. We liked that. Our tastes were not thin, or ethereal. We liked flesh in the Nineties. It didn't have to [be] bare, and it wasn't, but it had to be there. We muzhiks didn't see very much of her, but what we did see was ravishing. Maybe her waist wasn't so small as some of the others, but it looked ever smaller, her hips were so gorgeous and stately and her broad, white bosom so ample. She threw back her golden head and caroled coquettishly when the hero made love to her, she caroled severely at the villain, and she danced till the stage shook."

Whether the American Beauty risked adding to her figure following her triumph as the Grand Duchess at the Casino by going to a restaurant with Diamond Jim isn't known. The term for such after-theater meals of fowl and wine was bird and bottle supper. With shows ending between eleven and eleven-thirty, many members of their audiences made their way to restaurants such as Sherry's and Delmonico's or to those in nearby Broadway hotels. Actors, actresses, singers, dancers, and girls from the choruses arrived around midnight. When a headliner appeared, the orchestra broke out into whichever song was the star's in the show.

"It was a sight for the gods to watch the majestic progress down the room," recalled one observer. "The famous beauties, whose pictures were in the lobbies and whose names were in the feature stories in papers, knew just the right moment for an entrance. As a headliner appeared at the door with her escort, she was always so surprised and, finally, with every eye upon her, she walked slowly to a reserved table."

Such admiring gazes and hushed gasps never failed to accompany the grand entrance of Lillian Russell. Nobody basked in them more than the fat man in whose diamond-studded hand hers so frequently rested. The American Beauty was a vision of golden tresses, enchanting smile, hourglass figure, and stately carriage as the headwaiter led them to their table. Only then did Lillian slowly remove long white gloves and acknowledge acquaintances with a slight bow of head or a curtsy of eyelids.

Should Nell not be available for a midnight repast, Jim had no problem finding another partner, whether she was another star or a beauty from the chorus who'd peered over footlights at the fat man in the front row who sparkled with diamonds. He had become so familiar a figure in theaters that at some time during a performance someone on stage might give him a wave, wink at him, blow him a kiss, or shout "Hello, Jim."

By combining showy wealth gleaned from railroads with an engaging personality that was both natural and cultivated, James Buchanan Brady had created the celebrity called Diamond Jim Brady.

With salesmanship and luck he had become the personification of the essence of a city that more than ever separated Tony Pastor's Upper Ten Thousand from the Lower.

As Lillian Russell was thrilling Diamond Jim and other first nighters who flocked to the Casino to see her, a newspaperman who had taught himself how to use a camera was publishing a book of his photographs titled *How the Other Half Lives*. Caught in the glare of Jacob Riis's flash gun and recorded in black-and-white were stark images of living and working conditions of the city's poor. They had come to New York looking for better lives and now were hopelessly confined to squalid tenements. In the thirty-four years since Jim Brady's birth nearly 8 million people had passed through New York State's immigration station at Ellis Island. Although Jacob Riis termed them "the other half," they amounted to more than 50 percent of the city's population. They lived in overcrowded, unhealthy, crime-plagued, and gang-dominated sections known as Hell's Kitchen, the Five Points, and the Gas House District, where Clubber Williams had gained such esteem as a graft collector that his superiors at police headquarters rewarded him with better pickings of the

Tenderloin. Enriching himself from classy saloons, gambling dens, Broadway opening nights, and bird and bottle suppers, his figure became almost as familiar among the Upper Ten Thousand as the American Beauty's hourglass shape and Diamond Jim Brady's belly as they adorned plush banquettes of restaurants and dining salons of opulent hotels.

One such hostelry opened in 1890. Just six blocks north of the St. James, the Imperial Hotel at Broadway and Thirty-ninth Street was opposite the Metropolitan Opera House. Patrons entered a lobby with appointments rivaling the most extravagant settings in the Met's repertoire. Even more lush was the vast, green marble–finished dining salon called the Palm Room. There was so much gold leaf adornment throughout the hotel that a visiting Englishman said he feared that if he left boots in the hallway to be polished, "I'd find them gilded in the morning."

The opening of the Imperial marked the start of a decade of hotel building. In 1891 it was the Holland House on Fifth Avenue at the unheard-of cost of $1.2 million. Never to be outdone, William Waldorf Astor caught the hotel fever and began planning what he promised to be New York's most luxurious. At Fifth Avenue and Thirty-fourth Street and named for its owner, the Waldorf-Astoria would welcome its first guest in 1896. Not until the 1920s and 1930s would the island of Manhattan again witness such a splurge of hotel construction, including the erection of a new Waldorf-Astoria on Park Avenue in 1931 so the original hotel could be demolished to clear space for the Empire State Building.

While the new hotels of the 1890s provided the gourmand Diamond Jim additional places to eat, they provided James Buchanan Brady the salesman a new and more convenient means of courting customers for railroad equipment. Instead of going on the road to call on buyers, he was able to propose that clients combine business with pleasure by coming to New York. Should the railway executive take him up on the suggestion, Jim assured him, the business could be quickly completed and the cost of entertainment would be on him. Arrangements for the latter, he was quick to point out, would include a Broadway show with plenty of beautiful girls, followed by a bird and bottle supper at one of the hotels, or perhaps a more intimate repast with one or more of the girls in a palatial suite.

First, however, they'd have a fine dinner.

FOR OPULENCE in restaurants in 1890 Jim had two favorites, Sherry's and Delmonico's.

The proprietor of the former, Louis Sherry, although born in St. Albans, Vermont, built his reputation as restauranteur on being of French descent. He laid down an inflexible rule for his employees: "Never disappoint a customer." He'd learned the fine art of catering to the rich and famous in his teens in the dining room of the Hotel Brunswick and as maître d' at an exclusive hotel in Long Branch, New Jersey. Opening his own restaurant and confectionery shop at 662 Sixth Avenue in 1881, he soon impressed the hostesses of high society by arranging dinners and parties. When millionaire Robert Goelet vacated his mansion at Broadway and Thirty-seventh Street in 1890 for plusher digs farther uptown on Fifth Avenue, Sherry snapped up the building and converted it to large and small ballrooms, small restaurant, and confectionery shop. The new location afforded him a breakthrough when he arranged an affair celebrating the opening of the new opera house just across Broadway. This success was surpassed when he catered a gala for the Badminton Assembly held at the mansion of social style-setter Paran Stevens.

More than a decade before Louis Sherry went into the business of pampering the hungry rich, Lorenzo Delmonico had followed the movement uptown of his wealthy clients by shifting his restaurant from Fourteenth Street to Broadway and Twenty-sixth. His new neighbors were the opulent Brunswick and Fifth

Avenue hotels. The café, main dining room, and private salons were the biggest and most elaborate of the neighborhood. However, being upscale did not mean that the place could not from time to time take on the brawling aspects of a concert saloon. The most famous outburst involved Wall Street manipulator Edward "Ned" Stokes calling newspaper publisher James Gordon Bennett into the grand entry hall to settle a dispute with fists. Ned broke Bennett's nose. Nor did Delmonico's sedate atmosphere keep Oscar Wilde from noisily voicing a complaint about the steep price of his meal.

Whether at Delmonico's or Sherry's, each dinner served to Diamond Jim Brady was an occasion for the most careful consideration, lest he decide to eat elsewhere. The evening started with oysters. These were followed by soup. Next, the hors d'oeuvres: timbales, palmettes, mousselines, croustades, bouchées, and the like. A fish course was followed by the entrée. This might consist of terrapin, more oysters, crabs, lobsters, shrimp, or frog's legs. Then the meat course—roast beef, saddle of lamb, veal, mutton, venison, or fowl—accompanied by one or two vegetables. After a palate-cleansing sorbet, the game course was served. Final stages of a fourteen-course meal consisted of aspics, sweet dishes (hot or cold jellies, creams, blanc manges, or charlottes) and an array of fruits (fresh, preserved, and dried), bon bons, ice cream, cakes, and assorted pies with Turkish or French coffees. Throughout the meal his guests drank wines and champagne while he quaffed orange juice.

Jim customarily ordered a box of chocolates at the table and one to carry with him to the theater. Munching peppermint creams in his front-row center seat, he applauded the star actresses of Broadway: Ada Rehan, Maude Adams, Blanche Bates, Maxine Elliott, Mary Mannering, Rose Coughlan, and Fay Templeton. Headline actors were John Drew, Maurice and Lionel Barrymore, Nat Goodwin, Wilton Lackaye, De Wolf Hopper, and Richard Mansfield.

Tickets to see these performers became a vital part of Jim's treatment of the buyers who'd come across the country to meet with him. In the years since Cornelius Vanderbilt's intention to build a terminal on Forty-second Street was greeted with skepticism and even ridicule, the Commodore's vision of his Grand Central terminal becoming the hub of the city had been largely realized.

The main artery for this rapid uptown expansion was Broadway. Originally a path laid down by Indians, it began at the tip of Manhattan and ran its length for eighteen miles. For some blocks from Bowling Green to Astor Place, the roadway of the Dutch and the English who took over from them was laid straight. As the city expanded, the route veered at an angle to the northwest corner of the island. Walt Whitman wrote of it:

Thy windows rich, and huge hotels—thy sidewalks wide;
Thou of the endless, sliding, mincing, shuffling feet!
Thou, like the multi-colored world itself—like infinite,
    teeming, mocking life!
Thou visor'd, vast, and unspeakable show and lesson!

By 1892 Broadway was the heart of Diamond Jim's personal and professional lives, which were, in fact, the same. In the words of biographer Parker Morrell, "By some strange alchemy not known to other men he mixed the two until his life became a homogeneous pattern possessing some of the characteristics of each, and all of the characteristics of neither."

As Lillian Russell ruled the musical stages of Broadway, Jim made himself a star of commerce in restaurants and hotel dining rooms, at bird and bottle suppers, in the Tenderloin's gambling houses, and at after-midnight parties in private function rooms and suites. He played the role of genial host to the hilt. He did so believing that his grateful guests would be more apt to buy his wares at the end of an evening on the town than in his office at 26 Cortlandt Street.

At some point during a fourteen-course dinner, while enjoying the front-row spectacle of beauteous chorus girls in the latest show, while sipping champagne with one or more of them at bird and bottle suppers, or while getting even closer to them at a party that lasted till three in the morning, Jim could be counted on to turn to whomever he was courting for a lucrative contract affording him a one-third commission and exclaim, "Ain't it grand?"

ICING ON JIM'S CAKE in November 1892 was Grover Cleveland's reelection after a four-year hiatus from the White House. Having settled in New York during the term of Republican President Benjamin Harrison, the nation's twenty-second chief executive might have presented a challenge to Diamond Jim's title as the city's most famous fat man-about-town. However, the former president who took up residence with the beautiful young woman he'd married in the East Room of the Executive Mansion proved to be a homebody. Except for the occasional political dinner, between leaving office in 1889 and the November 1892 election Cleveland had ventured from his home only to go to the Broad Street law firm of Bangs, Stetson, Tracy and MacVeagh where he was "of counsel." Socializing became even more limited when Frances Cleveland gave birth to a daughter, "Baby" Ruth, after whom a savvy New York candy manufacturer named a chocolate-covered nut bar.

The major issue of Cleveland's campaign to replace the man who had defeated him in 1888 was repeal of the Sherman Silver Purchase Act. It required the government to purchase 4.5 million ounces of silver a month and issue notes that could be redeemed in gold. Cleveland saw this "dangerous and reckless experiment of free, unlimited, and independent silver coinage" as an invitation to unscrupulous businessmen to pillage the government's gold reserves. Indeed, by the end of 1892 they were depleted by more than $50 million.

In the interregnum between Cleveland's election in November 1892 and his inauguration as twenty-fourth president of the United States, his advisors urged that immediately after being sworn in he call a special session of Congress to deal with the gold drain by repealing the Sherman Act. European stock markets were in disarray and governments all over the world were looking for gold to bolster their solvency. Cleveland's men also urged action because violent fluctuations in the price of securities evidenced increasing uneasiness over business conditions. For months prices of staples such as cotton, corn, and iron had been declining.

Whether the national economy would be gold-based or "bimetallic" was of little concern to a man whose commissions awarded by customers for the grand time he'd showed them on the town in New York were quickly converted to diamonds. As long as the railroads were thriving, Diamond Jim Brady would go on selling them equipment and hoarding gems.

However, ten days before Cleveland was to be inaugurated, Diamond Jim was shocked to read in his morning paper that the Reading Railroad, to which he had sold $5 million worth of rolling stock a few years earlier, had announced debts of more than $125 million and declared bankruptcy. Much of the line's woes stemmed from fierce competition and uncertainties regarding labor.

Since the strikes of 1877, walkouts by employees had been few and of little importance. But groups of workers called "Brotherhoods" had been gaining strength under fiery leadership of union organizers such as Eugene Victor Debs. An ex-fireman on the Terre Haute & Indianapolis line, he was grand secretary of the Brotherhood of Locomotive Firemen. Now he was agitating among other brotherhoods to unite nationwide as the American Railway Union.

Jim's concerns about what consolidation of the country's rail unions might mean were sharpened on July 6, 1892, with news reports of a bloody clash at Andrew Carnegie's steel works in

Homestead, a small town on the Monongahela River near Pittsburgh. In an effort to break a strike, the steel mill had been
closed since July 1 by Andrew Carnegie's manager, Henry Clay
Frick. To protect the factory 270 heavily armed guards from the
Pinkerton Detective Agency had been sent to the plant. They'd
been met by 5,000 strikers. When the battle was over, ten men
were dead, more than sixty were wounded, and the defeated
Pinkertons were allowed to leave.

When Jim Brady was hired as a baggage smasher at Grand
Central, Commodore Vanderbilt and other owners of railroads
had had no reason to fear trouble from their workers. They
ruled a growing industry that provided enormous profits from
the actual running of the lines and even more from the practice
of manipulating stocks. Any slight negative effects on income
because of fluctuations in the national economy, such as the
Panic of 1873, could be overcome by questionable operating
practices, not replacing outworn equipment or maintaining tracks
and bridges, and cutting wages. If there was labor trouble, as in
the 1877 strike, and the Reading's problems notwithstanding,
Jim believed, railroads would survive and thrive because the
country needed them.

SINCE THE INTRODUCTION of trains, railroad companies had
sought to overcome trepidation among potential customers with
advertising promising convenient, safe, and comfortable transportation both for business and pleasure. Typical of these en-
ticements in October 1887 was a poster promoting the Boston
& Albany line. It depicted "four remarkably handsome drawing-
room cars" furnished with chairs and sofas of richly carved
mahogany, with metal work of statuary bronze, "many lit by
electricity."

When George Pullman created dining cars and sleepers, the
idea of long-distance train travel was promoted as affording all
the comforts of a grand hotel. Needs and wants of Pullman

passengers were attended by a staff of porters who were trained and employed not by railroad companies but by the Pullman Palace Car Company itself. The center of the company's far-flung empire was a company town near Chicago named for its owner and absolute ruler.

Americans with shorter distances to travel were sold on rail-roads on the basis of the time that would be saved. Those with leisure were invited to take trains to resorts at the seaside and in the mountains. Couples contemplating marriage were informed by the New York Central that there was no better place to honeymoon than Niagara Falls, reachable in comfort via its trains.

A westward-looking nation found enticing advertisements extolling the romance and adventure of cities and towns of the prairie, the Rocky Mountains, and California, most of which had been built by railroad companies. Thanks to government land grants and the enterprise of railway men, hardly any point in the United States was beyond the reach of trains.

Of course, there were risks. Now and then a train wrecked, and in the peculiar ways of American folklore, many of these calamities took on sentimental aspects. Nothing plucked the heart strings like a good wreck. When an excursion train of the Toledo, Peoria & Western line crashed in 1877 near the Illinois town of Chatsworth, killing eighty-two riders and the crew, an unknown minstrel had penned this:

> *From Peoria, town and hamlet,*
> *   There came a joyous throng*
> *To view the great Niagara;*
> *   In joy they sped along,*
> *The maiden and her lover,*
> *   The husband and the wife,*
> *The merry, prattling children,*
> *   So full of joyous life.*
> *But oh! how much of sorrow,*
> *   And oh! how much of pain*

Awaited those who journeyed
  On that fated railroad train.

As railroad companies hastened to point out that the frequency of mishaps had been greatly reduced through improvements in technology, another facet of rail travel that worried some would-be travelers came to their attention through newspaper stories and tales contained in dime-novel "westerns" about train robbers.

The first train robbery had taken place on October 6, 1866. Two masked men stuck up a train of the Ohio & Mississippi near Seymour, Indiana, and forced a guard in a baggage car to open a safe containing $13,000. Arrested but never tried were brothers John and Simeon Reno and one Frank Sparks. Almost a year later to the day, a train on the same line was robbed by Walker Hammond and Michael Collins. It was believed but not proven that they were part of "the Reno gang" that proceeded to rob other trains in Indiana until one night in November 1868 when vigilantes raided the jail at New Albany and strung up three Renos and an ally named Anderson. Five years later another pair of train-robbing brothers eclipsed the Renos by riding from Missouri to Adair, Iowa, and into history and legend. Frank and Jesse James aligned themselves with Coleman Younger on July 21, 1873, to pillage a train of the Chicago, Rock Island & Pacific. Their reign as America's most daring and admired (at least by dime-novel writers and readers) continued until April 3, 1882, when Bob Ford, "the immortal little coward" in the words of a popular song, drew a pistol while Jesse was hanging a picture in his parlor and shot him in the back.

Railroads of the "Wild and Woolly West" assured travelers that their chances of finding themselves looking down the barrel of a Colt six-gun in the hand of a young man with a bandanna hiding his face were almost nil. They also hastened to point out to still-wary potential customers that no such trepidation could be found in the ranks of the country's celebrities. The stars of the vaudeville stage routinely traveled by train. They called it taking their acts "on the road."

Since Abraham Lincoln went from Springfield, Illinois, to Washington, D.C., to be sworn in as president in 1861, the railroads boasted, every occupant of the White House had arrived in the capital by train for his inauguration.

So reliable and rapid were trains that in 1869 the federal government had established the Railway Mail Service to devise and put into effect an overall and systematic practice for handling the mail. Four years later the Post Office entered into a contract with the New York Central to provide trains to carry only mail. Diamond Jim's former employer built special mail cars and arranged schedules to clear the tracks for "Fast Mail" trains all the way to Chicago.

Fascination with the speeds of trains found its way onto the Broadway stage in the form of three plays in 1892, *A Mile a Minute, The Limited Mail,* and *The Midnight Special.*

On April 2 of that year newspaper reporters rushed to a railroad station in Baltimore to meet a politician who was passing through the city. Having breakfast in a Pullman dining car was Grover Cleveland. He was on his way back to New York City from a hunting trip to a friend's plantation in Louisiana. The journalists wanted Cleveland's views on an attempt by a rival in New York to convene a "snap" convention to block a movement to nominate Cleveland for president. The *New York World* reported that Cleveland seemed unperturbed and "the picture of innocent merriment" and "utmost good humor."

The interview is notable not for its political content but because it was the first time a press conference by a politician was held on a train. ("Whistle-stop campaigning" would not be introduced as a staple of presidential politics until Theodore Roosevelt barnstormed the country as William McKinley's running mate in 1896.)

Cleveland turned another page in history on May 1, 1893. He placed a plump finger on a golden button in the White House and sent an electrical signal to formally open a world's fair marking the 400th anniversary of Christopher Columbus's "discovery of America." Called the Columbian Exposition, the extravaganza sprawled along the shore of Lake Michigan in the city of Chicago. It offered the greatest electrical display in the world. A million bulbs lit up great white palaces devoted to shining achievements of American commerce.

Having made a fortune and a name for himself in a country that had reached a pinnacle of success on steel rails, James Buchanan Brady saw in the fair a once-in-a-lifetime opportunity to show a wider audience than the patrons of New York's theaters and lobster palaces the marvel known as Diamond Jim. He was also motivated by the fact that the star attraction for sixteen weeks on the fair's entertainment midway was to be Lillian Russell.

Anticipating cutting a swath with her through the exposition grounds and the restaurants and hotel dining rooms of a city that more than any in the world depended on railroads, Jim made plans to go to Chicago in June.

Unfortunately, his departure was delayed by a nasty surprise on Wall Street.

One of the stars of American industries being saluted at the Columbian Exposition was the National Cordage Company. At the beginning of 1893 it had declared a stock dividend of 100 percent. As a result, it was one of the speculative favorites of Wall Street, selling at the end of April at 147. But on May 4 the price wavered and by the end of the day had crashed. In very short order other stocks sank. As panic spread, the stock market spun downward. At the end of June it lay in ruins.

Across the country and particularly in the Midwest and West, individuals, manufacturers, and farmers who were already suspicious of banks withdrew $20 million from the New York financial institutions. Weaker banks went under. Gold flowed out of the country. Mines closed. Factories either shut down or went in receivership. Hundreds of thousands of men lost their jobs.

As the economic collapse that went into history books as the Panic of 1893 spread, Jim found executives of the nation's railroads painfully mindful of the bankruptcy of the Reading line and fearing the same fate. They had neither the money nor the desire to buy new equipment. After searching in vain for orders but with his own fortune unscathed by the tumult, he decided to ride out a storm that he expected President Cleveland and Congress to tame with the repeal of the Sherman Silver Purchase Act. His faith in that outcome was bolstered on June 30 when Cleveland announced that Congress would be summoned into session in August for that purpose.

With confidence in Cleveland and with spare time on his hands and plenty of cash, Diamond Jim booked a cabin of a Pullman Palace Car of the New York Central's daily *Lake Shore Limited,* packed his bags for a month's vacation, and headed for the world's fair.

6

The Earth for Fifty Cents

❧❦❧

A FTER A TWENTY-FOUR-HOUR TRIP, Diamond Jim stepped from the train at Chicago's Van Buren Street Depot and went by carriage to a State Street hotel most frequented by businessmen, the Palmer House. He was surprised that its lobby was bustling. Despite newspaper headlines and editorials screaming of financial panic and economic depression, people were pouring in from every state and territory, Mexico, Canada, and Europe and finding much to admire in the host city. Having risen from the ashes of the great fire of October 1871 that destroyed more than 17,000 wooden structures, Chicago was a city of brick and stone and the hub of a continent-linking system of railroads. Second only to New York in volume of trade and commerce, it had produced goods in 1892 worth more than half a billion dollars, including steel and iron, farm equipment, textiles, leather, Pullman Palace cars, and beer. The Union Stockyards' slaughterhouses and meatpackers accounted for sales of more than $150 million, making Chicago the nation's chief supplier of meats.

Hand in hand with industrial growth went a commitment by Chicagoans to culture, which included the founding of the American Conservatory of Music (1883), the Art Institute (1887), the John Crerar Library (1889), and the Chicago Symphony Orchestra (1891). Convinced that Chicago exemplified the spirit of the nation that resulted from Columbus's opening of the New World, the city fathers had carried on a vigorous campaign to have it selected as the site for the exposition marking the explorer's achievement.

A proposal for such a celebration had been made in 1880, but it had taken Congress nine years to authorize it and invite cities to submit ideas. Contenders were New York, Washington, D.C., St. Louis, and Chicago, whose businessmen pledged $500,000 to the fair, with a promise to double the amount if Chicago were chosen. Having succeeded and selected a site on the lakeshore, the city immediately engaged architects, artists, engineers, sculptors, painters, and landscapers to plan and build "the City Beautiful" on land encompassing two parks. Jackson Park covered 533 acres and had two miles of lake frontage. Nearby Washington Park was 371 acres. They were connected by a small strip of land. The main exhibition halls of the exposition were to be built on the parkland. Smaller buildings, concessions, and places of entertainment were to be on a linking land bridge called the Midway Plaisance.

Plans called for two hundred buildings, fourteen of which were exhibition halls. When a decision was made to paint them white, "City Beautiful" was changed to "The White City." Underlying themes of the Roman Imperial and Greek-style buildings were scale, harmony, and ensemble. Because most of the architects had been trained at the École des Beaux Arts in Paris, the style was called *Beaux Arts*. Correspondent Richard Harding Davis wrote in *Harper's* magazine that the White City "rose like a Venus from the waters of Lake Michigan." He called it "the greatest event in the history of the country since the Civil War."

The Exposition could be reached on foot and entered by way of the Midway Plaisance gates, by a scenic steamboat that docked at the Lake Michigan pier, or by special trains. After paying admission to "see the earth for fifty cents," visitors were greeted by an overwhelming cacophony of voices, shuffling feet, and music by the Columbian Orchestra and Chorus. Before them sprawled exhibitions of the forty-three states, twenty-three countries, and fourteen "great" buildings housing the main displays. The displays ranged from industrial marvels of Machinery Hall (the largest building in the world with acres of windows) to the Palace of Fine Arts (eight thousand exhibits, including works by John Singer Sargent, Winslow Homer, Thomas Eakins, Renoir, and Pissarro); the Fisheries Building (aquaria); U.S. Government Building (carrier pigeons and a redwood tree along with tributes to George Washington); and the Agriculture Building (farming equipment, a map of the U.S. made of pickles, two Liberty Bells of oranges and wheat, oats and rye, a Schlitz Brewery booth, and from Canada a "Monster Cheese" that weighed ten tons). On display in The Woman's Building was a manuscript of *Jane Eyre* in Emily Brontë's own hand, murals by Mary Cassatt, costumes from around the world, and a copy of the 1879 law allowing women to plead cases before the U.S. Supreme Court.

Exhibits of the states of the Union included a reproduction of John Hancock's house (the Massachusetts pavilion); the actual Liberty Bell from Pennsylvania; a 127-year-old palm and a fountain of California red wine beside a medieval knight figure made of prunes; and a Creole restaurant from Louisiana.

In the Transportation Building stood "John Bull," America's first locomotive; models of English warships; a representation of an ocean liner; bicycles; and a chariot from the Etruscan Museum in Florence, Italy.

So impressed was a reporter from *Harper's* with these displays that he wrote, "Even people of small means should not recoil from the expense of a journey which in these hard times they may consider an extravagance, and they should not fail to bestow upon their children the boon of enlightenment and ennobling impressions which this grand spectacle conveys, and which in all likelihood this will be the only opportunity in their lives to receive and enjoy."

But it was not the educational, uplifting, and inspiring or extravagant demonstrations of electric lighting that sparked the most excitement. The stars of the show were found along the Midway Plaisance. In its eighty acres was the first entertainment area ever offered by a world's fair. It provided "fakes" (side-shows), Hagenback's Menagerie, a tethered balloon in whose basket one could ascend to 1,500 feet, a reproduction of Blarney Castle complete with a stone to kiss, a German village, cider from a genuine French cider press, and "a street in Cairo" that offered a "world's congress of beauties." They included a veil-shedding "hootchy-kootchy" dancer known as Little Egypt. The president of the Society for the Suppression of Vice denounced both her and the midway's "vile dens and revolting performances" as the "worst violations of decency and virtue ever heard of." When asked to comment on "these shocking displays" of undressed women, Mark Twain opined, "Most men would rather see their nakedness than General Ulysses S. Grant in full-dress uniform."

A mechanical attraction even more startling than Little Egypt's hips was the work of a man named George Ferris. Towering 250 feet, the revolving round web of steel had thirty-six suspended gondolas that held sixty people each. Half a dollar bought two go-rounds. No one had ever seen anything like the "Ferris wheel."

"The Midway Plaisance," wrote one fair visitor, "seems to be a magnet of deepest and most lasting significance. It is the one quarter most talked about and investigated in the whole Exposition. There is the spice of adventure, something rakish and modestly questionable about this legalized harlequinade of other people's habits."

Among the attractions brought to the fair from overseas were an Algerian and Tunisian village, a panorama of the Swiss

Alps, a Chinese Theater, East India Bazaar, a model of the Eiffel Tower, South Seas Islanders, a bubbling and smoking representation of Hawaii's Kilauea volcano, a Brazilian Concert Hall, a model of St. Peter's Basilica, Venice-Murano glassblowing, an electric scenic theater showing landscapes under changing-colored lights simulating changing light as the day passed, and in the Java Lunch Room, pure Java coffee.

"One could spend many days in the Plaisance, always entertainingly, whether profitably or unprofitably," wrote another fair-goer, "but whether one visited the Samoan or Dahomeyan in his hut, the Bedouin and the Lap in their camps, the delicate Javanese in his bamboo cottage, or the American Indian in his tepee, one must be aware that the citizens of the Plaisance are not there for their health, but for the money there is in it."

The midway was so successful financially that without it the Exposition would have been a money loser. As to the lasting significance of the midway, every world's fair thereafter had to have an entertainment area, and "midway" went into the dictionary with that definition.

Other introductions at the 1893 Chicago World's Fair were: the U.S. Post Office's first commemorative stamp set and the picture postcard, the U.S. Mint's first commemorative coins (quarter, half-dollar, and dollar); Gray's Teleautograph, which reproduced handwriting at a distance (a forerunner of the fax machine); Thomas Edison's Kinetograph (precursor of the movie projector); a movable sidewalk carrying passengers at three to six miles an hour; first elevated electric railway; Cream of Wheat; Shredded Wheat; Aunt Jemima pancake syrup; Cracker Jack; Juicy Fruit chewing gum; Pabst Beer; carbonated soda; and the hamburger.

Despite the economic downturn, Americans flocked to see and enjoy these wonders. In an illustrated article for *Harper's* the artist Frederic Remington noted, "There is the muffled beating of tomtoms, the shuffling of many feet, the popcorn and lemonade, and thousands of dull, dusty, frowzy folks who stare and gape. The bulk of the throng have 'cornfield' written all over them."

As exciting as were the White City exhibits and as alluring as were the fakes and Little Egypt's writhing, the unquestionable main attraction of the Midway Plaisance for Diamond Jim was a woman who was born amid Iowa cornfields and raised in Chicago and had returned to star in the show at the Midway's Columbian Theater.

While Jim chose the opulent comforts of the Palmer House for his Chicago base, Lillian Russell had rented the John B. Jeffreys mansion on a fashionable South Side street. At thirty-two, neither married nor in love, she had arrived in the Exposition City in triumph and style and justifying her reputation as the American Beauty. To convey her to the theater and elsewhere in the city she had her own horses and carriage brought out from New York. Delighted to learn that her adoring and generous friend Jim Brady was ensconced in the luxuries of the Palmer House, she gladly joined him before and after her performances in exploring the gustatorial delights of both fair and city.

The food at the Exposition ranged from the cooked chopped beef served on a bun called a hamburger to the clam chowder, Boston baked beans, and pumpkin pie of the New England Clam Bake restaurant and the first corn crop served steaming hot and tender and dripping with melted butter churned that day on nearby farms. Lillian's favorite was luscious Country Gentleman corn whose tiny, snow-white kernels were sliced from the cob and sautéed in butter and heavy Jersey cream. If it was not available, she was happy to consume corn on the cob, in soup, or as fritters, puddings, and muffins.

Exotic food was available in abundance on the fairgrounds. The Brazilian Concert Hall had a restaurant, as did the Hungarian Orpheum, the Moorish Palace, the Persian Theater, and the Street in Cairo. Away from the Exposition, Jim and Lillian could dine in restaurants as fine as those in New York. The choices ranged from the very expensive dining room of the Richelieu Hotel to the moderately priced Thompson's on Dearborn Street and the cheap but filling fare of McEwan's Coffee House on Madison Street and Kohlstaat's Luncheon Rooms at three locations.

For elegance and superb feasting, however, no restaurant in the city and at the Exposition could hold a candle to Rector's. Nor was there a more amiable and knowledgeable host than the owner. The son of the proprietor of several frontier taverns in upstate New York, Charles Rector had become a restaurateur after organizing the kitchens of George Pullman's dining cars. When the first transcontinental train went from Boston to San Francisco in 1869, the travelers ate food prepared by him. By 1884 he was ready to open his own café in downtown Chicago. It proved so successful among Chicago's elite that when plans were drawn up for the Exposition, Rector was granted a choice location to create Café Marine. Although Rector was American, the atmosphere and menu of Rector's were French. He offered a *prix fixe* fourteen-course dinner that became one of the Exhibition's greatest drawing cards.

Diamond Jim was so enamored of the food and with an owner who shared his background in railroading that he pleaded with Rector to open a restaurant in New York.

As in Manhattan restaurants during the theatrical season, diners at Rector's and the other Chicago cafés and dining rooms could not help gazing in wonder when the famous Diamond Jim Brady and the celebrated Lillian Russell appeared to be engaged in a contest to determine which of them could eat more. Noting the superior capacity of his belly, the onlookers if asked to wager on the outcome would have put their money on Jim. He always won, but he conceded more than once, "For a woman, she done damn well."

That these friendly competitions added to Lillian's already generous figure didn't matter, for she was the reigning singing

star and actress in an age when pulchritude, as Clarence Day
was quick to point out, was judged and admired by the lady's
girth.

While the gentlemen of Chicago's elite found Lillian attractive and would have gladly changed places with Diamond Jim,
their wives turned up their collective noses at a "theatrical person" unworthy of admittance to a Chicago society of McCor-
micks, Armours, and Swifts ruled by Mrs. Potter Palmer, whose
husband owned the Palmer House. It was one thing to visit her
backstage, out of curiosity, or to observe her in a restaurant as
she made a regal entrance under one of her famous feathered
hats, but one did not invite a woman of "the stage" to tea or
dinner, even if she were residing in the Jeffreys mansion.

This snubbing of the American Beauty was most evident
during a highlight of the Exposition's social calendar, Derby
Day at Washington Park, held on a Saturday. A racing enthusiast, Lillian canceled a matinee performance to attend. She
arrived in all her glory in the clubhouse, only to find that her
appearance caused an uproar among "the ladies." Outraged,
they demanded that the president of the racetrack association
eject "that woman." Although he pointed out that Miss Russell
had every right to be there and that the city of Chicago would
look ridiculous if he asked her to leave, the women persisted.
Not wanting to delay the racing program further, he asked Lillian if she would mind watching the derby from a box in the
grandstand.

The result as she made her way to her seat was a roar of
enthusiasm from the crowd that newspaper reporters gleefully
noted. The *Chicago Tribune* noted that she had one of the best
boxes in the grandstand. The *Record* described her "holding a
levee between the races" and an informal reception for a throng
of admirers. Articles dealing with Derby Day gave more space
to her appearance at the derby than to the society ladies in
the clubhouse. The women who had turned her away discovered that in doing so they had made her a sympathetic figure

and provided additional publicity for her performances at the Exposition.

When Diamond Jim was not applauding Lillian from a front-row seat at the Columbian Theater or eating with her in restaurants of fair and city, he was exploring the Exposition and engaging in a spending spree. He spent days in the Fine Arts Building and disagreed with J. P. Morgan, who had declared that the paintings by Frenchmen Bougereau and Bourginnier appeared to have been done "by a committee of chambermaids." Jim liked them and bought a few.

Confident that the slumping economy would soon rebound and result in an upturn in the railroad business, he purchased fine Oriental carpets as gifts for presidents and other officials of the lines on whom he expected to be calling very soon. For $4,000 he bought a prizewinning gold and white grand piano.

His most spectacular purchase during his stay in Chicago was made from the A. H. Woods factory. It was an "automobile," but because it ran on an electric battery, not on gasoline such as those that had been built by American bicycle makers Frank and Charles Duryea, the machine was called an electric brougham. The first had been constructed by William Morrison of Des Moines, Iowa, and it had been bought by J. B. McDonald, president of Chicago's American Battery Company. He used it as an advertisement for his firm's products. During the Exposition, three of the noisy contraptions were roaming Chicago streets and scaring the horses. When Jim placed an order, he was informed that he could expect delivery of the hand-built machine in a year.

Among the attractions not directly associated with the fair that Jim enjoyed was Buffalo Bill's Wild West Circus starring William F. Cody. A plainsman and former Pony Express rider, Cody had crafted himself into a legend in his own time and then became a millionaire by putting on elaborate shows that featured cowboys, horses, Indians, and a sharp-shooting girl named Annie Oakley. Perhaps not as famous as Buffalo Bill, other personalities whom Jim found fascinating appeared at the fair as lecturers. Among them was political and social reformer Henry George, advocate of the single tax, and recently defeated independent candidate for mayor of New York. Other luminaries holding forth with their views in the course of the Exposition were William Jennings Bryan, John Dewey, Samuel Gompers, and Woodrow Wilson. The World's Congress of Authors presented Oliver Wendell Holmes, George Washington Cable addressing the subject of "The Uses and Methods of Fiction," and Frederick Jackson Turner discoursing on "The Significance of the Frontier in American History."

To Chicago in the causes of temperance and women's rights came Susan B. Anthony and Frances Willard. They hailed the work of the Anti-Saloon League as a noble mission. Had Jim been an imbiber, he could have quaffed in the saloons and beer gardens of the city or on the fairgrounds in exhibition halls of Germany, Austria, and other countries. Ironically, because of the fair, beer consumption in the city doubled, reaching 2.7 million barrels in 1893.

The foreign country's exhibition of most interest to Jim was the "Irish Village." Within its walls he found models of Blarney and Donegal castles and a representation of an industrial village where "colleens" made lace and linen.

Almost every day at the fair he ran into a friend or friends who, like him, had decided that the only logical thing to do until Congress convened in August to revoke the economy-crippling Sherman Silver Act was take in the Exposition. On such an occasion Jim invited them to drop in at his Palmer House suite that evening, or almost any evening, for a party.

But for even Diamond Jim Brady there came a point where enough was enough. After a month at the fair and looking forward optimistically to the convening of Congress, he said good-bye to Chicago and its delights, bade farewell to Nell, and headed for a spell of rest and recovery from the heat and overindulgences of the city in the shady glades and cool swimming pool of a spa in Virginia with the felicitous name Old Point Comfort.

Settled into the faintly bohemian atmosphere of the Hygeia Hotel, he took long swims in the ocean, sunbathed on the beach, and partook of leisurely breakfasts, lunches, dinners, and late suppers. In the evening as he sat in the hotel ballroom watching couples dance to the strains of the new popular songs "After the Ball" and "Say Au Revoir, But Not Goodby" or a medley of old Stephen Foster tunes, his expertly tailored attire was always adorned with the glittering emblems that justified his nickname. By comparison, other men who boasted social pedigrees and far more money in their bank accounts looked as plain and poor as barn swallows. Even naval officers in uniforms crusted with gold braid felt outclassed.

On August 7 Jim picked up a newspaper and read with relief of the convening of the special session of Congress to debate repeal of the silver-purchase law. Nine days later in a three-hour speech in the House of Representatives, America's most famous orator, William Jennings Bryan, railed against those who demanded strict adherence to a gold standard.

"On one side stand the corporate interests of the United States, the moneyed interests, aggregated wealth and capital, imperious, arrogant, compassionless," he said. "On the other side stand an unnumbered throng, those who gave the Democratic party a name and for whom it has assumed to speak. Work-worn and dust-begrimed, they make their mute appeal, and too often find their cry for help beat in vain against the outer walls, while others, less deserving, gain ready access to legislative halls."

The debate would continue in the House and Senate through October with President Cleveland defying members of his party such as Bryan and standing firmly for repeal. When it came to a vote in the Senate on October 30, the repeal passed forty-eight to thirty-seven. The *New York World* declared,

"Praise is due first to the Administration of Grover Cleveland, which has stood like a rock for unconditional repeal."

The *Times* predicted that, regarding the financial crisis of 1893, history would record that "at that moment, as often before, between the lasting interests of the nation and the cowardice of some, the craft of others, in his own party, the sole barrier was the enlightened conscience and the iron firmness of Mr. Cleveland."

By the time Congress acted, Diamond Jim was back in New York.

7

Sidewalks of New York

❦❧❦

T HE SHIFT OF the center of gravity of the lively side of
New York from the Bowery to the vicinity of Madison
Square was immortalized in 1892 by a popular song. The
waltz-time ditty by composer Percy Gaunt and lyricist Charles
H. Hoyt recounted the misadventures of a young man on his
first visit to New York. Having heard that the Bowery was the
center of fun in the city, but uninformed that its glory days
were past, he lamented in six verses how he had been bilked at
an auction, shocked by the bawdy nature of a vaudeville show,
and beaten up by a gang of toughs in a saloon. He vowed,
"The Bowery, the Bowery, I won't go there anymore."

While there remained islands of civility in the area, such as
McSorley's Ale House and Steve Brodie's, the places to go for
frivolity in the mid-1890s were uptown, and their epicenter was
west of Third Avenue between Fourteenth Street and Madison
Square. Dominating this entertainment center and taking up
the block between Madison and Fourth Avenue and Twenty-
sixth and Twenty-seventh streets was Madison Square Garden.
Designed and built by Stanford White, it contained an amphi-
theater accommodating fifteen thousand people, a theater, concert hall, ballroom, and rooftop restaurant seating four thousand.
A three-hundred-foot tower that contained White's apartment was
topped by a statue of a naked Diana by sculptor Augustus Saint-

Gaudens. Open to the public until 10 P.M. for twenty-five cents and reached by an elevator, an observation deck afforded the visitor a spectacular view of the city.

Immediately below lay the leafy, small, diamond-shape park surrounded by the heart of the theatrical district, including Koster & Bial's concert hall on West Twenty-third Street and the Casino on Broadway, and some of Manhattan's finest hotels. At the corner of Twenty-third Street was the Fifth Avenue Hotel, where Republican Party boss U.S. Senator Thomas Platt held court in an alcove known as Amen Corner. A block north was the Albemarle and two blocks farther, the Brunswick, the Victoria, and the St. James, where Jim Brady had been spotted as a promising youth by John Toucey.

Surpassing all these in opulence was the Hoffman House. Opened in 1864 at the corner of Twenty-fourth Street and renovated in 1890 at an unprecedented cost of $1.2 million it benefited from the shift uptown in large measure because of a magnificent "gentlemen's bar" where one of the bartenders had invented a bourbon and vermouth drink called a Manhattan. Running fifty by seventy feet and paneled in rich mahogany, the room had a heavily carved bar with brass-plated footrest and a floor that eschewed the sawdust of the saloons of the Bowery for Oriental rugs. But the barroom's chief decorative attraction hung on the wall behind the bar—an enormous oil painting, "Nymphs and Satyr," by the French artist Bougereau, famous for voluptuous nudes and whose works had enchanted Diamond Jim in the Fine Arts Building at the world's fair. The painting was so renowned that a reproduction of it appeared on the lids of boxes of Hoffman House ten-cent perfecto cigars sold by cigar stores all over the country.

Finding exactly the amenities required for both the entertainment of his clients and his own comfort, Jim had made the hotel his permanent home. He'd soon found himself almost as much an attraction in the barroom as the nymphs and satyr.

Although he imbibed root beer or lemon soda, he enjoyed the company of the accomplished men of commerce and politics who stayed at the hotel and drank at the bar. He also enjoyed feasting "gratis" on the daily "buffet," the Hoffman House's high-tone version of Bowery saloons' free lunches. Another innovation of the Hoffman House that Diamond Jim liked was called an "annunciator." Installed in every room, it was the "room service" of the 1890s. The device consisted of a circular card upon which were printed all items or services that a guest might need. An arrow was turned to whatever was desired, a button was pressed, an electric signal registered the request elsewhere, and a bellboy or maid promptly responded.

Back from the Columbian Exposition and the Virginia spa and again settled comfortably into these Hoffman House luxuries in September, Jim returned to his role as Mr. First Nighter by taking in *A Trip to Mars* at Niblo's Garden featuring a company of midgets (the Liliputians); *The Rising Generation,* a Park Theater show with "rollicking music" and a plot about a lowly Irish bricklayer who in true Horatio Alger fashion rises to success and riches as a contractor; and *The Woolen Stocking,* written by and starring Ned Harrigan in his own theater. Jim's favorite song was titled "Little Daughter Nell."

Concerning the woman he knew by that name, he was thrilled to learn in late September that his favorite actress and singer would grace a New York stage again in November.

"Lillian Russell will return to the Casino," noted *Town Topics.* "She has parted those scarlet, rapturous lips of hers and said so. No matter about Chicago, and all it did or did not do for her. She will expand and heave, throb, bloom and fascinate once again in our own vicinity."

Jim noted with satisfaction that the item made no mention of a rumor that had swept out of Chicago in late summer that Lillian Russell had fallen in love with and planned to marry a man who had been one of the attractions of the "fakes" of the Midway Plaisance. His name was Sandow and he had been billed by a brash young showman named Florenz Ziegfeld Jr. as "the world's strongest man."

Lillian dismissed the rumor. "I propose appearing again this season in opera," she said, "and, of course, I shall not marry, if at all, until my stage career is finished."

The vehicle for her return to New York was to be a musical about Rosa, a pretty Spanish cigarette maker who married a tobacco planter named Chicos. The title was *Princess Nicotine*. The plot followed the same formula for success that she had found in *Pepita, or the Girl with the Glass Eyes*. But the story was never the attraction in a Lillian Russell show. Audiences came to see her. Declared the reviewer for the *Tammany Times* after the show opened on November 24, "The fair Lillian herself is a delight to look upon and to listen to."

A month after the opening the newspaper reported that Lillian had a new tenor to play opposite her in the person of forty-year-old "Signor Don Giovanni Perugini." Vain and handsome and of medium height, he was actually an American named Jack Chatterton. Less than two weeks after their pairing on stage, the theater district was rife with a rumor that they'd fallen in love.

Lillian confirmed this on January 11, 1894, by stating nonchalantly that she had changed her mind about not marrying until her career was over. Perugini vowed that as man and wife, "We shall devote ourselves to opera comique. I say we, but it is Miss Russell that is the one; I put myself in the background."

No one was quicker in offering Lillian congratulations than Diamond Jim.

Without Nell to squire around town and with very little business to occupy him, Jim sailed off to England with the expressed purpose of inspecting the Leeds Forge Company's shops. His other aim was to satisfy an appetite for exploring the restaurants of Britain and France that had been whetted by their countries' exhibitions at the world's fair. In both places he was greeted by the natives with gasps and wondering gazes at his glittering display of diamonds. He carried on a shopping spree that surpassed his purchases in Chicago. The splurge might have continued if he had not been notified by cablegram that the automobile he'd ordered from A. H. Woods would be ready in a month. He cut short his Paris stay, returned to New York, and immediately headed for Chicago. By the time he arrived the machine was ready. However, there was a problem concerning shipping it to New York. Woods informed him that it was too tall to fit through the door of a boxcar. Not to be denied the pleasure of becoming the first automobile owner in New York, Jim arranged to place it on a special flatcar.

The vehicle was accompanied by a mechanic, William Johnson. A black man who knew how to run and fix it, he was hired away from Wood at a salary of $35 a week. Jim gave him a title he'd heard applied to drivers in France: *chauffeur*.

Because the electric machine was powered by storage batteries, Jim arranged for Thomas Edison's company to install charging equipment in a rented livery stable on West Fifty-seventh Street. With the batteries energized it had a cruising range of thirty-six miles. To be sure that it would operate on city streets without embarrassing breakdowns, Jim had Johnson take it for test drives on five successive days between three and four o'clock in the morning. Confident in his new toy, Jim then alerted newspapers of the impending debut of the city's first horseless carriage.

At three o'clock on a Saturday afternoon, dressed in a Prince Albert coat and top hat, he settled onto one of its two seats and told Johnson, decked out in a bottle-green uniform and a hat that a newspaper thought "would have shamed an admiral of the Peruvian navy," to go down Fifth Avenue to Madison Square. Amid ogles, whoops, and shouts of the stable's hostlers and the yapping of frightened coach dogs, the shiny machine emerged onto Fifty-seventh Street. It got to Fifth Avenue without difficulty. Only when they reached Forty-second Street, three blocks west of the Grand Central Depot, did they encounter people and horses in significant numbers. Passing the Croton reservoir, future location of the New York Public Library, the startling mechanical apparition caused at least five teams of horses to become runaways.

Traveling at eleven miles an hour, Jim found when he reached Madison Square that word of his progress had preceded him by the way of telephones. Beaming pleasure at his triumph, he directed Johnson to go around the park again and again. According to one report, "Each time the machine reached the upper side of the square, the horsey patrons of the Bartholdi Hotel, largely composed of members of the theatrical and sporting fraternities, leered enviously and wagered among themselves that Brady and his cart would come to grief before they made another tour of the circuit."

Disappointing them, Diamond Jim arrived at the Hoffman House, dismounted, ordered Johnson to wait, and entered the barroom. Followed by astonished and envious men, he bellied up to the long bar and asked for a lemon soda. He then invited the admirers to take turns sitting beside Johnson for rides around the square. The next day a newspaper headlined:

STARTLING HAPPENINGS IN MADISON SQUARE
JAMES B. BRADY DRIVES FIRST HORSELESS CARRIAGE
SEEN IN NEW YORK
APPEARANCE TIES UP TRAFFIC FOR TWO HOURS

To Jim's delight, an article described him as "a gentleman sportsman."

Worried about the effects of the newfangled machine on public order and safety, police ordered him not to bring it out in daytime. Jim obliged, but the respite from the automobile was short lived. Within a year of Jim's history-making display of motorized motion, the streets of the city were noisy with the sputtering of gas-powered engines, requiring police to impose a speed limit for the vehicles of ten miles an hour. But two years

"Gentleman Sportsman" Diamond Jim Brady accepts a silver cup trophy in a ceremony at Delmonico's restaurant for one of his Thoroughbreds' winning runs.

after the Brady demonstration, automobile enthusiasts threw the restriction to the wind by staging a Memorial Day race from City Hall to the suburban Ardsley Country Club during which Alfred G. Vanderbilt outraged the cops by going eighteen miles an hour in a big red touring car. Only when the car got stuck in a mudhole were they able to catch up and give him the first speeding ticket. Thereafter, the millionaire confined his fast driving to a racetrack in the form of an annual auto competition for the Vanderbilt Cup. Another "first" for the auto belongs to financier J. P. Morgan. When he knocked down a woman as she tried to cross Park Row, he became the first hit-and-run driver. His failure to stop to lend aid and comfort to the woman prompted the president of Princeton University, Woodrow Wilson, to denounce the reckless use of the automobile as a symbol of "the arrogance of wealth."

That showing off an automobile might be viewed by some as arrogance had not occurred to Diamond Jim. To him the machine served the same purpose as the display that gave him his nickname. Like sporting diamonds, lavish entertaining, being seen at theatrical opening nights, and having Lillian Russell as an eating companion, his introduction of the auto to the streets of New York had not been intended as an arrogant flaunting of financial good fortune but a good-natured exercise in Jim Brady self-promotion in the interest of doing business.

HAVING ATTAINED WEALTH that placed him firmly in the ranks of Tony Pastor's "Upper Ten Thousand" and having successfully competed with "the dudes," Jim believed he was entitled to be accepted as an equal by other men who had overcome their low beginnings to enter the pearly gates of "high society." He discovered, to his dismay, that neither money nor fine clothes, diamonds, and having a newspaper anoint him "gentleman sportsman" were sufficient to put him on equal footing with the Vanderbilts, Astors, Goulds, and Morgans. As Lillian Russell had been snubbed by "the ladies" of Chicago, he found himself socially ignored by the nabobs who resided in townhouses along Madison Avenue and mansions on Fifth.

In the Gilded Age, Mrs. Astor was queen of a domain that high society advisor Ward McAllister named the 400 (the number of people who could fit comfortably into her ballroom). But another realm of wealth and ostentation was a principality belonging to James Buchanan Brady. His was a demimonde centered on the hotels of Madison Square, Broadway theaters, and "lobster palace" restaurants that flourished in the nighttime and dissolved at dawn. It was populated by playboys, professional beauties, stars such as Lillian Russell, chorus girls, kept women, sportsmen, newspapermen, celebrities of the Bohemia of the arts, and businessmen from the hinterlands. Having heard the currently popular ditty by Charles Lawlor and James Blake, "Sidewalks of New York," they flocked into Manhattan hoping to meet Diamond Jim and "trip the light fantastic."

They discovered what one writer termed "a city of beautiful nonsense." It was a world of men gathered at the Hoffman House bar, the Astor House Rotunda, and a snug little grotto in the basement of the Normandie Hotel where "the boys" doffed silk top hats and Inverness cloaks to while away the hours until the showgirls arrived for bird and bottle suppers and whatever might ensue elsewhere.

When Mrs. Astor decided to remove herself from the Thirty-fourth Street mansion with the "400" ballroom and settle into a grander abode farther up Fifth Avenue, the site became the Waldorf-Astoria hotel. It immediately became what one newspaper writer called "the rallying point for big business." In the plush of its three-hundred-foot-long, amber marble, first-floor Peacock Alley, the formal-attire-only crystalline Palm Garden, and the Rose and Empire rooms a guest found himself rubbing elbows with similar men of commerce and magnates of industry, business, banking, and Wall Street speculation.

To these barons of an economy that was in what they trusted was a temporary slump, the only test of a man was whether he had sufficient banknotes on hand to join in high-rolling games of baccarat and poker presided over in a $20,000-a-year suite by a westerner by the name of John W. "Bet-a-Million" Gates. He'd earned the nickname by insisting that anyone who gambled in his company be willing and able to lose at least that sum. The story went around that when Gates informed Elbert H. Gary of this, the chairman of the board of U.S. Steel had politely demurred. While no one had ever been asked actually to pony up a million to get into a Gates game, a player had to ante $1,000 to be dealt a hand.

Wagering also took place in late afternoon under the high, ornately carved ceiling of the Men's Café. Two of Jim's companions in these lesser-stakes tests of skill and luck were James R. Keene, a Morgan partner and racehorse owner, and Anthony N. Brady (no relation), upstate streetcar magnate and capitalist.

Entering this monied milieu, Jim joined a pageant of the wealthiest, the most glamorous, and the most notorious of men and their women, some of whom were their wives. After observing this panorama on behalf of a midwestern newspaper, a reporter wrote:

> All around, in the vast, outstretching corridors, there swarmed and swirled in a bewildering maze of an endless, shifting crowd of men and women all attired in formal evening dress, the women resplendent in gorgeous creations of the dressmaker's and milliners arts. . . . From the big music gallery came the strains of a Strauss waltz, scarcely audible with the chatter of 5,000 voices, filling every nook and corner of the corridors. . . . The ten entrances to the hotel sang a steady song of whirring monotony. . . . Until two in the morning there was no let-up in the music, the popping of corks, the incessant chatter and babble of voices.

Presiding over the bill of fare in the Palm Room was an autocrat of the kitchen by the name of Oscar Tschirsky whose approval was even more important to Waldorf-Astoria patrons than an invitation to one of Mrs. Astor's balls. Admittance by Oscar or one of his headwaiters, said one historian of the era, "certified you as a 24-carat member of the conspicuous consumption club."

No Oscar of the Waldorf greeting was given more delightedly than that afforded Diamond Jim when he was accompanied by Lillian Russell. Nor was a chef more patient than he one night when Lillian could not make up her mind whether to have ice cream for dessert or the nonfattening cantaloupe. As Oscar awaited a decision, Jim said to Lillian, "Why not have both?"

Adding the half melon with a scoop of vanilla ice cream in its center to the Palm Garden dessert menu, Oscar called it "Cantaloupe a la Lillian Russell."

THAT THE AMERICAN BEAUTY hesitated in ordering ice cream reflected Lillian's concern that she was losing her hourglass figure. The wraithlike singer with peaches-and-cream complexion and pinched waist who charmed Tony Pastor and enchanted audiences for a decade and a half had grown noticeably fuller, expanding to a thirty-four-inch midriff, forty-two-inch bust, and 165 pounds. The voice was still there, but audiences were finding her more and more implausible playing innocent young girls. She was still the most famous woman in America, but there were moments when she dined in the public eye that she wished she were not a celebrity.

When a promising young actress by the name of Marie Dressler remarked, "It must be wonderful to be famous," Lillian had replied, "No, child. You ought to try to eat raw oysters in a restaurant with every eye focused on you. It makes you feel as though the creatures were whales, your fork were a derrick, and your mouth were the Mammoth Cave."

The only flaw in Lillian at the time, Dressler recalled, was that "she was none too clever about men."

The veracity of Dressler's observation was demonstrated following Lillian's declaration that she intended to wed her leading man in *Princess Nicotine*. When asked why she'd changed her mind about not marrying until her career was over, she replied, "Signor Perugini is a gentleman; he is a dear, good fellow, and he has asked me to marry him. That would probably be sufficient reason, but in addition to that I am tired of reading these reports in the papers of me marrying this man or that one."

She announced that the ceremony would take place on Palm Sunday at her Fifty-seventh Street townhouse. But she was reminded by her lawyer that a provision of the New York divorce she had obtained from Harry Braham prevented her from marrying again in the Empire State. She appealed to a court to void the limitation, but the judge upheld the divorce decree restriction. Her response was to defiantly announce that the wedding would proceed immediately. The date was set: Sunday, January 24, 1894.

The *New York World* asked in a headline, "Will It Be Bigamy?"

Rather than chance arrest, Lillian shifted the ceremony to the office of a justice of the peace across the Hudson River in Hoboken, New Jersey. Guests then took a ferry back to New York for the reception on West Fifty-seventh Street. One guest, George W. Lederer, recalled "a jolly little supper." His account continued, "Somewhat to my astonishment, the fair Lillian suggested we all sit down to a game of cards. We got out the cards and chips and presently were in the midst of a friendly game of poker. Around two-thirty in the morning, Perugini got sleepy and retired. I made several suggestions that we stop the game, but Lillian insisted that we continue. We kept on playing and playing. I began to think that our hostess's habitual politeness prevented her from getting rid of us, so I suggested to her as politely as I could that she boot us out bodily. Whereupon she looked at me very sweetly and said, 'Not at all. I wouldn't think of it. I *always* play cards on my wedding nights.'"

Within a week, according to Marie Dressler, members of the *Princess Nicotine* company were whispering that Miss Russell was a "kissless bride." This perception was based on Lillian's invitations to people in the show to go home with her. "It was evident that she did not want to be alone with Perugini," Dressler recalled. "I think she was afraid of him even then."

The *Town Topics* noted, "It has been an open secret for weeks that Lillian Russell and her latest husband were not radiantly happy together. Indeed Miss Russell and Perugini were the only two persons in the world that believed before the marriage ceremony was performed in the possibility of their having a joyful married life."

Broadway buzzed with whispers that the groom was homosexual.

When the inevitable separation was announced, Lillian gave a long statement to the *New York Herald* in which she admitted that she realized on the morning after the marriage that she had made a terrible mistake.

"He began to show a disposition to rule me," she complained, "and to dictate who should be my friends, who should enter my home, where I should go and what I should do."

She reported having "quarrel after quarrel" until she could stand the situation no longer, especially when she was "the breadwinner." Such a woman, she said, should be "respected, not nagged at."

Perugini retorted in print, telling the *Tammany Times* that Lillian was an abusive prima donna who didn't want him attaining stardom. "She once told me she saw no reason why I cared for fame," he said, "as I would be sufficiently honored through the applause she would receive."

Not satisfied with an accusation of professional jealousy, Perugini declared that Lillian "laces [uses corsets] and wears false hair and is horribly made up, and is not the least bit pretty off the stage."

The marriage ended four years later when Perugini filed for divorce on the grounds that Lillian had abandoned him.

Thrice divorced, Lillian was denounced from lecture platforms, in newspaper editorials, and in church pulpits as "the most eminent of fallen women."

She sought and found solace in the company of the one man in the world she had learned would never criticize her, embarrass her, feel jealous of her successes, make trouble for her in the press, break her heart, or try to upstage her. To the contrary, being seen with Diamond Jim Brady had given her a bonanza of publicity.

While he showered her with examples of his hallmark, she knew that no matter how many diamond pins, bracelets, and necklaces he bestowed, she need not worry about having to fend off amorous advances in the cab ride home. She saw in Jim, and rightly so, a man who lived to eat as other men existed only to paint, write, go into politics, and accrue fortunes in industry.

For James Buchanan Brady, Lillian Russell was a flesh-and-blood diamond forming the centerpiece of his collection of gems which proclaimed that he had climbed out of his father's saloon to dominate at least a portion of the life of a city where flash mattered. When he wore her on his arm, he evoked the looks of men who were handsomer, cleverer, wittier, and far richer, and in so doing he became the most envied man in the pleasure palaces of Broadway.

TWO DECADES AFTER Grand Central opened on Forty-second Street, a New Yorker could pay a nickel fare to ride on steel rails on the ground or those of the "Elevated Railroads" to any spot on the island. To go north or south a traveler had a choice of fourteen car lines; if the destination was "crosstown," there were twelve. The cars ran every few minutes. Transfers were free. Four "L" systems carried 200 million passengers a year. Except for the business hours when they were, as the 1893 Baedeker guide to the United States warned, "disagreeably crowded," the L provided "a very pleasant mode of conveyance."

A twenty-three-year-old journalist named Stephen Crane, who in 1893 had pseudonymously published a naturalistic New

York novel, *Maggie: A Girl of the Streets,* observed cable cars running on Broadway that "by force of column and numbers, almost dominate the great street, and the eye of even an old New Yorker is held by these long yellow monsters which prowl intently up and down, up and down, in a mystic search."

He described the trolley car sweeping "on its diagonal path through the Tenderloin . . . the place of theaters, and of the restaurants where gayer New York does her dining [and] in evening dress the average man feels he has gone up three pegs on the social scale."

The entry fees into this Broadway world, wrote John Burke in *Duet in Diamonds,* "were plenty of money vulgarly displayed and a reckless disregard of the effect of overeating and over-drinking on the human constitution. A genuine rounder also spent ten hours of his time, from nightfall to dawn, to make sure he touched all the bases. There was no creeping down dawn streets in fear of muggers, but there was a plentiful assortment of pickpockets, con men, prostitutes, pan handlers and drug addicts."

Overseeing the Tenderloin in terms of maintaining law and order was the policeman who had named it, Inspector Alexander "Clubber" Williams. He was supervised from headquarters at 300 Mulberry Street by the most famous "copper" in America, Chief of Police Thomas J. Byrnes. Born in Ireland, a veteran of the Civil War, and a New York policeman since 1863, he was fifty-five years old. Among his contributions to crime detection were "mug shots," "rogues gallery," and "the Third Degree," which he saw not as physical maltreatment of suspects but psychologically leading a suspected criminal to confess. He told an interviewer, "My business is shrouded in mystery, and the more difficult it is to unravel the harder I work."

He also worked hard at swelling his bank accounts by taking graft. No one on the police force labored more diligently at picking such morsels from the saloons, gambling dens, and houses of prostitution of the Tenderloin, aided and abetted by the avaricious Clubber Williams.

If the average New Yorker who rode a trolley or took the L to his job every day had not known that the police department was riddled with graft, he learned what was going on at 300 Mulberry Street by reading a newspaper on Monday, February 15, 1892. The day before, from the pulpit of the Madison Square Presbyterian Church, a slight, respectably bearded, scholarly, soft-spoken minister, the Reverend Charles Parkhurst, had said in outraged tones that the city's elected leaders were "a lying, perjuring, rum-soaked, and libidinous lot of polluted harpies feeding day and night on the city's quivering vitals."

Even worse, Parkhurst railed, were "the guardians of the public peace and virtue, vulgarly known as the police." The men in blue uniforms and "plain clothes" detectives were a force of corrupt bribe takers."

Challenged to prove these accusations, Parkhurst did so by going "under cover" with the aid of an ex-policeman. When he returned to his pulpit with the evidence, the result was formation of a state senate committee to investigate his charges. As witness after witness substantiated the extent of bribery and other graft, primarily gleaned from the Tenderloin, an outraged citizenry organized to throw the offenders out of office and into jails by backing a "fusion reform ticket" in the mayoral election of 1894. The insurgents' hopes immediately centered on a young politician who as a Republican had earned a reputation as a reformer in the state legislature and was at the moment a member of the federal Civil Service Commission, Theodore Roosevelt. After he chose not to run, pointing out that he'd lost a bid for the mayoralty in 1886, the nomination went to businessman William Strong.

When the reform slate won by more than 42,000 votes, the *Times* headlined: "The Tammany Tiger Has Been Flayed Alive." Cynically assessing the Democratic defeat, the party boss, Richard Croker, said, "One trip of inquiry into Tammany ward would have told you that [our own people] were going to vote against us this year. Our people could not stand the rotten police corruption. They'll be back at the next election. They can't stand reform either."

Public interest turned immediately to whom Strong would select to take charge at 300 Mulberry Street and clean out the crooks. Although the overwhelming favorite was Roosevelt, it was not until April 1895 that Strong gave the job to the man an admiring public called "Teddy" and those who were closest to him addressed as "Theodore" and "TR."

Although by no means an intimate of the new president of the four-man board of commissioners in charge of the police department, Diamond Jim had often crossed paths with Roosevelt at dinners and other occasions attended by the city's business leaders. While the son of a saloon owner who had lived a Horatio Alger life had little in common except closeness in their age with a politician whose wealth and status were inherited, Roosevelt had earned a reputation for "square dealing" that appealed to a man whose only dishonesty had been in bilking members of a German band in the matter of train fares fifteen years earlier.

At some point these two contrasting figures, one a settled family man who was physically fit and a proponent of "the strenuous life" who liked to exercise by boxing and the other a fat man whose only exertions appeared to be in lifting a food-laden fork, found commonality in the heavyweight boxer John L. Sullivan.

In 1882, when twenty-six-year-old Jim Brady was perfecting his salesmanship and twenty-four-year-old Theodore Roosevelt was in Albany, New York, making a name as a reform-minded legislator, John Lawrence Sullivan of Roxbury, Massachusetts, age twenty-eight, had won the bare-knuckles heavyweight championship. He used a devastating right punch to knock out Paddy Ryan in nine rounds in Mississippi City, Mississippi. Since then, the "Boston Strong Boy" had taken on all comers while winning adherents not only to his prowess in the ring but to his swashbuckling personality. He'd fought and won the last of the bare-knuckle bouts in 1889 by subduing Jake Kilrain in seventy-five rounds, again in Mississippi. In fights wearing gloves and conducted under the Queensbury Rules in New Orleans in 1892, he'd lost to James J. Corbett.

At a time when Lillian Russell was the most famous actress in America and recipient of admiring stares whenever she entered a restaurant, "the Great John L." found himself a superstar of sports and beneficiary of all the free drinks he could handle in New York's hotel barrooms and any saloon he entered. But as the number of drinks mounted, the ex-champion grew increasingly pugnacious. Usually around one in the morning, this belligerence reached a point where he was a menace to everyone around him. If patrons of the bar or saloon were lucky, Diamond Jim would be on hand to rescue them and the furnishings from devastation. Jim often averted damage by dangling before John L.'s eyes a diamond ring, watch fob, or stick pin. If Jim was not present, someone made a mad dash out to the street in hopes of finding a policeman. More often than not, a squad would have to be summoned from Mulberry Street headquarters to subdue him.

That Diamond Jim was the only man in the city who could quell the Boston Strong Man without resorting to force was not lost on Police Commissioner Roosevelt. Jim quickly became accustomed to getting a telephone call from TR or finding a cop at the door with a request from the commissioner to go somewhere and get John L. home to bed before he wrecked the place. He also came to expect a next-morning inquiry concerning a report of any fracas in a hotel bar that had landed on TR's desk. Even if Roosevelt knew Jim had not been present, he assumed that Jim had already gotten an account of the incident that was likely to be more complete and accurate than the police report. TR knew enough about Diamond Jim Brady to appreciate that although Jim did not drink, he was the ablest barfly of them all. It was well known in the Tenderloin district, and therefore at 300 Mulberry Street, that no barroom rendering of "The Sidewalks of New York" was complete without Diamond Jim's basso profundo and no respectable brawl took place unless he was there to serve as referee.

If Roosevelt dispatched a copper to enlist Jim's assistance in the summer of 1895, the address given to the officer was at the corner of Broadway and Fifty-seventh Street. After years of dividing his time between hotels while on the road and the Hoffman House when he was in town, Jim decided to become an apartment dweller. In keeping with his newly acquired reputation as gentleman sportsman and needing space to display objects of art, furniture, and other accouterments expected of a man of his wealth, he rented and connected two six-room suites in a fashionable building named the Rutland. It was close to Lillian Russell's townhouse.

A splashy feature of the layout was in step with a current architectural fad in decorating at least one room in an Oriental motif. Some aficionados called it the Turkish Room. The style required at least one divan strewn with burnt leather cushions, numerous pillows, heavy tasseled draperies, hand-painted coal scuttles, and renderings in watercolor, charcoal, and oils of exotic locales, turbaned men, and beautiful women in veils and diaphanous gowns, most of which were the imaginings of artists who had never seen the Near or Far Easts.

The apartment also provided Jim with easy access to the stable where he stored his automobile and an array of old-fashioned forms of transportation, including three horse carriages: a Brewster trap, a brougham, and a victoria specially built to sustain his weight by the most noted carriage maker of the time, Peter Martin. To draw them he bought two perfectly matched teams, one of which cost $3,000.

In charge of the carriages were coachman Mike Clancy and footman Steve O'Donnell. If Jim chose to go out in the victoria, the men wore uniforms to match its green upholstery. Should he prefer the plum-colored brougham, they were clad accordingly. To Jim, arriving at a theater or restaurant in a coach with servants whose uniforms did not match it was as unthinkable as showing up without a dazzling display of diamonds.

On the advice of his physician, Dr. J. A. Bodine, who told Jim that if he insisted on eating so much he had better engage in some form of exercise, he also acquired saddle horses, which he took to riding in nearby Central Park in the morning before breakfast. He quickly discovered that becoming an equestrian not only enhanced his image as gentleman sportsman, it provided a new avenue of approach to the more elevated society that he yearned to join. But this newborn enthusiasm for sitting astride a horse quickly waned.

Instead of gaping at the astonishing display of a 240-pound man astride a horse, people strolling the sidewalks of New York were treated to Diamond Jim Brady riding the country's latest fad.

8

Big Wheeler-Dealer

❧❦❧

IT WOULD HAVE BEEN unlikely that Diamond Jim Brady or anyone else in New York City in 1895 could have answered the question "Who was Baron Karl Drais von Sauerbronn?"

Yet the desire of the chief forester of the duchy of Baden to facilitate his inspection tours of the woodlands for which he was responsible in 1816 had resulted in a device that had men and women of the Gilded Age spinning—literally. The baron invented a mode of getting around that he called the *draisine*. Tinkering with two-wheeled machines by men such as Scottish blacksmith Kirkpatrick MacMillan, Ernest Michaux and Pierre Lallement in France, H. B. Smith of New Jersey, H. S. Owen of Washington, D.C., and James Stanley of Coventry, England, had turned the baron's feet-on-the-ground contraption into the pedal-powered "bicycle." Other inventors added brakes, adjustable handlebars, and, in 1891, the inflatable rubber tire.

The following year songwriter Henry Dacre sat at a piano in his room in an office of a music publishing firm in Tin Pan Alley and took note of a "craze" for bicycles by writing:

> *Daisy, Daisy, give me your answer do;*
> *I'm half crazy, all for the love of you;*
> *It won't be a stylish marriage;*
> *I can't afford a carriage;*
> *But you'll look sweet upon the seat*
> *Of a bicycle built for two.*

People who rode bicycles were called wheelers. Everyone who had the price (from $9 to $21) wanted one. Doctors recommended them for fitness. Some ministers said they were good for the soul. Societies and clubs were formed, among them the Michaux Club on Broadway near Fifty-third Street. Its members sported Tyrolean hats. Women had specially tailored outfits.

Observing the increasing numbers of wheelers, the man who had introduced New York to the automobile decided that if he were to get on one of the machines, it could serve not only as a means of getting the exercise demanded by his doctor but as another advertisement for Diamond Jim Brady. He inquired into bicycle manufacturers and determined the best was the Columbia. It sold for $19. But James Buchanan Brady was not interested in an ordinary model. He wanted a bicycle capable of supporting his weight and upholding his reputation as a man with flash. No standard plain coloring would suffice. His Columbia must be painted in the brightest and finest enamels. The firm also equipped it with a horseshoe-shape seat not only large enough to accommodate Jim's posterior but inflatable for maximum comfort. Jim was so pleased that he promptly ordered two dozen.

"With the whole country going crazy over this bicycle idea," he explained to a former circus rider he'd hired to teach him how to wheel, "I'll have to have enough for everyone when I give parties."

He wanted them to have gold frames and silver spokes. For decorating handlebars and frame he would provide "a few diamonds and rubies."

When Harbert Haberele of Columbia replied that a frame of gold could not support the weight of even an average-size man, but that a steel frame could be gold plated, Jim arranged to have them delivered to an electroplater named William Mock on John Street in New York. Mock built a special tank that plated three at a time.

Deciding to improve on the bicycle built for two of Henry Dacre's song, Jim asked the Columbia bike makers to build a three-seater with "drop frame" front and center sections to accommodate ladies' skirts. But on most outings he took the front seat, dressed in a plaid "cycling suit." The woman occupied the center seat. His trainer, Dick Barton, took the rear and did the hard pedaling. When Jim was not wheeling alone with a female guest, he provided bikes for five or six couples on Sunday outings to Coney Island or Bayonne, New Jersey.

If he decided on the latter destination, the party met at his apartment house at ten in the morning and were taken in his carriages to the ferry slip at Forty-second Street, where the bicycles and a private boat were waiting. The first pause en route to the seaside was at a German beer garden in Guttenberg, where Jim fortified himself with pig's knuckles and sauerkraut. He did the same at Elizabethtown.

These Sunday sorties took on aspects of a day of picnicking by a feudal lord surrounded by his courtiers. They were held when the weather permitted, except when Lillian Russell was in town. On those occasions Jim's cycling outings were within city limits, either in Central Park or via Riverside Drive to Dorlando's restaurant. While Jim wore his plaid cycling suit, Lillian was clad in a white serge outfit. But it was her bike that elicited gasps. A gift from Jim, it had a heavily gold-plated frame studded with diamond chips. The handlebars were mother of pearl. Tiny diamonds, sapphires, rubies, and emeralds gleamed and twinkled on silver spokes and hubs. When it was not on the road, it was carefully tucked into a blue lush-lined case. The talk of the town held that it had cost Jim $10,000. He'd actually paid only $1,900.

While Police Commissioner Roosevelt's force of foot patrolmen expected that Central Park and Riverside Drive on fair Sunday mornings would be crowded with wheelers, neither they nor TR had been prepared for the sensation created by New York's most famous duo as they ventured forth either on separate bikes or on Jim's triseater with Dick Barton at the rear. If they took the latter, strapped to the frame behind Barton was a double-walled box. Between the outer and inner walls was crushed ice to keep jugs of orange juice cool. Reaching Eighty-sixth Street, the trio dismounted, and as a crowd watched, Jim and Nell sat on a blanket on the grass of Riverside Park and Barton poured.

When the famous wheelers resumed their outing, they found themselves part of a procession of other cyclists and pedestrians, all trying to get close to the celebrated duet. Everyone in the crowd of followers had heard about Lillian's diamond-studded bike and wanted to see if the story was true. More often than not, the police officers had to clear a path for Jim and Lillian to continue.

Commissioner Roosevelt's rules against cops taking gratuities notwithstanding, Jim invariably rewarded their efforts with crisp, new $5 bills.

The challenge to the police as the cycling craze showed no sign of waning was "reckless wheeling." The problem became so acute that Acting Police Chief Moses Cartright asserted, "There are so many thoroughfares of the city where the traffic on vehicles of all kinds, and especially bicycles, is so great that it is necessary for the protection of life and limb that such traffic should be properly regulated."

The result of this concern was creation of a two-man police bicycle patrol. "If the policemen on bicycles are a success," said TR's co-commissioner, Avery Andrews, "we shall organize a bicycle squad."

The pair of biking cops rolled out of the West Eighty-sixth Street station house at six in the evening on December 12, 1895. Three months into the experiment, the police department declared that the service had been of "great benefit to the public." Theodore Roosevelt wrote of the bicycle squad in his autobiography: "They frequently stopped runaways, wheeling alongside of them, and grasping the horses while going at full speed;

and, what was more remarkable, they managed not only to overtake but to jump into the vehicle and capture, on two or three occasions, men who were guilty of reckless driving, and who fought violently in resisting arrest. They were picked men, being young and active, and any feat of daring which could be accomplished on the wheel they were certain to accomplish."

None of these daring young men on wheels had to worry about undue speed or recklessness on the part of the fat man and the stout star of show business as they made their way along the bike paths of Central Park or en route to Dorlando's. The only problem presented by Diamond Jim and the American Beauty was in the form of the traffic jams that their passage caused as other wheelers pedaled to keep up with them.

Every week more people were caught up in the bicycle craze. So many factories went into the business of manufacturing them that when the Madison Square Garden held a bicycle show in January 1896, the *Times* headlined:

BICYCLE BOOM CONTINUES
Not Room Enough for the Big Madison Square Show

———————

EVERY INCH OF SPACE TAKEN
The Biggest Exhibition of Wheels
and Their Attachments Ever Given

"If the Garden had been three times as large," said the exhibition's James C. Young, "we could have rented every available space."

Of course, none of the bicycles displayed matched the grandeur of those belonging to Jim Brady and Lillian Russell. But it's more than likely that many of the people who bought bicycles did so because of the boost given to the craze by the country's most famous unmarried couple. Countless women who took up wheeling also fitted themselves out in cycling attire patterned on Lillian's costume of white serge with leg-of-mutton sleeves.

That women embraced the bicycle may also be attributed to its endorsement by women's rights advocates such as Susan B. Anthony and Frances Willard. Cycling by women, they felt, was doing more to liberate women than any number of street demonstrations because being on a bike put a woman on equal footing with men. The feminists were pleased with the change in the public's view of what was suitable in women's clothing. Because a woman could not pedal her bicycle wearing voluminous petticoats, did it not make sense to put on divided skirts?

Female wheelers had become so numerous that on November 19, 1895, at the Grand Opera House on Broadway, the audience was afforded a performance by Nellie McHenry in Louis Harrison's *The Bicycle Girl*. The plot dealt with "the new man," "the new woman," and, of course, the bicycle. A reviewer from the *Times* noted, "A bicycle woman with fin de siecle taste in bicycle costume would enjoy the various bloomer styles that are shown by the young women who say things that give Nellie a chance to sing and talk."

Many women were delighted to find that wheeling was also a pleasurable means to lose weight. Indeed, eventually that was Lillian Russell's sole motivation. She was pleased that her wheeling resulted in much-desired publicity, but she was thrilled to discover that she was losing pounds. With every ounce shed, her enthusiasm grew. If pedaling a bicycle on Sundays produced that result, she reasoned, how much more excess weight might she eliminate if she went out every day? Her daily companion was not Jim Brady but her friend Marie Dressler.

"Every morning, rain or shine," wrote the pug-nosed and pudgy actress in her autobiography, "we would climb on our wheels and, bending low over the handlebars, give an imitation of two plump girls going somewhere in a hurry."

Lillian had reason to worry about her figure. An artist named Charles Dana Gibson had presented a new ideal beauty in drawings of slim-hipped young women. They were soon known as Gibson Girls. At the same time in the fickle world of show business Lillian found a competitor in a vivacious singer who had been brought from France by the ambitious impresario who had given the world's fair Sandow the strong man. Florenz Ziegfeld's discovery was a doll-like creature with big eyes and wispy figure that tipped the scales at a mere ninety pounds. Her name was Anna Held. Another contender for the title of reigning Broadway beauty had caused a sensation as a chorus girl in *The Belle of New York*. The alarm was sounded for Lillian in *Town Topics*. "Edna May," the writer noted, "is now what Lillian Russell was when I first saw her at Tony Pastor's on Lower Broadway in *Pinafore*."

Lillian also found that she could no longer count on receiving rave reviews. When she appeared at the Abbey Theatre in an operetta produced by her own company, the Lillian Russell Opera Company, one critic sniped, "Miss Russell's company is not an organization which it is possible to praise. She doesn't want pretty women [around her on stage] and she doesn't want clever women to dim her own luster."

Another reviewer offered this backhanded compliment: "Lillian Russell is an affable, kindly creature. She shows her audiences all they can expect for their money. She is as filling as a plum pudding stuffed with plums. When you go to Abbey's, you'll see not only her diamonds, but some ultra-gorgeous gowns, and as much of her pectoral flesh as she can reasonably be expected to exhibit."

While this carping by Broadway critics was disconcerting enough to motivate Lillian to take up wheeling to trim down, she remained widely and wildly popular. Her picture adorned the inside of lids of boxes of cigars named for her. A photograph of her, looking like a Gainsborough painting, was a collector's item. It was so broadly distributed that one of them had been carried by a cowboy in Nevada named Dave Colfax. He'd gunned down another cowpoke for claiming that Mexican dancer Lola Montez was more beautiful and shooting a hole in Lillian's picture. The jury that deliberated a charge of murder against Colfax compared the two pictures. They found that even with a bullet hole, Lillian was more beautiful than Lola. They acquitted Colfax on grounds of justifiable homicide.

Lillian might also have pointed out to her detractors that a man in Niagara Falls named Hippolyte Schneider had become so despondent at not being able to leave his wife and child to marry the American Beauty that he stood at the lip of the falls, shot himself, and plunged to his death in the roiling waters of the cataract.

If Lillian still needed a comforting word and a shoulder on which to rest her head, she could venture to the Rutland apartments or invite the building's most famous tenant to pay a call at her new townhouse twenty blocks north on Seventy-seventh Street.

Having grown weary of living out of suitcases on the road and in hotels when she came back to New York, and with earnings of $2,300 a week, which put her on a financial par with many tycoons and captains of industry, she'd bought the four-story house after her return from the Columbian Exposition in the autumn of 1893. Close to West End Avenue, the dwelling was convenient to a small park where her daughter Dorothy and a governess could stroll. Settled into it, she invited reporters to tour its lavishly furnished and extravagantly decorated rooms.

In the first-floor parlor they found and marveled at divans and chairs built for her hefty figure, a huge table of rosewood and brass, a grand piano, two enormous tiger-skin rugs, and an array of bric-a-brac. A reporter's quick inventory of the items included miniature musical instruments, a collection of souvenir spoons under a glass dome, numerous porcelain snuffboxes and decorative china plates. A collection of jeweled cigarette holders attested that Lillian Russell was a smoker, a fact that if known by the public would have in the minds of some people vindicated their belief that every woman who went on stage was "fallen."

Adjacent to the drawing room on the first floor was a dining room with leather-covered walls, red velvet hangings, Chippendale sideboard, palm trees in tubs, and a huge fireplace. The second floor was Lillian's bedroom and bath. The large brass bed was draped with satin ribbons and flanked by mirrors. On the third floor were rooms for Dorothy and several guests. The fourth had ample space for several servants.

This was at a time when three-fourths of New Yorkers lived in dismal tenements. They labored in sweatshops for eighteen hours a day. If a worker could somehow raise thirteen cents, he could go into a restaurant on Orchard Street and have a dinner of soup, stew, bread, pickles, pie, and a schooner of beer. Men such as Jacob Riis and women such as Lillian D. Wald and Mary M. Brewster, who had opened a "settlement house" for the poor on Henry Street, warned that if the dismal plight of "the other half" who lived downtown continued to be ignored by those who resided uptown, the future of American democracy was in jeopardy.

THAT THE DEPRESSION that had begun after the 1893 stock market crash carried with it the possible fulfillment of such warnings had been driven home to Diamond Jim Brady by a pair of unsettling events in 1894. In March newspapers were suddenly full of stories about a disgruntled farmer in Ohio named Jacob Coxey. A short, bespectacled man with a wife (Lucille), a daughter (Mame), and a son Jacob called "Legal Tender," Coxey was a "silverite" with an idea that he believed was the solution to the country's economic mess. The way out of the depression, he had proposed in a petition to Congress, was for the U.S. government to issue $500 million in paper money for highway construction and other public improvements.

When Congress dismissed his formula, Coxey organized like-minded folks for a march from Ohio to Washington to confront the nation's leaders with "a living petition." He called them the Army of the Commonwealth of Christ. Headline writers christened it Coxey's Army.

The trek took more than a month, but when Coxey's footsore, bedraggled, and exhausted soldiers appeared on the capital's streets on May 1, they numbered less than five hundred and were vastly outnumbered by amused spectators and wary ranks of policemen. As the marchers approached the Capitol, they were arrested for the misdemeanor of treading on the grass. The next week Coxey was found guilty of trespassing and given twenty days and a $5 fine.

While Jim and most Americans were amused by the episode, no one found pleasure in an economic protest that had begun in the town of Pullman, Illinois, where the undoubted lord of the fiefdom was the inventor of the sleeping car. Anybody who had dared to defy him met ruthless resistance and ended up by being bought out or being broken in costly litigation. The result was that by 1894 the Pullman Palace Car business was a monopoly with a capitalization of $36 million. The firm held surplus profits of about $25 million. In the previous fiscal year it had paid shareholders, including mercantile mogul Marshall Field, $2.5 million in dividends.

As the "Cleveland depression" deepened and the company claimed to be suffering from a loss of business, Pullman joined other industries in slashing workers' wages. It did not, however, lower rents in the company town. When a committee of workers appealed to Pullman in May 1894 to either raise wages or cut rents, they were refused and three of the committeemen were fired.

The act outraged the man who headed a new railway labor organization. Eugene Debs had formed the American Railway Union. The men fired by Pullman were members. Debs warned that unless the Pullman Palace Car Company rehired the men by June 26, ARU members on all rail lines would refuse to handle Pullman cars and equipment.

This immediately thrust the ARU into conflict not only with Pullman but with railroads contracted with Pullman. These rail companies were not a group of disorganized and unrelated operations; they had a kind of union themselves. Eight years previously, the heads of twenty-four of them either centered in Chicago or terminating there had formed the General Managers' Association to coordinate operations. At the heart of these activities were switchmen, who handled coupling Pullman cars to trains. The Managers' Association had agreed to pay wages on an agreed scale, then proposed that similar scales be imposed by all member railroads. This proposal was regarded by unions as unacceptable. With the ARU threatening to pull its members off their jobs over an issue that did not involve the railroads directly, the association backed Pullman. When June 26 passed without Pullman's compliance with the union's demand, Debs gave the order for the boycott.

What started as a dispute affecting a single firm and four thousand workers suddenly mushroomed into a nationwide capital versus labor crisis affecting many thousands more in twenty-seven states and the territories. It was also a genuine threat to a nation of millions who had grown dependent on the flow of goods by rail. And it happened in the midst of an economic depression that Americans largely blamed on President Cleveland's economic policies.

On June 27 Cleveland, just back from a fishing trip to Chesapeake Bay, perused morning papers at breakfast and read with alarm that the union ultimatum and its rejection by the Pullman company had precipitated a strike that one newspaper reported had "assumed the proportions of the greatest battle between labor and capital that has ever been waged in the United States."

The number of walkouts in Chicago was estimated at twenty thousand. Debs's union headquarters figured another forty thousand men had quit or struck elsewhere. Freight and passenger traffic into and from Chicago was at a halt. The Post Office Department found itself forced to stop mail service all over the West.

When the U.S. attorney reported on June 30 that the previous night a group of strikers had stopped mail trains in the suburbs of Chicago, the U.S. marshal requested he be authorized to employ a force of special deputies on trains to protect the mails and to "detect the parties guilty of such interference." With the president's approval, Attorney General Richard Olney gave the order for "prompt and vigorous" action. He also designated Chicago attorney Edwin Walker to act as special counsel for the government in any subsequent legal proceedings. Inflaming this crisis were newspaper stories filled with what Illinois governor John Peter Altgeld termed distorted, exaggerated, distorted, and often baseless information. On July 1 the *Chicago Tribune* headline blared "Mobs Bent on Ruin." The next day the U.S. attorney reported to Olney that Judges Peter S. Grossup and William A. Woods had signed an injunction ordering the union to "refrain from interfering with or stopping any of the business of the railroads in Chicago engaged as common carriers." Debs's union was also told to cease persuading employees to stop working. The U.S. attorney then announced that the injunction extended to all union members and disobedience could subject individuals to arrest.

On the afternoon of the issuance of the injunction, a crowd of union members in the town of Blue Island, Illinois, attacked a federal marshal and 125 deputies, one of whom was stabbed. In a veritable state of panic the marshal telegraphed Olney, "In my judgment it is impossible to move trains without having the Fifteenth Infantry from Fort Sheridan moved here at once. There are two thousand rioters here and more coming."

Federal troops were ordered to Chicago. They arrived on July 4, causing some residents to assume the infantry, cavalry, and artillery were there for an Independence Day celebration. The U.S. attorney told the press, "We have been brought to the ragged edge of anarchy, and it is time to see whether the law is sufficiently strong to prevent this condition of affairs. If not, the sooner we know the better."

Eugene Debs warned, "The first shots fired by regular soldiers at the mobs here will be a signal for civil war. Bloodshed will follow, and ninety percent of the people of the United States will be arrayed against the other ten percent. And I would not care to be arrayed against the laboring people in the contest, or find myself out of the ranks of labor when the struggle ended."

Like a self-fulfilling prophecy, the simmering crisis exploded into warfare on the seventh. In a pitched battle between mob and soldiers seven men were killed. The next day, without notice to Governor Altgeld of Illinois, President Cleveland put the city under martial law. The edict banned all unlawful assemblages. Cleveland vowed, "There will be no vacillation in the punishment of the guilty."

Two days later a grand jury indicted Eugene Debs and others on seventy-one charges, including obstructing the mails. At the outset of the Pullman strike thirty-seven-year-old lawyer Clarence Seward Darrow rushed to Debs's cause by quitting a lucrative position as legal counsel to the Chicago and North Western Railroad. He'd been practicing law in Chicago since 1887 and had been a partner of Governor Altgeld.

Although Cleveland felt justified in using troops, the irate governor sent off a tart letter to the president. "Surely the facts have not been correctly presented to you in this case or you would not have taken the step," he wrote. "Waving all questions of courtesy, I will say that the State of Illinois is not only able to take care of itself, but it stands ready today to furnish the Federal Government any assistance it may need elsewhere."

The president retorted that in order to keep the mails moving, "and upon abundant proof that conspiracies existed against commerce between the States," it had been clearly "within the province of the Federal authority" to send in troops.

Costs of the strike to railroads for destroyed property and hiring of guards was $685,308. Loss of earnings as a result of interruptions of train service totaled $4,672,916. Earnings lost by 31,000 Pullman employees was estimated at $350,000. People had been shot and killed. More than twelve thousand persons had been arrested by police on charges of murder, arson, burglary, assault, riot, and lesser crimes. Seventy-one men had been indicted on charges of obstruction of the mail, conspiracy in restraint of trade, and conspiracy to injure, threaten, or intimidate.

On December 10, 1894, Eugene Debs and others were sentenced to jail for six months. But the issue of greater moment for Debs and his lawyer, Clarence Darrow, was not defiance of the injunction but what authority the federal government, or any government, had to seek such a restraint and a court to grant it. The U.S. Supreme Court affirmed that the U.S. government "may remove everything put upon highways, natural or artificial, to obstruct the passage of interstate commerce, or the carrying of the mails" and in doing so had a right to enjoin those who interfered with the railroads.

Debs served the six months and left prison to find his ARU destroyed but himself in the role of a national hero in the cause of organized labor.

A result of these events in 1894 was Cleveland's enemies' portrayal of him as a strike-breaking capitalist lackey. Critics of Cleveland's administration viewed the ordering of the army to end the crisis by moving against the strikers as further evidence of the government's ineffectiveness in dealing with the continuing depression and to characterize its policy toward working men as at best indifferent and at worst cruel.

Being on the side of the railroad companies, Diamond Jim Brady disagreed.

9

I Can Always Start Over

❧❧❧❧

IN JUNE 1893 the newly established Interstate Commerce Commission reported that 192 railroad companies owning almost 41,000 miles of roadway were in receivership. They included the Reading, Erie, Northern Pacific, and Union Pacific. Struggling to avoid bankruptcy were the Santa Fe and the Baltimore and Ohio. To rail industry figures such as Diamond Jim Brady, these troubled firms were cause for worry.

For the country's most famous and arguably most detested financier, they were ripe for picking. Born in Hartford, Connecticut, on April 17, 1837, John Pierpont Morgan had gotten his education in mathematics in Germany and learned the skills of high finance with the Wall Street firm of Duncan, Sherman and Co. and as New York agent for his father's London-based Junius S. Morgan and Co. Gold speculation and financing of a scandalous arms-profiteering scheme in the Civil War had provided him a springboard for plunging into the postwar railroad frenzy.

In the 1880s he reorganized a number of struggling rail lines through a process that became known in the industry as Morganization. Finding inefficient management, inflated security structures, and unrestrained and cutthroat competition, he provided new capital and restructuring of bonds and other indebtedness. Doing so assured him firm control of future financing and placed

J. P. Morgan,
arguably the nation's
most hated financier.

him on boards of directors. By not actually taking control of these companies, he kept his focus on what he knew best—finance—and guaranteed himself and his company far greater profits than he could ever earn by running railroads.

J. P. Morgan's interests extended into almost every industry, from organizing U.S. Steel to providing backing for Thomas Edison's electric light, resulting in the illumination of Morgan's house on Madison Avenue and his Wall Street offices, and the eventual formation of General Electric and the Niagara Falls Power Company.

Through his interlocking directorates across the spectrum of American industry, he and his associates came to control the biggest commercial banks in New York. All of this made J. P. Morgan a legend in his own time. He was the central figure of two stories that made their way around Wall Street and the nation. In the first, a new millionaire looked admiringly at Morgan's yacht *Corsair* and asked how much the vessel had cost. Morgan replied, "If you have to ask, you can't afford it." The second yarn had a young businessman asking Morgan for a loan. Morgan refused but said, "I'll let you be seen walking down the street with me on my way to lunch." The sight proved more than sufficient to ensure the young man's credit elsewhere.

So powerful was J. P. Morgan in the Gilded Age that his critics called him Pierpontifex Maximus. His intervention in a dispute among competitors was usually enough to settle it, especially regarding railroads. When industry warfare had threatened to break out in 1885 regarding competition on routes to Chicago, he summoned the officials on both sides to a conference on New York's East River aboard the *Corsair*. No one was allowed ashore until an agreement had been hammered out to settle the dispute. Newspapers hailed the result as the Great Railroad Treaty of 1885.

Thereafter, railway barons found themselves repeatedly summoned to Morgan's office, or the yacht, to hear Pierpontifex Maximus lay down the law. One such meeting in 1886 resulted in the creation of associations to set a uniform rate structure that the fledgling Interstate Commerce Commission and the 1890 Sherman Antitrust Act were unable to prevent.

During the period of financial stresses and upheavals in the railroad business following the Panic of 1893, Morgan turned his keen eyes toward the status of railroading in New England with the intention of Morganizing it. The focus of these efforts was the New York & New Haven Railroad.

Organized in New Haven in 1844, the line ran westward to the New York state line and was designed as a passenger service. Its chief competitors were two small railways and several steamship services. Through mergers and leases and strenuous efforts to curtail or inhibit construction by rivals (no less than 203 separate small lines), the New Haven became the dominant rail service in New England. Yet it actually owned only 141 miles of track and held leases for an additional 503.

Assessing this complex and bewildering situation and declaring it unacceptable, Morgan set out to make the New Haven the dominant rail service in New England by smashing its main rival, the New York & New England. Its general manager, Charles Spangler Mellen, had started out like Jim Brady, as a ticket clerk. As head of the New York & New England, he found himself battling against the formidable Morgan in one of the most vicious fights of a pugnacious and omnivorous era of unrestrained rivalries to form and maintain industrial monopolies.

Years later, in a trial of New Haven directors for conspiracy, Mellen was asked about the state of competition between the New Haven and the New York & New England when he was the latter's general manager. Mellen answered, "It was the worst form of cut-throat competition I ever had any experience with in forty-four years. It was one man cutting the heart out of another, except they were two railroads."

Shrewdly discerning that the heart of the New York & New England was Mellen, Morgan saw to it that Mellen was lured away from the line. In 1892 Charles P. Clark, the president of the New Haven, on orders from Morgan, offered Mellen the post of second vice president of the New Haven at a much higher salary.

With Mellen gone from the New York & New England, the New Haven launched a plan to deprive his former employer access to New York. This was achieved when Morgan bought a small railroad that had been leasing its New York trackage to the New York & New England.

Morgan soon discovered that he and Mellen had much in common. Although Mellen was nowhere near Morgan in riches, he came to the New Haven Railroad a fairly wealthy man. In coming years he would rise to the presidency of the line and boast a palatial house in New Haven and a large estate in Stockbridge, Massachusetts, with lakes and woods populated by his prized swans, peacocks, ducks, pheasants, and fancy fowl of all kinds.

The Wall Street tycoon found Mellen to be as tough as himself and, should the situation require it, as cold as a bar of U.S. Steel. Deceptively soft-spoken, Mellen was described by his contemporaries as "arrogant and domineering, possessed of granitic gravity, and a man of iron will." He had a facile tongue and a predilection for sarcasm that sometimes overawed those with whom he came in contact.

Yet in his rise in the railroad business this frequently off-putting figure had become not only a valued customer of Diamond Jim Brady but friend to the gaudy, Irish, jovial, hale-fellow-well-met gourmand. Eventually Mellen would use that friendship to his advantage in several schemes of questionable legality. One involved buying $100,000 of common stock in Jim's name in the New England Investment & Securities Company. The deal put Mellen in control of the $20 million firm without anyone outside the firm knowing it.

In Jim's mind, fronting for Mellen seemed the least he could do, considering that Mellen's positions with several railroads had resulted in lucrative Brady contracts for equipment purchases. The first deals had been made when Mellen was a purchasing executive with a small Massachusetts line, the Boston & Lowell. The professional and personal relationships continued when Mellen was general manager of the New York & New England, as purchasing agent for the Union Pacific and the Northern Pacific (both controlled by Morgan), and then as second vice president and ultimately president of the New Haven.

A MEETING OF THE BOARD

Diamond Jim felt no qualms about secretly holding stocks for
friends, such as Charles Mellen, president of the New Haven
Railroad. The arrangement became known during investigations
by the federal government. The scandal became fair game for
newspaper cartoonists such as Rollin Kirby of the *New York World*,
who depicted the New Haven's board of directors wearing
bandits' masks.

For a twenty-year period (1894 to 1914), Mellen saw to it
that Diamond Jim's equipment-manufacturing companies received more than $36 million in contracts for 28,660 freight
cars and 709 passenger carriages, without having to submit bids.

Jim would learn just how great a friend Mellen could be
one day in 1902 when the latter was running the Northern
Pacific. In a hurry to get back to New York for a race in which
he had a horse entered, Jim burst into Mellen's office and
blurted, "Charlie, I ain't got a lot of time. I'm here to sell you
some cars and you have to take 'em without any argument."

Without hesitation, Mellen replied, "Name your best price."

In addition to using Jim's name to conceal stock ownership, Mellen arranged for Jim to be placed on the boards of directors of several corporations. For several years when Jim was the president of the Providence Securities Company, he admitted that he had no idea what the firm did. (It owned trolley lines.) The only time he put in an appearance at a meeting of the board of directors was to collect his annual salary.

None of these arrangements struck Jim as unusual. Had they been known outside the financial world, the general public would not have been surprised. Since the end of the Civil War the reunited nation had been in the throes of breathtaking industrial expansion. During the 1870s there had been a process of consolidation in the form of cartels. These soon became trusts. The most notable was Standard Oil, in which eighty-six separate entities accounting for 90 percent of the oil-refining and oil-transporting capacity of the country turned their properties over to the trust that had been hammered together by John D. Rockefeller.

Although there were numerous governmental investigations, denunciations in some antitrust newspapers, and an occasional adverse court ruling, Standard Oil persisted, aided by a federal government led by sympathetic Republican presidents as well as by corrupt members of the Congress in both parties. Should a federal or state legislative committee convene to question the power of a trust, its efforts were greeted by an onslaught of lawyers and publicity agents working for the trust who attacked the investigators' patriotism. During a probe of alleged collusion by railroads in setting freight rates, Chauncey Depew, president of the New York Central, accused the committee chairman of being a communist.

Apologists for the trusts asserted that slums, poverty, sickness, hunger, and unemployment were merely unfortunate but transitory side effects of a dynamic new economy. If government kept its hands off business, they argued, business would lead the nation into a period of unprecedented prosperity. Few men in government dissented from this point of view even following the Panic of 1893 and the subsequent depression. Although fifty years would go by before the president of General Motors, Charles Wilson, would declare, "What's good for General Motors is good for America," the belief that government should not interfere with industry was the prevailing sentiment in the era of J. P. Morgan, John D. Rockefeller, Andrew Carnegie, and Diamond Jim Brady.

Hundreds of thousands of men who labored in those industries responded to the absence of governmental concerns about their plight by unionizing. Although there had been attempts to organize labor immediately after the Civil War in the form of the Knights of St. Crispin and the Noble Order of the Knights of Labor in the 1870s, it was not until Samuel Gompers created the American Federation of Labor in 1881 that workers were able to join a well-organized union and make their collective voices heard. And, as has been noted, railway workers had flocked to the banner of Eugene Debs's American Railway Union. The result of this joining ranks by the nation's workers between 1881 and the end of the century was almost 39,000 strikes and lockouts of more than a day's duration.

While labor was uniting for a battle with capital, the components of the national economy were also split geographically between the industrial eastern states and the agricultural states of the South and West. This division manifested itself politically in the form of a third party. Formed in May 1891, the People's, or Populist, Party had put up a candidate for president in 1892. James B. Weaver ran against Republican incumbent Benjamin Harrison and Grover Cleveland, trying for a second nonconsecutive term. The Populist platform favored improvement in conditions of laborers (enforced by the government), free and unlimited coinage of silver, a graduated income tax, postal savings banks, direct election of U.S. Senators, a single term for president and vice president, ballot initiatives and referendums, recall elections, breaking up of trusts, revocation of land grants to railroads, government ownership of telephone and telegraph systems, and nationalization of the railroads.

One of the Populist proclamations declared, "Corruption dominates the ballot-box, the Legislatures, the Congress, and touches even the ermine of the bench."

It continued, "The fruits of the toil of millions are boldly stolen to build colossal fortunes for a few, unprecedented in the history of mankind; and the possessors of these, in turn, despise the Republic and endanger liberty. From the same prolific womb of governmental injustice we breed two great classes—tramps and millionaires."

In 1894 no American had embodied the idealism of the Populists more than Jacob Coxey, but his march on Washington had resulted only in his arrest and a fine for trespassing. Not long after the dispelling of Coxey's Army, a bitter joke went around the country concerning President Cleveland gazing out a White House window and finding a man crawling on hands and knees on the north lawn. Rushing out to him, Cleveland asked, "What are you doing?"

The man replied, "I'm out of work and I'm hungry, so I'm eating grass."

Cleveland said, "Well, go around to the south lawn, the grass is longer there."

Cleveland held the view that the proper relationship between the government and business be in line with the hands-off policy of his Republican predecessors. He'd been voted into office in 1884 and 1892 with no mandate to go after trusts or to otherwise hinder the means by which American business conducted itself. Regarding the laborer, however, he became the first president to seek legislation recognizing the rights of workers to organize and enter into collective bargaining with capital. Yet when Texas farmers appealed to the government for aid in the aftermath of a disastrous drought, Cleveland vetoed a measure to provide funds for them to buy seed. In rejecting what twentieth-century economists would call a "bailout" bill, he said, "The people support the government. The government does not support the people."

In the fourth year of his second term as president, Cleveland found himself not only the butt of grass-eating jokes but blamed for bringing on the depression that came in the wake of the Wall Street crash of 1893 because of his steadfast insistence on maintaining gold as the foundation of the economy. As a result of the depression, the Republicans had taken control of Congress in the 1894 elections. And in a speech to the House of Representatives, a Democrat from Nebraska with a reputation for oratory, Williams Jennings Bryan, had taken to the floor for three hours to speak against gold and in favor of silver.

Sounding like a Populist, he declared that the nation stood divided with "the corporate interests of the United States, the moneyed interests, aggregated wealth and capital, imperious, arrogant, compassionless" on one side and on the other was "an unnumbered throng, those who gave the Democratic party a name and for whom it has assumed to speak. Work-worn and dust-begrimed, they make their mute appeal, and too often find their cry for help beat in vain against the outer walls while others, less deserving, gain ready access to the legislative halls."

Bryan did not invoke the Populist imagery of a country of tramps and millionaires, but he later delivered one of the most ringing statements in the annals of American politics—not once but twice. On December 22, 1894, at the midpoint of Cleveland's second term, he told the House, "I shall not help crucify mankind upon a cross of gold. I shall not aid in pressing down upon the bleeding brow of labor this crown of thorns." Two years later, when he'd gained the Democratic nomination for president, he galvanized the party's convention by telling the backers of the gold standard, "You shall not press down upon the brow of labor this crown of thorns. You shall not crucify mankind upon a cross of gold."

Taking note of Bryan's gilded oratory, Diamond Jim Brady, the devoted adherent to the party line laid down by Tammany Hall, the man who'd been named after a Democrat president, the jolly fat fellow who counted himself a friend of several millionaires, the super-salesman and gentleman sportsman who had no problem taking on the role of "dummy director" at the behest of Charlie Mellen, looked at the 1896 nominee of his beloved Democratic Party with alarm.

When Charles Moore told Jim that if Bryan were elected "we might as well shut up shop because there won't be a wheel turning on any railroad in the entire country," Jim had to agree that the only alternative to Bryan's dangerous Populist ideas was the Republicans' presidential nominee, the fifty-three-year-old governor of Ohio and "sound money man," William McKinley.

Moore asked Jim to give McKinley more than his vote; he asked for a contribution to the McKinley campaign coffers. Jim insisted that whatever assistance he provided McKinley be done secretly. "Whatever I do, you'll have to keep it quiet," he said to Moore, "because it wouldn't do me any good with some of the people I do business with at Tammany Hall if the fact gets out."

INCLUDING $100,000 given by Jim on the promise that its donor would not be identified, money raised for McKinley by his campaign manager, Mark Hanna, exceeded $3 million, the largest election war chest to that time. Although McKinley honored the tradition of presidential candidates not taking to the hustings by remaining at his home in Ohio, the Republican's surrogates barnstormed the country. They painted a bleak picture of what the nation could expect should Bryan be elected. Bankers and businessmen were warned that Bryan in the White House meant inflation and federal controls on industries.

Workers were told that if the Democrats won, factories would be closed.

Wholeheartedly committed to a McKinley victory, Jim let employees of the Fox Solid Pressed Steel plant know that he would never fire a man for voting the way the man wanted, "but if any of you fellers vote for Bryan, I'm going to be mighty displeased."

On November 3, 1896, James Buchanan Brady for the first time in his life abandoned his fealty to Tammany Hall by marking a ballot with an X beside the name of a Republican. By the end of the day nearly 14 million votes would be cast, the paper ballots tallied by hand in towns and cities from coast to coast, and the results reported to an anxious, depression-plagued nation by telegraph. In New York City newspapers reported the presidential returns to throngs gathered in parks by posting them on bulletin boards. The tallies were relayed directly by telegraph to the headquarters of the parties at Madison Square. Republicans were ensconced at the Fifth Avenue Hotel. Democrats were nearby.

"At the great bar of the Hoffman House—the traditional stronghold of Democracy in New York," wrote an observer, "men found it almost a physical impossibility to wriggle their way to a point where they could shout their orders for drinks."

The official bouncer for the hotel, Billy Edwards, was placed in charge of holding money bet on the outcome of not only the presidential contest but for any other election that stirred the interests of men with dollars to wager. As official stakeholder that night he would have more than $400,000 stuffed into his pockets.

Men with a zeal for betting on the balloting who could not shoehorn themselves into the barroom were able to place wagers in the Ladies' Parlor (temporarily turned into a male domain). Eager to handle the bets were two of the biggest professional bookmakers in the city, George Wheelock and Matty Gorham. Among the gamblers were "Bet-a-Million" Gates; James

R. Keene, with unlimited funds earned in his position with J. P. Morgan; Theodore A. Hostetter, "the Bitters King"; an assortment of Pittsburgh steel millionaires; and Diamond Jim Brady.

As the evening wore on, none of these men paid attention as Jim excused himself from time to time to battle his way through the throng, disappear for a few minutes, and then return to propose bets on returns from particular states or districts. Nor did anyone question his uncanny luck—or attribute to him an amazing talent for political analysis—when he won.

Jim's success was the result of neither. When he briefly left the Hoffman House, he went to the Republican headquarters in the Fifth Avenue Hotel where an accomplice waited to provide him with electoral results well in advance of their public release.

When all the results of the presidential contest were in, McKinley tallied slightly more than 7 million votes, giving him a popular vote majority over Bryan of nearly 600,000 and an Electoral College tally of 271 to 176.

Diamond Jim came out of the election with a cash surplus of $180,000 in wagers won.

With his personal fortune improved and Bryan defeated, Jim breathed a sigh of relief and looked forward to the rapid recovery of the national economy under McKinley. Rejecting doomsayers who predicted the depression would continue, he became a proponent of what economists of the Ronald Reagan years would term the "trickledown theory" of wealth.

Asserting confidence in the future, he said, "Nothin's wrong with this country that ain't only just temporary."

He sold securities valued at $139,000 and declared to a friend, "I'm gonna spend every God damn cent of it buildin' goodwill. If it works, I'm gonna clean up bigger than any man ever has before or will again—and if it don't, I can always start over."

Two months before the presidential election of 1896, the railroad whose bankruptcy in early 1893 had been a harbinger of the Wall Street crash emerged from receivership. With extra money in his pocket thanks to his election-night winnings, the man who once planted himself in the office of the president of the Reading Railroad in order to tell him to go to hell, and landed a multimillion-dollar contract as a reward for his audacity, saw opportunity in the Reading line's return to life. In November, dipping into his election-night windfall, he purchased two thousand shares of Reading stock.

On the morning he placed his order the stock rose four points. He bought more, and he went on buying until the price reached $26. Holding his shares, he waited until the stock traded at $68, then sold out. The sudden dumping sent the value plummeting and nearly ruined one of Jim's friends, the gambler Richard Canfield. He'd also been pyramiding Reading stock. Diamond Jim Brady's profit of $50 a share left his bank accounts swollen by $1,250,000.

With Christmas approaching, Jim said to Lillian Russell, "I'm gonna do things in a big way from now on. There's a lot of fellas who ain't been gettin' much from me lately, on account of the depression—and this bein' Christmas season, it's as good a time as any for me to give 'em something."

After putting together a list of friends and business associates, he sent an assistant to the Washington Market to buy "all the fixin's" for a Christmas dinner for everyone on the list. Each box contained a huge turkey, sweet potatoes, chestnuts, cranberries, celery, dates, dried fruits, and jellies. Exactly one week before Christmas, they were sent by fast freight to points in almost every part of the country. The recipients were chief clerks, secretaries, section foremen, engineers and firemen, and conductors of railroads that he traveled and with whom he did business.

In the city, on Christmas eve, Jim's coachman delivered boxes to the homes of firemen, street cleaners, and police officers who had happened to come to Diamond Jim Brady's attention.

Many of the startled recipients had not realized that he knew their names.

Others whom he knew very well received other kinds of presents. Customers got costly neckties. (Jim bought twelve hundred at one of his favorite haberdashers, Budd's.) Each package of ties came with a note: "If you don't like these, take them back and exchange them for some that you do."

Said Jim to Lillian, "This is a hell of a lot of fun. If I'd known I was gonna get so much fun out it I'd've started the idea sooner."

He continued the practice to the end of his life.

10

Rogues, Rascals, and Railroaders

❧❦❧

A MONTH BEFORE Wall Street took the nosedive that triggered the Panic of 1893 and sent the nation reeling down into its worst economic depression in history to that time, theater in New York had made a leap of faith and geography. On May 22 the American Theater opened doors to audiences at 260 West Forty-second Street in a former farmland area of the city called Long Acre. The new theater's first offering was *The Prodigal Daughter*. The opening proved to be less than auspicious. Theatergoers were reluctant to travel "that far uptown" to a district that in the daytime was the city's horse-trading center. They would change their minds two and a half years later with the opening of an entertainment center between Forty-fourth and Forty-fifth on the west side of Broadway. Touted in advertisements as "the grandest amusement temple in the world" and called "Olympia," it was the idea of a friend of Diamond Jim Brady, the theatrical impresario Oscar Hammerstein.

A German orthodox Jew born in 1847, Hammerstein had made his fortune by inventing a cigar-making machine that eliminated hand-rolling and greatly reduced the cost of manufacture by increasing the output of the men, women, and children who worked in tenement sweatshops. The device rolled and cut twelve cigars at once, far beyond the capacity of any individual worker.

Having been in love with show business all his life, Hammerstein once wagered $100 that he could write a complete opera in twenty-four hours. The result was titled *The Kohinoor Diamond*. When he produced it at his own (great) expense, it was a flop. He'd made his first venture into theater-owning with the Harlem Opera House, the first theater built north of Central Park. In 1892 he'd opened the Manhattan Opera House at Thirty-fourth and Broadway in partnership with Koster and Bial. It was there that "Mr. First Nighter," Diamond Jim Brady, had met him and immediately liked him for his rakish, even roguish, personal style.

Among the most endearing of Hammerstein's behaviors was his practice of seeing his productions from a seat in the audience. If he didn't like what he saw on stage, he expressed his views by hissing. When this practice was called to the attention of Koster and Bial, they took Hammerstein to court in an effort to get a judge to order him to cease and desist. The court ruled that Hammerstein's right to hiss was guaranteed by the First Amendment. The thwarted partners then paid Hammerstein $370,000 to end their relationship.

With those funds and an additional $2 million, Hammerstein built the Olympia. Under its one roof New Yorkers would be able to enjoy the offerings of a great music hall, a concert auditorium of "noble design and ample proportions," a theater named the Lyric built on "unique lines" to accommodate comic opera and burlesque, and a "rooftop garden" with an Oriental café. It provided smoking rooms, a billiard parlor, and lounges. The music hall offered 128 boxes and general seating for 2,800. The precursor of twentieth-century "multiplex" cinemas had a capacity in its various venues to seat six thousand people. The ticket price for admission to all these theaters would be the same as the amount paid "to see the world" at the Columbian Exposition—a mere fifty cents—although the very best seats went for a $1.50.

With great fanfare in newspaper ads, on billboards and in handout sheets, Hammerstein announced that the Olympia would open on November 25, 1895, with a burlesque on the stage of the Lyric Theater. The star was to be the singer/actress who was the main rival of Lillian Russell, the beautiful, younger, but not much slimmer Fay Templeton. Born in a theater on Christmas day 1865 in Little Rock, Arkansas, she'd spoken her first lines at age three, as Cupid. At eight she was Puck in *A Midsummer Night's Dream* in her New York debut. At age fifteen she was a prima donna with romantic leads in musicals such as *Evangeline, The Mascot,* and *Billie Taylor.*

Like other female stage luminaries such as Ada Rehan, Maude Adams, Blanche Bates, Maxine Elliott, Mary Mannering, Rose Coughlan, and Lillian Russell, Templeton found herself a recipient of an admiring Diamond Jim Brady's gifts, though never as many nor as lavish as those Jim presented to Lillian.

In *Excelsior, Jr.,* Templeton would be in the title role. It was a period in which women musical stars portrayed men in what were known as "trouser roles." Unfortunately, on the opening night no one saw her perform.

Although her name alone would have assured a huge turnout, a nervous Hammerstein had oversold the house. More than ten thousand tickets had been sold or given away. Complimentary ducats had been handed out to the most notable of the dudes, first nighters such as Diamond Jim, and a long list of luminaries that included Senator-elect Jacob A. Cantor, New York District Attorney DeLancey Nicoll, and brewer Jacob Ruppert Jr.

On the rainy night of November 25, hansom cabs and private carriages delivering men dressed in evening clothes and women in dresses with puffy sleeves (the latest fashion fad) appeared to make their way through a mob of excited New Yorkers who had trekked uptown by cable cars or on foot. By eight o'clock their numbers thronged Broadway and side streets and attempted to force their way into the Olympia in what a reporter for the *New York Times* called "a modern gridiron, with nobody to retire the injured from the field and nobody to count the yards of gain or loss."

Griped one embattled ticket-holder who'd tried to push his way inside, "I played football and you can get a fair show for a rush in that game. You can't get it here."

The news report described puffed sleeves wilted, ladies' crimped hair that had become "hoydenish" in the crush and rain, ripped dresses, stepped-on toes, and first nighters' and dudes' evening wear splashed with muck. Those lucky enough to get inside the theater found other hazards in the form of walls, stairway bannisters, and doors with wet paint. Elihu Root was seen with green and yellow stripes lacing the back of his coat. District Attorney Nicoll's swallow-tailed coat picked up a rainbow of hues.

The *Times* man gazed upon a "denser mass than was ever the crowd at an international wedding." One woman who was observed being "shot like a cannon ball" through a door was heard to exclaim to her husband, "Gracious, Harry, I'm glad I didn't wear anything good."

Barely heard above the din, Hammerstein shouted, "Close the doors. Call the police."

Not since a riot outside the Astor Theater in 1849, when Americans had protested the appearance of an English actor, had the police been summoned to quell a disturbance at a place of entertainment. Struggling against the crowd, the burliest men of Police Commissioner Theodore Roosevelt's force managed to close the doors, but at ten o'clock the crush was as great as ever.

It would be four days before Fay Templeton would finally take to the Lyric stage. But Oscar Hammerstein soon discovered that his dream had been too big. The Olympia was simply too large to fill and too costly to run. In 1898 he found himself bankrupt. Undaunted, a year later he was back in business at Broadway and Forty-second with a new theater, the Victoria. Managed by his son Willie, it soon became the vaudeville center of the city and marked the beginning of a new theater district around Times Square that future generations would identify as Broadway.

AMONG THE FRIENDS of Diamond Jim Brady who'd found their evening wear and patent leather shoes ruined by the wet paint and mud on November 25 was New York's most famous architect, Stanford White. Three years older than Jim (born on November 9, 1853), he had been educated in private schools. Entering the Boston architectural office of Gambill and Richardson in 1872 as an apprentice, he'd worked on the design of Boston's Trinity Church. After studying in Paris with Augustus Saint-Gaudens (1878–1879), he returned to New York and joined in a firm that became known as McKim, Mead and White. Their specialty was luxurious homes for the rich in New York City and Newport, Rhode Island. White's forte was designing furniture and interiors, but he'd also created the pedestals for many of Saint-Gauden's sculptures, including a heroic statue of Admiral David Farragut in Madison Square Park.

Opposite it, White had designed the city's largest site for theatrical presentations, sports events, and expositions. Opened in 1890, it occupied the whole block between Twenty-sixth and Twenty-seventh streets and Fourth and Madison avenues. It took its name from its site: Madison Square Garden. At the pinnacle of the structure's most dramatic feature, a tower that had been copied from the Giralda in Spain, was a controversial statue of a nude Diana rendered in gold by Saint-Gaudens. The sprawling building also featured on its uppermost floor a restaurant called the Madison Square Garden Roof.

Considered one of the most dashing men in the city, White was a dapper figure with a red handlebar mustache. He was known to his closest friends as Stannie. When and where he and the fat, diamond-studded railway equipment salesman became acquainted is not known. They probably met on a night at the theater. Possibly they had been introduced by a mutual friend, Freddie Gebhard, for whom Jim had arranged a special train for Lillie Langtry's tour of the American West. However White and Jim came together, they promptly formed a bond that left observers scratching heads in amazement.

In background, culturally and socially they were polar opposites. White was educated and suave and had been raised to be a gentleman. Jim had a rough-hewn quality that no display of diamonds could ever overcome. Yet throughout the 1890s the two were constantly seen in each other's company, evidently enjoying their friendship.

As a stockholder and the organizer of Madison Square Garden's entertainment programs, White had a spacious apartment in the tower. He also had a studio nearby at 22 West Twenty-fourth Street in which the dominant furnishings were not his desk and drawing tables but an enormous canopied bed surrounded by mirrors. Hanging from the ceiling was a swing with its ropes and seat covered in red velvet. White installed it to be used by beautiful blondes and brunettes whom he invited to the studio and persuaded to entertain him by swaying on it in the nude.

Swings were also a feature of a party White arranged for Jim to host for two of Jim's out-of-town customers. It was held in a banquet room atop Madison Square Garden. The guests were seated on divans inspired by stories of the bacchanals of ancient Rome.

Dangling from the ceiling before each sofa was a swing with white velvet ropes and seat.

As Jim, the two men, and White waited for the meal to be served, perhaps wondering about the absence of tables, they drank freely of White's best wines. (Jim sipped sarsaparilla.) On White's signal, four naked girls entered the room. Each carried a silver serving tray holding a plate of food, the utensils, and a napkin. As the girls sat on the swings, the guests who understood they would be asked to provide business to Diamond Jim in the morning realized with whoops of delight that they were expected to grab their dinner from the trays held on the girls' laps as they swung to and fro on the swings.

A bevy of bare beauties would also be the highlight of a stag birthday party that White decided to throw for Jim. (The year being celebrated isn't known.) The location was a small banquet room in Madison Square Garden known as the Hall of Mirrors. Including Jim and White, twelve men dined lavishly on fourteen courses, but seated around a broad table. Three waiters served. When it was time for dessert (always Jim's favorite part of a meal), he expected them to bring in a huge birthday cake with blazing candles.

One of White's servants, who referred to White as "the Governor," left this anonymous account of what followed:

Then, a twinkle in his eye, the Governor gave a signal and the waiters entered the room bearing aloft a huge Jack-Horner-Pie. They carefully placed it in the center of the table, and then handed each of the gentlemen a white silk ribbon. Mr. Brady's ribbon, I noticed, differed from the others. It was a red one. After making a little speech reminding all those present that it was Mr. Brady's birthday and that the pie was in lieu of a birthday cake, the Governor suddenly said 'Pull!' and all the gentlemen pulled on their ribbons. Then the pie fell apart revealing a beautiful and entirely nude girl nestled in the middle of it. Mr. Brady kept pulling on his red ribbon which, I could see, was fastened to the girl's arm. And as he continued to pull, the girl got up and danced down the table to where he was sitting. She then climbed down off the table and onto Mr. Brady's lap where, after kissing him several times, she proceeded to feed him his dessert.

The other guests were rather envious of Mr. Brady's good fortune, and they proceeded to show their envy with loud wails and groans. After he had let them do this for a few minutes, the Governor smiled and suddenly clapped his hands. The doors opened and in came eleven other nude young ladies who also proceeded to feed the guests their dessert.

It was a very pleasant evening.

Stanford White's rival in staging such parties was Jim's pal Freddie Gebhard. Because his considerable private fortune left him with no need to work for a living and a great deal of time on his hands, he thrived on planning more and more extravagant and increasingly outrageous fetes. As a result, he welcomed opportunities to assist in entertaining Jim's clients. Most of those affairs were held at a hotel at Broadway and Twenty-ninth Street. They became known—and notorious—as the Gilsey House parties.

Aided by a tolerant and indulgent management, the team of Brady and Gebhard staged what one observer called "high old times" in the private dining rooms, starting after the theaters let out and sometimes lasting until dawn. The guests were Jim's customers. The entertainers were chorus girls from the nearby theaters. They happily attended because they knew they would be rewarded by Diamond Jim with $100 bills tucked under their dinner plates. Whether a girl would garner more money, or perhaps a sparkling trinket, from one of Jim's grateful guests in a more intimate setting in one of the Gilsey House rooms was entirely up to the customer and the girl. As Jim explained, "It wasn't so much what happened while a party was going on that he cared about, as it was what went on when it ended."

Should one of his guests choose to stay the night in the hotel, Jim provided a suitcase containing everything a gentleman might require for passing a comfortable night, including a couple of bottles of wine and a nightgown for the lady. Understood in all this was that the next day the grateful customer would put his John Hancock on a Brady contract.

When he pursued his salesmanship by plying customers with food, drink, and amenable young women, he was being a man of his time. "Jim's methods were not subtle, nor in the best of taste," wrote a historian of the era. "He would have been the last man to affirm that they were. But they were productive."

In this approach to doing business and in his easygoing attitude toward the morality of such dealings, the James Buchanan Brady whose public persona was "Diamond Jim" accepted the current norms of a gaudy, freewheeling era. Its history would be strewn with the names of brash, bold men whom many people saw as great builders and innovators, but others viewed as ruthless robber barons, rogues, and rascals.

Among Diamond Jim's friends who cut a flamboyant swath was Herbert Barnum Seeley, a nephew of one of the most colorful men of the era that immediately preceded and had laid the foundation for the Gay Nineties. When P. T. Barnum died in 1891, the showman and circus impresario bequeathed Herbert $444,444.40. Five years later when his brother, Clinton Burton Seeley, announced that he was getting married, Herbert decided to give him a bachelor dinner at which no expense would be spared.

The date was Saturday, December 19, 1895. The venue was an upstairs private dining room of Sherry's restaurant. Guests numbered twenty, including Diamond Jim, Freddie Gebhard, and Stanford White. The menu consisted of Sherry's finest repasts. As the festivities unfolded, a door flew open to admit three lovely, exotically clad dancing girls. But all eyes centered on one of them. Dark-eyed and voluptuous with diamonds in her garters, Little Egypt had thrilled and scandalized the midway crowds of the Columbian Exposition by introducing belly dancing. For the delighted men upstairs at Sherry's she began undulating clad in a Zouave jacket and a pair of lace pantaloons.

To the astonishment of the ogle-eyed guests, shortly after Little Egypt began dancing, the door to the private room opened again, but the figures barging into it were men in the blue uniform of the New York Police Department. Equally as surprising to the men was the leader of the raiders, Captain Chapman of the Thirteenth Street Station, whom the men knew to be a copper who had never shown an interest in exhibiting such diligence in enforcing the city's public morals ordinances. Whatever the captain's motivation, Little Egypt, the other girls, and the guests escaped arrest because the police broke into the party at a moment when the women were fully clothed. Unable to charge anyone with public lewdness, Chapman's men departed.

When the story of the raid was headlined in the newspapers, an uproar of public outrage forced District Attorney Nicoll to convene a grand jury. As organizer of the scandalous event, Herbert Barnum Seeley was indicted for conspiracy "to induce the woman known as Little Egypt to commit the crime of indecent exposure." But in the face of the testimony of Little Egypt and the others at the party that she had not shed so much as a veil, the case collapsed.

Speculation quickly turned to why the morally myopic Captain Chapman had swooped into Sherry's that night. The most popular theory held that he had been informed that among the guests enjoying the undraped gyrations of Little Egypt the raiders would find none other than the very person who as head of the board of police commissioners had been carrying on a crusade to clean up police corruption and enforce the laws against selling alcohol on Sunday by forcing the police to close the saloons. Theodore Roosevelt's enemies on the police force, who had made a living by taking bribes from saloon owners to be allowed to stay open, had hoped to undercut his authority by showing him to be a hypocrite and forcing him to resign.

To anyone who knew Theodore Roosevelt the idea that he would attend such a party and wish to watch women dancing naked was preposterous. Told by newspaper reporters that this apparently had been the motivation behind the raid, Commissioner Roosevelt thundered, "What! And I at home with my babies!"

Police department connivance in fostering the flesh trade as another means of lining police pockets with bribes contributed to a revolt at the ballot box in 1894 that had resulted in Roosevelt's mandate to clean up the police department. Principal leader of the demand for reform, the Reverend Charles Parkhurst of the Madison Square Presbyterian Church, had said of rampant prostitution in the city in the 1890s, "Social vice has been so protected and encouraged by the filthy officials who control the [police] department that the number of abandoned women and disorderly houses now existing in the city is no measure of what it would be if we had no police force, from top down, who conceived of sexual crime as an evil to be suppressed, not as capital to draw dividend from."

Roosevelt viewed having to deal with the prostitution as "one of the saddest features of police work." But he did not limit his policemen to rounding up the women. He ordered police to treat the women's customers "on an exact equality for the same act." He favored a proposal put forth by the Reverend Charles Stelzle of the Labor Temple that called for publication of the names of the owners of property used for immoral purposes, after the individual had been given ample time to stop the practice. He backed prosecution of keepers and backers of brothels, men and women, and demanded their punishment "as severely as pickpockets and common thieves." Fines would not suffice. They must go to jail.

In assessing the motivation of women to go into prostitution, Roosevelt concluded they did so because they found wages in lawful work "inadequate to keep them from starvation, or to permit them to live decently." He declared, "The employers and all others responsible for these conditions stand on a moral level not far above the white slavers themselves."

Although it seemed to some that Diamond Jim's moral standing in paying chorus girls to attend the parties for his customers was shaky as regards to using vulnerable women for profit, he saw himself in the role of helping them. None was ever ordered to earn $100 he'd placed under her dinner plate by providing sexual favors to his guests. If a girl decided to do so, it was her decision alone. If approached on the street by a prostitute, Diamond Jim never bought her services. He handed her money "to tide you over until you can find decent work."

Horrified friends who learned that he doled out cash to every woman who handed him a hard-luck story—two or three thousand was a conservative estimate—upbraided him for being a sucker. His usual reply was "Why shouldn't I help them along a little bit, even if it does make an easy mark out of me?"

As a result, he found himself waylaid not only on the street but in hotel lobbies, at the theater, and even when he rode the elevated trains. As one disapproving friend put it, "Any gal with a sob story could get a steak or a stake out of him."

He certainly could afford it. As the only Republican for whom James Buchanan Brady ever voted swept to victory in the presidential election of 1896, Diamond Jim was raking in a windfall from his decision to buy stock at $50 a share in the restructured Reading Railroad, resulting in a Brady profit of $1.25 million. Confident that "sound money man" William McKinley would defend the gold standard and lead the nation out of "the Cleveland depression," Jim looked forward to a healthy rebound of the railroad business.

His optimism was based on a change in the construction of railway cars.

SINCE TRAINS FIRST took to the rails in America, freight and people had been carried to their destinations in cars built of wood. This limited the size of the cars, dictated the weight of their cargo, and limited the shippers' profits. With business declining during the depression, the railroads desperately needed every train to pay as much revenue as possible. Consequently, a demand rose for freight cars with a greater capacity than that afforded by wood frames. The ideal structure, it seemed to the man who'd made millions by introducing and making pressed steel undercarriages, would be an all-steel freight car.

In association with an official of the Carnegie Steel Company, Charles L. Taylor, who had studied the use of all-steel cars in Europe, Jim's Fox Solid Pressed Steel Company took up the challenge in the spring of 1894. A few months later the company delivered seven all-steel flatcars with a bearing capacity of 80,000 pounds to the Carnegie company—the first such cars in America. Encouraged (and enriched), Jim formed the Fox Pressed Steel Company. Incorporated in Pennsylvania on February 8, 1896, it immediately entered into collaboration with the Pennsylvania Railroad on all-steel hopper cars. They were designed to carry 80,000 to 100,000 pounds of coal, but a test with wet sand showed that the cars were capable of hauling 125,000 pounds.

Delighted with the design, Taylor informed Jim that he would exhibit the hopper cars at the Master Car Builder's Convention at Saratoga, New York, in the fall of 1896. Seeing a rich opportunity, Diamond Jim announced that he would also be at Saratoga with his order book in hand. And in true Diamond Jim Brady fashion, he would place at the disposal of his potential customers three cottages staffed by twenty-seven Japanese servants. More important delegates got letters inviting them to stay with Jim for the duration of the convention. To ensure that no one would be disappointed, he brought along hundreds of bottles of beer, wines, ales, and the finest whiskies. Thousands of pounds of food ranged from corned beef and cabbage to caviar and *pâte de fois gras* with truffles. Havana cigars were available by the box. Conventioneers who partook of this open-house hospitality entered Jim's cabin and found on display in the foyer one silver-plated Fox truck and an example of one of his famous gold-plated bicycles.

While Jim had no problem selling Fox trucks and other equipment, he discovered that the giddy railwaymen were reluctant to give him orders for the all-steel cars. The men admired them, and they admitted that someday all the railroads would be using them, but they were not ready to buy them at that moment.

Jim's only consolation was that neither was anyone buying steel cars being offered by a competing, but much smaller, firm. The Schoen Pressed Steel Company had been founded at about the same time as Fox by a former Philadelphia postman, Charles T. Schoen, and a nephew, William. The tiny plant in Allegheny, Pennsylvania, had never been considered by Diamond Jim to be a serious contender in the railway equipment business. But three weeks after McKinley was inaugurated as president of the United States, J. T. Odell, vice president and general manager of the Pittsburgh, Bessemer and Lake Erie Railroad, announced a contract with the Schoen firm for a thousand steel coal and coke cars at a price that was very little over the cost of manufacture.

Shocked and outraged, Jim bellowed at his secretary, "They'll ruin the business. The God damned fools will spoil everything before it's even started."

He received a second shock when he learned that Schoen had used the contract to obtain a bank loan to increase the capacity of the Allegheny plant to four times its original size. The new facility would allow the company to build and deliver five hundred steel cars in 1897.

But Schoen's triumph proved a boon to Diamond Jim's car-building plans. When J. T. Odell's P. B. & L. E. line found that steel cars required much less maintenance, resulting in greater profit per carload of coal, other railroads recognized the value in steel cars. Jim's company soon found itself swamped with orders.

Delighted with this turn of events, Jim took a leaf from the books of other industrialists and decided to forge a monopoly in steel cars by either driving Schoen out of business or making Schoen an offer he couldn't refuse. When he offered to buy out the competitor, Schoen countered with an even better idea. He proposed that Jim and Sampson Fox come in with the Schoens in the form of a trust. By combining, Schoen argued, they would create one gigantic entity that would dominate the steel car business. After two years of complicated negotiations that involved pooling patents and hammering out details of the partnership, the new Pressed Steel Car Company was incorporated under the laws of New Jersey on January 12, 1899. Its purpose was to manufacture freight and passenger cars, street cars, trucks, frames, and all kinds of pressed steel equipment and specialties. Capitalized at $25 million, making it the largest company of its kind, its issues of 125,000 shares of preferred and 125,000 shares of common stock were split among the Schoens, the Fox people, and a few of their intimate friends. Charles Schoen became the new company's president, nephew William vice president, and Brady men as secretary and treasurer.

In keeping with his view of himself as America's greatest salesman of railroad products, Jim took charge of the new firm's sales. As always, he declined a salary in favor of a commission on the gross business. During the first year, the company made and Jim sold 9,624 cars and other equipment for a gross of $13,965,000.

The amount that went into Diamond Jim's pocket is not known, but he treated himself with a small part by buying a twenty-five-carat emerald for a stick pin.

AS OSCAR HAMMERSTEIN'S Olympia had signaled the start of an uptown shift of the New York theater district, a change was under way in the nature of shows. French *opera bouffe* that had been the reigning musical mode and the route to stardom and riches for Jim's best friend Lillian Russell was being supplanted by a style Broadway impresarios called musicals. Their ascendency was marked by the appearance of Ada Rehan early in 1897 in a revival of a vehicle titled *Meg Merriles*. The new production was promoted not as a "romantic melodrama" but a "romantic *musical* play." *Opera bouffe* and operettas were of European origin. The musical comedy offered a brisker, less sentimental, American idiom.

One of the stars of the former who achieved success in the latter, De Wolf Hopper, said of the difference, "The European flavor of light opera was, no doubt, one of its weaknesses in America and an explanation of why it [would be] all but driven from our stage by musical comedy. The former was purely romantic and far removed from American life. Musical comedy was of our own soil, its wit native, its book topical, its music generally livelier, if cheaper, and it bore down heavily on comedy."

The leading developer of the musical comedy was George W. Lederer. Although Lillian and he had engaged in a lengthy contract dispute some years earlier, in the fall of 1896 Lederer had presented her in an operetta, *An American Beauty*. Despite its title, it was a show in the old style, set in Europe. The opus delighted audiences in the Midwest and was scheduled to open in New York on October 11, 1896. While playing the title role in the just-opened New Century Theater in St. Louis, Lillian received a telegram informing her of the death of her beloved father. Although he had continued to live in Chicago, he had never missed one of his daughter's opening nights in New York. He had given her a nickname, "Airy Fairy Lillian," which clung to her all her life. Although Lillian wanted to attend her father's funeral, to do so would mean closing the production, thereby jeopardizing the future of the show, and putting more than seventy people out of work. After consulting by telegram with an uncle and sisters, Lillian decided not to travel to Chicago. The

Theatrical poster for Lillian Russell in *An American Beauty* (1896). When she did not close down the show in St. Louis to attend the funeral of her father in Chicago, she was savagely criticized by the press. She explained that if she did so, the large cast would have lost a week's pay, and that her father was such a nice man that he would have approved.

show went on and Lillian was scolded in newspapers in St. Louis, Chicago, and New York for being a heartless actress.

The criticism notwithstanding, Lillian opened in *An American Beauty* at the Casino in New York on December 28, 1896. She played Gabrielle Dalmont, a young lady who goes riding, forgetting it is her wedding day. In her most spectacular scene she entered on an elephant. The show proved successful financially in New York and on tour.

While still heralded as the American Beauty, Lillian's position as the greatest female star in the country was challenged by a newcomer to the stage, Edna May. Daughter of a postman in Syracuse, New York, she attracted such attention and acclaim as a standout petite chorus girl in *The Belle of New York* that a writer in *Town Topics* asserted, "Edna May is now what Lillian Russell was when I first saw her at Tony Pastor's on Lower Broadway in *Pinafore*."

Lillian also felt challenged by Anna Held and Edna Wallace, a fast-rising American actress who later became Mrs. De Wolf Hopper.

In noting these rivals for the crown of America's favorite actress, *The Standard*'s theatrical commentator wrote, "For the life of me I cannot believe that Russell is done for, as the prophets of the theater insist she is."

That Lillian's claim to supremacy on the stage might be slipping was indicated when she returned to the Casino in April 1897. The production was another operetta, *The Wedding Day*. But Lillian was not the show's only star. For the first time in her life she shared billing equally. Her costars were Della Fox and Jefferson de Angelis. It was the first time in musical comedy history that three such high-salaried personalities appeared together in one company. The show proved financially successful in New York and would do the same on the road.

In that spring of 1897, as the McKinley administration took up the vexing problems of an ailing economy and the debate over gold versus silver, or a combination, as its basis, demands were being voiced by imperialistic "jingoes" for American intervention on the side of rebels in Cuba who were fighting to overthrow Spanish rule. A leading proponent of the United States going to war with Spain was Theodore Roosevelt. The

When producer Florenz Ziegfeld discovered the singing beauty Anna Held in Paris, he borrowed $10,000 from Diamond Jim to sign her to a contract and bring her to New York. "Flo" and Anna were eventually married.

bellicose police commissioner who had become nettlesome to the New York political establishment because of his enforcement of the Sunday saloon-closing laws had been appointed assistant secretary of the navy by a reluctant McKinley, who feared Roosevelt would provoke a war the president did not desire.

While attention turned to the affairs of the new administration in Washington at the time Lillian's status in the hearts of theatergoers was slipping, and James Buchanan Brady was in contention with the Schoens to build all-steel railroad cars, know-it-alls and gossips in the hotels and lobster palaces of New York were agog over stories that the American Beauty and Diamond Jim both had fallen in love. The word was out that Lillian's heart had been given to a copper magnate and Diamond Jim's had been captured by a policeman's daughter.

11

The Girl's a Lady

❧❧❧

THRICE MARRIED AND DIVORCED, forty years of age, getting stouter in figure and thinner in her vocal qualities, and no longer unchallenged queen of comedies, Lillian Russell continued to be the darling of men who possessed the means to express their admiration with gifts. Unfailing in devotion was Diamond Jim Brady, whose only demand on the American Beauty continued to be her companionship at the table and on bicycle outings. But just as persistent was a friend of his, an heir to a copper fortune. Small, dark, and almost fragile in his appearance, Jesse Lewisohn had gotten to know Jim because of their passion for gambling.

Understanding that Jim was not interested in becoming Lillian's lover, and certainly not in being her fourth husband, Lewisohn had been as generous as he in showering Lillian with costly trinkets. Every opening night of a Lillian Russell performance was observed with delivery to her dressing room of a huge floral piece containing his card. Tucked amid the flowers was a jewel to vie with whatever Diamond Jim had sent.

Any doubt that Lewisohn may have harbored regarding Jim's intentions toward Lillian was dispelled in the summer of 1897 when lobster palaces, bars, and gambling rooms of the Madison Square hotels and the Waldorf suddenly buzzed with gossip that Diamond Jim had fallen hard for a twenty-year-old,

168

(*top*) This is the only known photograph of Edna McCauley. Diamond Jim wanted to marry the former shop girl, but Edna fell in love with copper tycoon Jesse Lewisohn (*right*), who happened to be the man Lillian Russell hoped to marry. Both Jim and Lillian were shocked and heartbroken, but got over it.

blond, gold-digging, social-climbing department store salesgirl from Brooklyn by the name of Edna McCauley.

She had met Jim in the Waldorf's Peacock Alley, the story went, through the artifice of dropping her handkerchief. Picking it up and presenting it to her, Jim supposedly had said, "It is a beautiful handkerchief, but not nearly as beautiful as the owner."

When he invited her to tea at his apartment, Edna accepted.

According to those who claimed to know all about her, the second daughter of a policeman had been born in Brooklyn and had received a decent education. Upon reaching working age, she'd crossed the Brooklyn Bridge and found employment as a salesgirl in a department store for $8 a week. Not long after taking the job, she was noticed by one of the sons of the store owner. He took her to dinner several times and eventually was rewarded with far more intimate evenings, for which he expressed his gratitude by promoting her to the store's perfume counter at $10 a week.

One night he took Edna to dinner at the Waldorf, where he made the mistake of pointing out another man having dinner. "See that fat fellow sitting over there by himself?" he whispered. "He's the notorious Diamond Jim Brady. He spends every afternoon here gambling and then has a huge meal at that same table."

Soon after, possibly the next day, Edna returned to the hotel. She found her quarry having his dinner. Passing Jim's table, she let the lacy hanky float to the floor.

Whether this story was true or the result of someone's romantic imagination was of no concern to those who heard it. How Edna McCauley came to Diamond Jim Brady's attention and into his life was immaterial. All could see that she was obviously the apple of his eye. It was a turn of events that left everyone astonished.

No one proved more amazed at the success of a salesgirl's audacity than Edna herself. She found New York's most famous and wealthy man with a reputation for enjoying being in the company of women, but never allowing them to think for a moment that they might marry him, telling her of the wonderful things that were going to happen and of the plans he was making for their future life together. She had expected her charm would win a certain response, but she never imagined that there would be anything more than an affair. Instead, Jim asked her to move into his Fifty-seventh Street apartment. When she did, he welcomed her by presenting a diamond tiara with a center stone that weighed eleven carats. Then came rings, brooches, bracelets, gold mesh bags, and earrings. He handed her $1,000 a month in "pocket money" to buy anything she wanted.

When a friend questioned all this extravagance, Jim retorted, "The girl's a lady, and I'm going to put her into Society."

MONARCH OF THAT "SOCIETY" was Caroline Webster Schermerhorn Astor, wife of William Astor, second son of William Backhouse Astor. Her reign had begun at the southwestern corner of Fifth Avenue and Thirty-fourth Street in a four-story mansion built at a cost of $1.5 million and furnished for $750,000. Although William disliked social life, Caroline not only adored it, she made up her mind to dictate its style and tone. Her device in this ambition was a grand ball. Held on the third Monday of every January, it became the capstone of the social season.

What Mrs. Astor lacked in brains and beauty (she wore a black wig because her hair was falling out), she made up in adornments. Festooned with as many jewels as possible, including a triple necklace of diamonds and a famous brooch said to have belonged to Marie Antoinette, and resplendent in gems and floor-length gown, she greeted her guests in front of a life-size portrait of herself. Once welcomed and having demonstrated obeisance, guests entered the ballroom. When her "chamberlain" and secretary, Ward McAllister, explained to a reporter that the size of the assemblage was dictated by the number of people who could fit comfortably into the ballroom, McAllister coined the phrase that immediately became synonymous with the elite of New York society.

"There are only about four hundred people in fashionable New York society," he said. "If you go outside the number you strike people who either are not at ease in a ballroom or else make other people not at ease."

Among those who could never be counted among "the 400" was the flamboyant figure with the flashy nickname whom McAllister dismissed as "that impossible Brady person."

Although Jim longed for admission to the 400, the closest he came to Caroline Astor's ballroom was a hotel that was built on a corner opposite her mansion in 1892. Thirteen stories high with 530 rooms and 350 private baths, it was constructed by her nephew, William Waldorf Astor, great grandson of the Astor patriarch, John Jacob Astor. Know-it-alls and gossips stated with certainty that he had decided to raze his house at Fifth and Thirty-third and build the hotel so that it would block the sun from his aunt's home. William named the hotel the Waldorf.

Less than a year after it opened, the sunless Caroline surrendered by engaging architect Richard Morris Hunt to design and build her a new mansion farther up Fifth. Her son, John Jacob Astor IV, saw an opportunity in Caroline's decampment to embarrass cousin William by tearing down her mansion and building a hotel of his own, the Astoria.

Familial competition eventually yielded to common sense and smart business practice, resulting in combining of the hotels and their names. The Waldorf-Astoria became the world's largest, costliest, and most magnificent hostelry. It offered 1,000 rooms and 765 private baths, the first hotel roof garden, a huge four-sided bar, and Peacock Alley, where Jim Brady and men like him who also were excluded from the 400 met for high-stakes card games. Modeled on the grand salon in King Ludwig's palace in Munich, the hotel's dining room was called the Empire. It was there that Edna McCauley had let her dainty handkerchief flutter to the floor within Jim's easy reach.

Under the management of George C. Boldt, the "hotel with the hyphen," as it was called, quickly became the mecca of men who were uncrowned monarchs of a financial empire whose center was miles downtown. After three in the afternoon, these men trekked up from Wall Street to "meet at the Waldorf." They assembled at the bar and around heavy oak tables, each seated in a luxurious leather armchair, to compare how well, or not so well, shares had traded on the day. Only J. P. Morgan sat aloof and alone, silently drinking scotch, ever the unapproachable, godlike, and unmatched in power.

Seated in quiet alcoves or clustered in adjacent rooms were the gamblers, such as John W. "Bet-a-Million" Gates, playing poker for "one a point." When a young novitiate won several hands, he expected to pocket $330. Only when he received a check the following morning for $330,000 did he realize he'd not been playing for a dollar a point but for a thousand.

Although Jim occasionally sat in on such games, he preferred quiet rounds of poker with men he regarded as cut from the same cloth as he. How much might be won or lost was not as important as companionship. Among them was his chief competitor in the bestowing of gifts on Lillian Russell.

Having settled into a romantic relationship with Edna McCauley, Jim was pleased to note that Lillian appeared to be enjoying a settled period herself, primarily because of attentions paid to her by the copper heir. Knowing that the only music that appealed to Lewisohn, aside from Lillian's singing, was the click of poker chips and the whir of a roulette wheel, Jim gave Lillian's affair with Lewisohn his blessing. Referring to her failed marriages, he told her, "Thank the lord Jesse is not another of those damned leeching musicians."

But as Jim was romancing Edna, he and Lewisohn found themselves for a time without Lillian's companionship. Following her stint in *The Wedding Day* in which she had shared star billing, she had sailed away on the liner *Teutonic* for Germany and a theatrical tour in which she intended to yield the limelight to no one.

WITH HER SISTER SUSIE as traveling companion, the American Beauty was greeted with an enthusiasm that surpassed anything she'd enjoyed on Broadway and on tour across America.

But she found herself unable to reciprocate. She discovered little to like in Germans. She found the country's steel barons and heel-clicking, hand-kissing army officers "overbearing."

Nor did she care much for the pushy attitude of Prince Henry of Pless. Having observed her debut at the Winter Garden through a monocle, he expressed "admiration" in the card that he sent to her dressing room with a seven-foot, purple-and-white floral piece. On the following nights his cards accompanied a huge bouquet of violets and an enormous basket of red roses. The third night brought a pin in the shape of a dragonfly. Sprinkled with diamonds and rubies, it was unmatched by anything she'd gotten from Diamond Jim and Jesse Lewisohn.

Deciding she could not accept it, she told her Germany attorney to return it. The lawyer replied that he did not want to risk offending the nobility.

The next morning, as Lillian and Susie were having breakfast in their hotel suite, the door opened and in marched two Prussian grenadiers, followed by a man in full morning clothes who introduced himself as Count Honlau. The prince's factotum, he clicked heels, bowed, and asked the startled American Beauty from Iowa by way of Chicago, Brooklyn, and Tony Pastor's on the Bowery, "Have I the honor of addressing the celebrated and most high-born and beautiful Miss Lillian Russell?"

Lillian assured him that he was in the right suite.

"Prince Henry of Pless presents his esteemed compliments," continued Honlau, "and he desires her company in Parlor L at twelve o'clock this evening to take supper with him."

Such a scene was common in the operettas that had made Lillian Russell a star and a rich woman. But this was real life and she felt offended. She answered, "Tell the gentleman that I do not know him, and I never take supper with anyone whom I do not know."

Assuming that would be the end of the prince's attentions, she was astonished the next morning by Count Honlau again appearing with his guard of honor, this time bearing a note in

Prince Henry's hand. She read, "Miss Russell should take her golden bicycle. She should ride out to the Grunewald at eight o'clock tomorrow morning. She should ride the North Drive and she will see an officer in green uniform on a white horse, who if she descends from her bicycle when she sees him, will dismount from his horse and speak to her. Harry."

Deciding that this real-life operetta had become a farce, she said to the count, "Tell Henry I would not get up at eight o'clock in the morning to watch George Washington cross the Delaware. You can also tell him that I am an American and not obliged to obey his royal commands."

She rose from her breakfast and went to her dressing table. Taking the diamond-and-ruby dragonfly from a drawer, she carried it to the count.

"And," she said, taking his hand and dropping the pin into his palm, "give him this."

A few days later, to underscore her citizenship, she invited forty American girls who were studying in Berlin schools to a *kaffee-klatsch* in the Tiergarten. This was followed by treating the dazzled girls to an all-American luncheon at the Hotel Bristol, featuring sweet corn on the cob imported from Hungary and pork and beans from London.

Her displeasure with Germany was exacerbated when she learned that her $3,000-a-week salary was subject to a 10 percent income tax. And after she gave a command performance for Kaiser Wilhelm III and his family in Potsdam, for which the emperor rewarded her by allowing her the pick of the stock of the royal jeweler on the Unter den Linden, she was dismayed to find the choices appalling.

She declared to the jeweler, "These are the most terrible-looking diamonds I've ever seen. How could His Highness offer this junk to anyone?"

With an expression of shock, the jeweler replied that he supposed the kaiser believed that just to have a souvenir from him was sufficient.

"Well, *Mein Herr*," Lillian replied, "it ain't."

The most infuriating occurrence during the German sojourn was a claim by a woman in Hamburg that Lillian Russell was her mother. Had Lillian not been forced to retain a costly German lawyer to refute the allegation, the episode might have been funny. The woman who asserted she was Lillian's offspring was grossly overweight, bore no resemblance to Lillian, and was just two years younger than her claimed parent.

Lillian wrote of the episode, "No imagination could picture me as a German frau with a big, fat and forty-year-old daughter."

After fulfilling engagements that met with tepid approval of German audiences and critics, she stayed on in Berlin to take a ride in a Zeppelin. She pronounced it the only really enjoyable part of her tour. Returning to the United States, she looked forward to a triumphant and warm reception from American audiences and reviewers.

Her vehicle was Offenbach's *La Belle Helene*. Instead of receiving accolades, she found herself compared unflatteringly to a younger and slimmer cast member. Especially upsetting was this from Alan Dale in the *New York Journal*: "Lillian has no beauty beneath the chin. She could not possibly wear three-quarters of a yard of silk and corset lace with the confident effrontery of Edna Wallace Hopper, and she moved with the soft heaviness of a nice white elephant."

Offended, Lillian announced she would not be in the show when it went to Philadelphia. She changed her mind when threatened with a lawsuit by producer George Lederer. As if being compelled were not bad enough, she found that Edna Wallace Hopper took the stage in costumes that as the engagement continued got scantier and flimsier. In the balcony seats, University of Pennsylvania boys who whistled and cheered Hopper gave Lillian catcalls and hisses.

Outraged at being upstaged, Lillian quit the production and returned to New York with a trail of breach-of-contract lawsuits from the producer. All were dropped when she threatened to reveal that Lederer had borrowed $600 from her to meet the payroll and that the only reason he had been able to get a lease on his Casino theater was her guarantee that the rent would be paid.

Waiting in New York to smooth her ruffled feathers were two men to whom she would always be the brightest light in the theatrical firmament.

Among solaces that Jesse Lewisohn's friendship provided was a great deal of money she had earned when she followed his advice and put some of her savings in copper stocks. As she was fending off Prince Henry's advances, finding the kaiser's gifts unworthy of her, being insulted by newspaper writers, and hearing the hoots of derision from a Philadelphia balcony, a flurry of enthusiasm for copper had provided her a Wall Street windfall.

Stalwart and undemanding Diamond Jim welcomed her back with a suitably bejeweled gift and a formal introduction to his girlfriend.

Lillian was so impressed by Edna McCauley's pretty looks and winning ways that she offered to use her influence with theatrical producers to get Edna a job as the understudy to Ada Rehan. Painfully aware of the disdainful attitude of "Society" toward actresses and recalling how "the ladies" of Chicago had given the cold shoulder to Lillian at the Columbian Exposition, Jim would have none of it.

His intention, he informed Lillian, was to spend the summer with Edna at the fashionable New Jersey seaside resort of Belmar. Amid the ocean breezes in a cottage he'd rented for the season, he expected, Edna's beauty and charm would win her friendships that would smooth the way for her acceptance, and his, into High Society.

When Jesse Lewisohn announced that he would have to travel to Europe for the summer on business, Jim happily extended an invitation to Lillian to come to Belmar and stay with him and Edna at the cottage. In keeping with the "sensibilities" of the era, Edna would be passed off as Jim's niece. While the men who summered at Belmar went along with the pose and thronged to parties Jim gave at the cottage, their we-know-better wives demurred.

Undaunted, Jim took Edna with him to the even more socially rarified Newport, Rhode Island. His purpose in going was to attend a railroad conference, but he hoped that by showing Edna off as hostess at parties, he would enjoy the success that had eluded him at Belmar. To his delight, Edna was a credit to him. Coupled with her good looks and fashionable clothes was a sweetness and pleasant manner that won her admiration. If one of the convention delegates tried to be too friendly, he found himself rebuffed, but in a charming way. Jim discovered that Edna brought to his parties a quality that he lacked, that elusive virtue he called "class."

So pleased was he with Edna's success at Newport that he hoped to refine her manner, poise, and assurance by introducing her to the graces of Europe.

With thirteen trunks, nineteen pieces of hand baggage, Jim's valet-masseur, and Edna's maid, they sailed for France on August 1, 1898, on the steamship *Normandie*. Also in the party was young Gerald Merchant, son of the general manager of the Buffalo, Rochester and Pittsburgh Railroad. He was booked onto the luxury liner as Edna's brother.

This ruse worked during the crossing. But when they arrived at the Continental Hotel in Paris and Jim registered for the seven rooms he had reserved, he told the clerk that Edna was his niece and Merchant his secretary. Because this did not accord with their travel papers, the clerk summoned a *gendarme*. A 1000-franc note slipped into the policeman's palm and a Brady wink, along with an explanation that there'd been a mixup in language, disposed of the matter. Determined to avoid other mistakes, Jim hired an interpreter. Edna became his "daughter."

Sixty years after Diamond Jim Brady introduced the former department store salesgirl to the most sophisticated city in the world, the American songwriting team of Alan Jay Lerner and Fritz Loewe painted a portrait of Paris in the Gay Nineties for movie audiences. They did this by adapting a story by Colette in which a young French girl, Gigi, was groomed to be a courtesan. Diamond Jim's purpose in taking Edna to Paris was to polish her as a gem cutter shaped and smoothed a diamond in the rough. Edna McCauley would be as brilliant an adornment to him as any of the treasures in his jewelry trays. On the road for Manning, Maxwell and Moore he had dazzled customers with his display of the stones that gave him his nickname. Edna would now sparkle for clients who called on him in New York. He would use her to help him entertain them at parties. But not as his wife. At some time, perhaps. But not yet.

As word spread among Americans in Paris, especially the many actors and actresses who happened to be visiting the City of Light, that the fabulous character Diamond Jim Brady was ensconced at the Continental, Jim and Edna found themselves besieged by men and women who were eager to help them discover and partake of the joys of the city (knowing that if they did so it would be Jim who paid the bill). One actress who sought him out did not have to concern herself with who paid. She was Anna Robinson. At the height of her stage career, power, and glory, she was so famous for her diamond-enhanced beauty and infamous allure to men that when she entered a restaurant, wives led their husbands out. She was so rich that she'd once taken $90,000 from Jim at poker and dismissed her winnings as "pin money." She became a frequent companion to him, Edna, and Merchant as they traveled around France.

Another person whom Jim had known in New York was Count Boni de Castellane. He was described by one of Jim's acquaintances as a "golden-haired, doll-like little fop." But Jim liked him. One day the count announced a party in Jim's honor.

"I have been royally feted by you in your New York," the count explained to Jim, "and now I beg you to do me the honor of returning the favor in my beloved Paris."

Jim knew that it would not be an ordinary affair. The count's parties were famous for their opulence. He'd recently given one at which his garden was illuminated by eighty thousand Venetian lanterns. Lest guests get their shoes dirty, the grounds were covered with nine miles of red carpet. Music was provided by two hundred musicians. Entertainment was offered in the form of a special ballet performed by eighty dancers.

The reception for Jim was held in the count's rococo pink marble mansion on the Avenue du Bois de Boulogne. When Jim arrived, de Castellane exclaimed, "As the greatest party impresario in all of France I salute you, Monsieur Brady, my most worthy American rival."

Rarely at a loss for words, Jim was so flattered that he stammered, "Why, uh, it's damned nice of you to say that, Count."

The nature of the lighting provided by the count was not recorded. Whatever it was, its illumination was brilliantly reflected by the greatest display of diamonds seen on one person in Paris since the time of Marie Antoinette.

Not present at the affair was the count's American wife. The former Anna Gould, she made an excuse of not feeling well. The truth was that she shared New York's High Society's view that Diamond Jim Brady was a vulgar nobody, notwithstanding the fact that the Gould fortune had been accumulated by means of her father's embezzlements and corporate piracy.

If Jim was offended by the snub, he kept quiet about it.

Keenly aware that nothing amused Jim Brady more than a great meal in a fine restaurant, the count advised Jim to dine at Café Marguery. His reward, said the count, would be a filet of sole with an exceptional sauce.

Jim tried it and declared, "*Exquiz-eet*." He demanded that he be given the recipe, but the chef respectfully declined to share the secret of his success. For the first time in the life of James Buchanan Brady an offer of money got him nowhere.

As he had done on his first visit to Europe, Jim went on a buying spree. Tracking down the Paris buyer for New York's Wanamaker's department store, he gave him $20,000 to "buy a few knick-knacks that I can take home to my friends." He then had to buy more trunks and luggage to contain the results.

Having gotten his fill of Paris and French food, Jim escorted Edna across the channel to England. His purpose was to visit Leeds to see his partner, Sampson Fox, and survey the works that had made them both rich. The quiet little man who'd had a feeling that American railroads were ready for pressed steel trucks was now squire of a vast manor house on a sprawling estate.

Jim and Edna found themselves surrounded by acres of deer parks, streams stocked with salmon, and every quarter of a mile in any direction an al fresco bar disguised as a tree stump. With the touch of a button, a door opened to reveal bottles of liquor, glasses, and buckets of ice.

Learning that the American actor and Brady buddy Nat Goodwin was appearing in a play in London's West End, Jim took Edna to see him. When they entered their box, Jim was decked out in his favorite jewelry and assorted gems purchased in Paris. Dazzled English theatergoers gasped at a display of gems that eclipsed anything sported by His Royal Highness, the Prince of Wales.

Informed just before going on stage that Diamond Jim was in the audience, Goodwin left the audience even more agog by stopping the show to speak directly to the fat man in the box and make a date with him for supper after the performance.

Hoping to call on Mrs. Langtry, Jim was informed that the actress was not in London at the time. She was spending the summer in the company of Sir Hugo Gerald de Bathe, whom all who claimed to be in the know predicted the Jersey Lily had set her sights on remarrying. (The prediction came true the

next year.) Running into Oscar Wilde for reminiscences of raucous nights at Harry Hill's was out the question. Oscar had
fled from England after his release from a two-year term following a conviction for sodomy. But London was buzzing with
talk of the imminent publication of a long poem Oscar had
written while incarcerated, titled *The Ballad of Reading Gaol*. A
British friend explained to Jim that "gaol" was the English
spelling for "jail." Two years later Jim would learn that Oscar
died in Paris on November 30, 1900. The most outrageous of
the dudes who had told a New York customs man that he had
nothing to declare but his genius succumbed to cerebral menin-
gitis, a disgraced, lonely, beaten, and broken spirit.

Deciding he'd had his fill of Europe, Jim said farewell to
Sampson Fox and boarded a train with Edna for Liverpool to
sail home on the pride of the Cunard Line's fleet, the *Campania*.
She had been built in Glasgow, Scotland, and launched in
March 1893. Two months later, on the return leg of her maiden
Atlantic crossing, she had won the Blue Riband from the
Inman Line's *City of New York* by sailing from Sandy Hook, New
Jersey, to Britain in five days, seventeen hours, and twenty-
seven minutes with a record-setting pace of 21.09 knots. With
a length of 622 feet, she offered her passengers three decks for
promenading and 300 third-class, 200 second-class, and 526
first-class cabins. Jim booked three in first, for him, his "daughter" Edna, and Merchant.

Arriving in New York with thirty-six trunks and twenty-
seven pieces of hand luggage, he discovered that he was not an
Oscar Wilde who could clear customs inspection with a bon
mot. Rather, he found his baggage being opened and gone
through thoroughly. Outraged, he blared, "What the hell do
you think you're doin'? I declared everything I've got."

With protestations ignored, he demanded that someone
telephone the mayor, Robert van Wyck, and the boss of Tammany Hall, Dick Croker. While neither of those men appeared,
an official of the Cunard Line observed the fuss and stepped

forward to demand an explanation from the customs officer why the upstanding citizen Diamond Jim Brady was being rudely detained.

The customs inspector explained that he and his men were acting on a tip from Paris that Mr. Brady had been observed buying in such a wholesale way that he had to be a smuggler. No one, the tipster in Paris had said, would ever pay duty on so many purchases.

Persuaded that Jim was indeed on the up and up, the customs officer waved him through.

Greeted by reporters who asked him how he had enjoyed his long continental holiday, Jim replied, "I've seen everything that Europe's got to offer, and I've traveled all over America, too, and all I can say is this—for my money, give me little old New York every time."

12

"This Is Where I Live"

❧❧❧❧

A S DIAMOND JIM helped Edna into a sturdy four-wheeler cab at dockside, he startled her by telling the driver to take them to Central Park West and Eighty-sixth Street. When the carriage arrived, he directed the cabbie to pull up in front of a new four-story brownstone house.

Looking puzzled, Edna asked, "Why are we stopping here?"

"From now on," Jim replied with a broadening grin, "this is where I live." Taking her hand, he added, "I should say, my dear, that this is where *we* will be living."

Having grown tired of his Fifty-seventh Street digs, and anticipating acquiring whatever struck his fancy in the galleries and furniture emporiums of Paris and London, he'd bought the house for $87,000 in cash. To decorate it and transfer many of the items he chose to keep from the apartment he'd retained interior designer Collins Marsh. Jim's instructions were to furnish it in the most elaborate style.

The bill for the Marsh touch came to $320,000.

Among the prized possessions that were carted the twenty-nine blocks uptown was a billiard and pool table that had been made to order by the Brunswick-Balke-Collender Company. Made of mahogany, it had sides and legs ornamented with carnelians, lapis lazuli, and other semiprecious stones. Illuminated by electric ceiling lamps with leaded-glass shades by Tiffany, it occupied the center of a front basement game room with wood-paneled walls. In a corner of the huge space stood a roulette wheel and table. Chips for playing were of mother of pearl and onyx. Scattered around the room were tables and chairs for poker, faro, and bridge. For diversions that were less stressful there were tables with inlaid chessboards. A portion of one wall was reserved for darts. Though the owner of the house remained an abstainer, a long bar supplied any kind of liquor his guests might desire.

Adjoining the game room was a wide hall that led to the kitchen. It rivaled those of the city's best lobster palaces and ranked second to none of those found in the mansions of Mrs. Astor and her favored 400. Walls and ceiling were of green and white marble. The combination was repeated in waterproof floor tiles. On racks above and around two enormous stoves hung gleaming copper pots and pans. Half of a wall was devoted to iceboxes.

All furnishings not fixed in place were built for ease of movement so that the floor could be scrubbed and washed down with a hose. But the immaculate cooking area had one amenity not found in any of the kitchens of the city's restaurants and millionaires' mansions on Fifth and Madison avenues. Behind a large Italian marble screen that stood on bronze legs was an alcove equipped with a bathroom. With a shower and the finest porcelain tubs and basins, the facility was for the servants. A condition of their employment was that they use it at least once a day.

Beyond the kitchen door lay a backyard that Marsh had laid out in a garden of flowers, gravel paths, and shade-giving cedar trees.

To guard against anyone who might attempt to enter the house in search of items that had given the owner his fabulous nickname, the ground-level windows were rendered inviolate by thick steel bars.

On the first floor, facing Eighty-sixth Street, was the living room. The furniture was entirely in Louis XIV. The elegant chairs would provide Jim's guests with yet another reason to wager with one another. They bet for or against the probability that if Jim sat in one of them, it would collapse. Aware not only of the sport at his expense, but of the cost and limited supply of the antique chairs, Jim occasionally joined in the betting and dared the consequences by sitting in one, but only after he had secretly tested the chair's tolerance. Walls were hung with tapestries. The floor coverings were Oriental carpets. Placed around the parlor were teakwood stands and tables to show off his collection of bronzes in the form of fauns and laughing boys and girls as they picked thorns from their feet. Breakfronts exhibited another of his passions as a collector, Dresden and Tangara figurines.

Large pocket doors provided access to a dining room of extra-large dimensions. Table and chairs were of hand-carved San Domingo mahogany. The carpets were the best of the Orientals that Jim had purchased at the Chicago World's Fair. Statuary was wild animals—boars, deer, elk, tigers, elephants, and a huge bull. On the recommendation of Stanford White, who had told Jim about rites of banquets in Ancient Rome during which diners had access to baths, a screened-off alcove of the dining room also contained a bathroom. The amenity gave rise to a tale that may or may not be true that a then-unknown English actor named Charlie Chaplin became so tired of the seemingly endless courses at a Jim Brady dinner that he sneaked into the bathroom to take a nap in the tub. A maid found him still sleeping there in the morning.

The house's second floor was bedrooms. The one in front was the Turkish Room. Even more opulent than the one in Jim's apartment in the Rutland, it offered three divans about the size of a standard bed. Brocaded drapes could be closed to provide each with privacy. A fourth divan was equal in space to two double beds. Statuary reflected the room's hedonistic purpose. The bronzes depicted nude women or scantily garbed couples. Three of these voluptuous works by Rodin were estimated to be worth more than $50,000.

Between the Turkish Room and Jim's back bedroom was a large hall lined on one side with closets for Jim's wardrobe of fifty suits and twenty-five overcoats. When a closet door was opened, an electric light went on—an innovation not found in Mrs. Astor's mansion. On the opposite wall were maple chests of drawers. One held shirts, another socks. A third was filled with silk underwear. The fourth had neckties. The fifth was for handkerchiefs.

Between the last of these chests and the door to Jim's bedroom was a wall paneled with maple veneer. It concealed a vault where he kept his jewelry. The door to it was in Jim's room and was concealed by a tapestry. Dominating the large rear room was a bed large enough to sleep three men the size of its owner. The bed, tables, and chairs were in San Domingo mahogany. In a corner by a window stood an object that would not be found in any bedroom in New York City, or probably anywhere else. Standing in front of a mirror and placed to benefit from the morning light was a barber's chair.

Said Jim to Edna McCauley as she first gazed at it in wonder, "It ain't beautiful, I know, but it's gonna be damned convenient and comfortable when I shave every day."

On the third floor of the house was the Tiger Room, so called because its walls were of highly polished satinwood whose grain looked like the stripes of a tiger. Continuing the motif, the floor was scattered with tiger-skin rugs. The bed's headboard was carved with tiger heads with mother-of-pearl fangs, ruby eyes, and opal claws. Other furniture was carved in the form of wild beasts and inlaid with fire opals, small emeralds, rubies, and petrified wood known as tiger eyes. Because of Sampson Fox's interest in animals, the room was reserved for his use when he came to New York.

The townhouse on West Eighty-sixth Street was sumptuous in its decor: (*top, above*) the living room; (*bottom, above*) the Porcelain Room, decorated with examples of Diamond Jim's extensive porcelain collection; (*top, facing page*) the Turkish Room; and (*bottom, facing page*) the Dining Room.

A bath joined the room to one in the rear that was furnished in bird's-eye maple and soft blue hangings. With Chinese rugs, nearly $20,000 worth of bronzes of horses and other animals, and a bric-a-brac cabinet for more of Jim's collectibles valued at over $10,000, the bedroom was intended for the use of a lady. A third guest room was in tones of red with cherry-wood furniture.

The fifth room on this floor was Jim's office. Adjoining the Tiger Room to the left, it had oak-paneled walls covered from ceiling to floor with pictures of Jim and his friends. More than twelve hundred of them showed Jim as gentleman sportsman, Mr. First Nighter, and the world's greatest salesman of railroad equipment.

On the top floor were quarters for servants and a gymnasium that Jim intended to use to lose weight and get into better physical shape. It shared the fate of Jim's bicycle exercising. The gym would be used only by his valet-masseur, Max Stadler.

IN THE SUMMER OF 1898, while Jim and Edna were in Paris and London and the house on Eighty-sixth Street was being readied for their return, the country they'd left behind was in a war with Spain over the future of Cuba. President William McKinley had labored to avoid American intervention in a long-standing rebellion against Spanish rule of the island. The president sought a negotiated settlement, while his assistant secretary of the navy, Theodore Roosevelt, did all he could think of to bring about war and to see that the navy was fit to win it. McKinley's efforts at peaceful resolution sank when the U.S. battleship *Maine,* on a "peace mission" to the island, was mysteriously blown up in Havana harbor. The American rallying cry for war was "Remember the *Maine.*" Soldiers soon sailed for Cuba to wreak revenge.

When Diamond Jim's doctors told him he needed to exercise, he equipped his Eighty-sixth Street townhouse with a state-of-the-art gymnasium. Like many Americans who decided for health and fitness to "work out" a century later, Jim quickly lost interest in using it.

By the time Jim and Edna returned to New York in the fall, the Spanish-American War was over; Cuba, Puerto Rico, and the Philippines were under the Stars and Stripes; and Roosevelt was the most famous man in the country because of heroic leadership of his "Rough Riders." In July he'd led a valiant and victorious charge up San Juan Heights, overlooking the strategic city and port of Santiago de Cuba. Although the primary reason for the Spaniards' surrender in what a U.S. diplomat called "a splendid little war" was destruction of its Pacific and Atlantic fleets by the U.S. Navy, the hero to the folks at home was "Teddy." When he arrived at Montauk, Long Island, for demobilization of the Rough Riders, he found himself offered the Republican nomination for governor. He accepted it.

As U.S. soldiers and sailors had headed off to realize the desire of Roosevelt and other "jingoes" to validate the Monroe Doctrine by kicking Spain out of the Western Hemisphere and grabbing as much Spanish territory as possible, they had done so to the jaunty cadence and words of a popular new song, "There'll Be a Hot Time in the Old Town Tonight," and to a new march by the nation's most famous band leader and patriotic composer, John Philip Sousa. "The Stars and Stripes Forever" proved so uplifting of Americans' spirits, and so in keeping with the idea that the United States had a "manifest destiny" to dominate the hemisphere, that many Americans thought Congress should declare it the national anthem.

A member of another American force that had landed in Cuba with Teddy Roosevelt's Rough Riders and other equally valorous, but less celebrated, units was newspaper correspondent Richard Harding Davis. Like Stephen Crane, another New Yorker who'd gone to Cuba as a war reporter, Davis was a novelist. In 1897 Crane had followed up *Maggie, A Girl of the Streets* with a Civil War novel, *The Red Badge of Courage.* Davis's book, *Soldiers of Fortune,* was illustrated by Charles Dana Gibson. The story involved a pair of red-blooded Americans in charge of a mine in a fictional Central American republic. As the men reminisced about life in the United States, one of them said, "What I'd like to do now would be to sit in the front row at a comic opera, *on the aisle.* The prima donna must be very, very beautiful, and sing most of her songs at me, and there must be at least three comedians, all good, and a chorus entirely composed of girls. I never could see why they have men in the chorus, anyway. No one ever looks at them."

The America of the late Gay Nineties that Davis's expatriate characters missed was not that of the brutal "other half" depicted at the beginning of the decade by Teddy Roosevelt's devoted friend and publicist, Jacob Riis, but the America of "Diamond Jim" Brady and Lillian "the American Beauty" Russell. It was an America of bicycles. Of newfangled and increasingly evident automobiles. Of Sunday-school picnics, boys and girls "spooning," lawn tennis, football, and a new game called baseball. Its gentlemen sported cutaway coats, gracefully draped watch chains, top hats in winter, and, in summer, rakishly tilted straw "boaters." Ladies donned big feathered hats, full skirts, and blouses with billowy sleeves. Beneath them they wore tightly laced corsets in a generally futile attempt to mimic the vogue of pinch-waisted beauties in Charles Dana Gibson's drawings.

It was also the America in which comic operas, the new style musicals based on the American experience, and Tony Pastor's vaudeville shows were finding competition in diversions called burlesque. New York audiences were rocking with laughter at these raucous mixtures of sentimental and witty songs, acrobatic acts, big all-girl chorus numbers, parodies of successful plays (known as "travesties"), and largely improvised comedy sketches, usually featuring a pair of comedians. None was better at it than the team of Joe Weber and Lew Fields.

Billed by their last names in that order, they were products of the Lower East Side slum tenements of Riis's book. They'd started in show business at age nine at the Turn Hall on East Fourth Street but were booed off the stage. Failing to impress Tony Pastor with their act, they landed at the new Chatham Square Museum. At $6 a week for both, they did eight shows a day. Performing a "Dutch act" in oversize, pillow-padded clothes, pasted-on whiskers, and exaggerated accents, they made their entrance singing "Here we are a jolly pair."

The years, persistence, and experience eventually paid off with Tony Pastor changing his mind and offering them $250 a week in one of his summer shows. But it was Oscar Hammerstein's signing them for $500 at his Olympia Theater that established them as stars. Suddenly "the toast of the town," they took over the Imperial Music Hall at Broadway and Twenty-ninth Street and became impresarios of shows in which they topped the bill. Changing the name of the theater to Weber and Fields' Music Hall, they hired the cream of musical theater:

Ziegfeld competitors in staging elaborate shows were the comedy team of Weber and Fields. They persuaded Lillian Russell to give up her career in operettas and appear in their kind of entertainments. Lillian became an even greater star.

Fay Templeton, David Warfield, Peter Dailey, Bessie Clayton, Truly Shattuck, Mabel Fenton, and Frankie Bailey. The shows were directed by Julian Mitchell. Their songs were written by Edgar Smith and John "Honey" Stromberg.

A problem for Weber and Fields was in holding onto such stars. Because their theater had only 665 seats, with tickets selling from half-a-buck to $2, they found themselves unable to match financial offers from other producers. Time and again they lost their best headliners.

After one such occasion occurred with both the departure of Fay Templeton for a bigger show and the retirement of Mabel Fenton to a farm she'd bought in New Jersey, Lew Fields ran into Jesse Lewisohn at Sheepshead Bay racetrack. Having heard that Lewisohn was an almost constant companion of Lillian Russell, and knowing she was "at liberty," the comedian found the nerve to ask Jesse, "Do you think Miss Russell would consider a star role in our Music Hall?"

Lewisohn said, "Why don't you ask her? Come over to our box and I'll introduce you."

Seizing the chance of a lifetime, but expecting to be laughed out of the box, Fields posed the query to her. While she did not laugh, she replied, "I would require twelve-hundred-and-fifty dollars a week, guaranteed for a season of thirty-five weeks, and all gowns and costumes to be paid by you. You yourself can see that it is beyond your means, especially in your tiny theater."

Fields astounded her, Lewisohn, and himself by replying "We'll expect you in August."

To help meet Lillian's salary, Weber and Fields came up with an idea that appealed to the men who did not find themselves invited to an Astor ball but who had no lack of money. When they learned that box seats for the debut of Lillian Russell at Weber and Field's Music Hall were to be auctioned from the stage, they thronged the theater. Two boxes were bought by Lewisohn for $1,000. Other successful bidders were Stanford White, restaurateur Louis Sherry, Tammany Hall boss Richard Croker, newspaper tycoon William Randolph Hearst, and others who made the trek uptown after trading on Wall Street to gamble at the Waldorf-Astoria. None bid with more zest than Diamond Jim in acquiring a box for himself and Edna. The ploy by Weber and Fields resulted in a publicity bonanza and an opening night box office of more than $10,000.

For the occasion the comedians had redecorated the Music Hall in subdued tones of a delicate pink and buff in keeping with the soft beauty of their star. When the curtain went up for *Whirl-i-Gig,* a mix of vaudeville acts, Weber and Fields' Dutch comedy, and a "travesty" of a hit Broadway farce titled *The Girl from Maxim's,* the audience found Lillian Russell in bed in what seemed to be a nightgown. When she threw back the lacy coverlet, she was dressed in a low-cut evening gown. The audience roared approval.

What no one knew was that they were witnesses to the transition of Lillian Russell from queen of the comic opera to a new style of entertainment in which she would be a star well into a new century.

WHEN A TRANSPLANTED VISIONARY from Massachusetts named Andrew H. Green first proposed in 1868 an amalgamation of Manhattan, Brooklyn, the Bronx, Queens, and Staten Island into one metropolis to be called the City of New York, the idea met stiff resistance, especially from the residents of Brooklyn. Those who took pride in living in snug houses amid parks and at low taxes in "the city of churches" looked with horror on the noisy, dirty, sin-ridden, and seemingly ungovernable Manhattan island, which they called "the city" (and still do). But closer ties had become inevitable in 1883 with the opening of the Brooklyn Bridge. Further impetus for the marriage of the two cities came in the 1890s from the boss of New York's Republicans, U.S. Senator Thomas Platt. He saw in the merger of areas surrounding the Democratic stronghold of Manhattan a way to wrest political control from Tammany Hall. Because Republicans controlled the state government in Albany, the legislature dictated a new charter for the city. Signed into law by Governor Frank Black on May 4, 1897, it called for creation of five "boroughs" and their consolidation as the City of New York. The governor's pen to paper also made it, as of January 1, the largest city in the country, with a population of

3,393,252 inhabitants in a territory that ran 36 miles north–south and covered 320 square miles.

An editorial in the *New York Tribune* joyfully noted that the sun would rise on January 1, 1898, "upon the greatest experiment in municipal government the world has ever known."

Less enthusiastic about the merging of five governments into one, the elected officials of each planned nothing in the way of ceremony except a few speeches. But when word of this low-key event reached William Randolph Hearst, the newspaper owner saw an opportunity to boost his *New York Journal* by sponsoring the biggest public event in the city since the dedication of the Statue of Liberty in 1886. He announced plans for a party featuring bands, marching societies, singers, dancers, military units, bicycle races, and fireworks. To help foot the bill he tapped the wallets of the old city's richest men, from J. P. Morgan to all the Waldorf-Astoria card players.

When Diamond Jim learned that Tammany Hall's boss, Dick Croker, had contributed $500, he dug into his pocket and matched him. And when a throng gathered in rain and snow at Union Square to march down to City Hall to watch the city's new blue-and-white flag go up the flagpole (on a signal sent by telegraph by the mayor of San Francisco, site of Will Hearst's first newspaper), followed by fireworks at midnight, Jim happily fell into step and joined in singing "There'll Be a Hot Time in the Old Town Tonight."

The day after, Hearst's chief New York journalistic rival, the *Tribune,* admitted that it had been the "biggest, noisiest and most hilarious New Year's Eve celebration that Manhattan Island has ever known."

Still residing on Fifty-seventh Street, Jim invited his closest men friends to continue the party in his apartment in the company of a bevy of chorus girls.

In greeting 1898 he had more to be pleased about than having become a resident in a city that by political fiat had been elevated to largest in the nation. In the nine months since his man in the 1896 presidential election, William McKinley, had taken the helm of the government, the national economy had been in upswing and showed no sign of stopping. Not even the talk of war and the subsequent invasion of Cuba, which ousted the Spaniards, had dimmed the prospects, as Jim saw the situation, of a complete recovery from effects of the Panic of '93 and the Cleveland Depression. Throughout 1897 and 1898 McKinley had remained steadfast on keeping gold as the underpinning of the economy. Industries were back in business, and the things they made were being shipped in growing quantities on the greatest and most efficient network of railroads in the world. To make matters even better as 1898 drew to a close, for the first time in Diamond Jim's life he had a magnificent house of his own in the greatest city in the world and a pretty, vivacious young woman to share it.

The only cloud on the horizon was his mother.

ENSCONCED IN a comfortable home that Jim had bought for her on Lexington Avenue, Mrs. Brady found herself alone. Her daughter and first son, Dan, were married and counting on their wealthy bachelor brother to take care of their aging parent. Jim's money had provided her a stylish wardrobe, a box of jewelry, and a well-stocked and frequently used liquor cabinet. When he acquired the Rutland apartment, she'd expressed disapproval of what she saw as a waste of money when there was ample room for both of them on Lexington. Following Jim's move to Eighty-sixth Street, she had expected to be invited to take up residence there. With the realization that she would not be moving, she complained to Dan in the hope that he would intervene with his brother.

Instead, Dan indulged longtime jealousy and resentment of Jim's financial successes. He informed her that Jim's purposes in taking the large house were to feather a love nest for him and his young mistress and to use it as a harem for the entertainment of visiting railroad tycoons.

Mother Brady reacted by railing at Jim for callously abandoning her for "that trollop," forsaking their religion by becoming a voluptuary and libertine, and bringing disgrace to the Brady name. With steely patience, Jim endured the outbursts of vituperation and attributed blame to sibling rivalry and his mother's increasing recourse to the contents of the liquor cabinet.

A few days after Jim settled into the house on Eighty-sixth Street, he went downtown to his Cortlandt Street office and found his mother marching back and forth on the sidewalk and yelling at startled pedestrians that her son, the famous Diamond Jim Brady, was a rotten man who had abandoned his mother in her old age. Embarrassed and alarmed, Jim consulted the family physician. After paying a call at the house on Lexington, Dr. Paul Otterbridge opined that Mrs. Brady's behavior resulted from an extreme case of "nerves" exacerbated by many, many years of overindulgence in alcohol. He recommended that she be placed in a sanitarium until both conditions improved.

When Jim began court proceedings to do so, he was met with resistance from Dan and his sister. They alleged that their brother's purpose in wanting their mother institutionalized was to get control of her money. It was a preposterous charge because all her money had come from Jim. Yet the assertion was enough for the court to hold a hearing. It lasted for days and drew embarrassing, snickering, and damaging attention of newspapers, which were in the full flower of an era of scandal-mongering, sensation-seeking stories, reports of horrible crimes accompanied by lurid pictures, and garish and shocking headlines known as yellow journalism.

Jim was appalled to discover that reporters who'd been delighted to write about the jolly, jewel-bedecked fat man and perennial escort of Lillian Russell could suddenly turn on him and depict him as a heartless cad concerning his aging mother. But he understood that they had been doing their job and, appreciating that the character "Diamond Jim" relied on getting attention in the press, he forgave them. The people he could not, would not, and did not forgive were his brother, sister, and mother. After Mrs. Brady was placed in the care of a board appointed by the court, Jim severed relations with his family for the rest of his life.

BACK IN FAVOR with reporters, Jim granted an interview with one who was left agog when Jim asserted with a straight face, "The trouble with our American men is that they overdress."

The newspaperman realized that his leg was being pulled as Jim continued, "Now, I take it that I am considered a handsome man and one who would be called well dressed. Never by any chance do I permit more than seventeen colors to creep into the pattern of my waistcoat. Moreover, I consider that twenty-eight rings are enough for any man to wear at the same time. Others may be carried in the pocket and exhibited as occasion requires. Diamonds larger than doorknobs should never be worn except in the evening."

Despite the Wall Street crash and ensuing depression, the Gay Nineties had been a good decade for James Buchanan Brady's thirst for flashy adornments. As he made plans to welcome a new decade (the 1900s were already being called "the naughts"), the concealed vault in the house on Eighty-sixth Street held hundreds of thousands of dollars' worth of jewelry. To ensure that he did not have to wear the same items more than once a month, his safe's velvet-lined drawers contained thirty matched sets consisting of a watch, watch chain, ring, scarf pin, necktie tack, shirt studs, collar buttons, cuff links, belt buckle, and vest- and suspenders-button covers. Each set also had a jeweled mechanical lead pencil.

Every set had its own motif. The most expensive was the Number-one Diamond Set. Its ring held a diamond weighing twenty-five and a half carats. The scarf pin's single diamond:

thirty-three carats. Two five-carat stones were set in the watch. Its chain contained eight diamonds of four carats each. Cuff links had four ten-carat diamonds. Tie clip: twelve carats. An eyeglass case's diamond: fifteen carats. On the clasp of a pocketbook, a five-carat stone. The pencil was crusted with five diamonds with a total weight of fifteen carats.

The most expensive array was the Transportation Set. Created to his design at a cost of $105,000, it consisted of platinum pins studded with diamonds and rubies in the shape of a Pullman car, a tank car, a bicycle, an automobile, and a locomotive. The little steam engine sparkled with 210 diamonds in a set consisting of 2,518 gems.

The Racing Set was horse figures, saddles, and bridles. A Sporting Set paid tribute to Jim's favorite games. The U.S. Coin set was actual coins set in gold and surrounded by gems. Another set was the initial "B" done in various stones.

Completing the inventory were sets that Jim classified according to the main stones: Diamond, Pearl, Emerald, Ruby, Cat's Eye, Sapphire, Marquise Diamond, Opal, Turquoise, Garnet, Topaz, Abalone Pearl, Moonstone, Coral, Sardonyx, Amatrice, Jade, Thompsonite, and "Plain White."

The most valuable item in the vault was a ring with a twenty-three-carat cabochon emerald the size of a Ping Pong ball. It was surrounded by six three-carat diamonds. Also in the safe drawers were a scarf pin containing a seventeen-carat pearshape emerald, watch fob with a twenty-carat emerald, watch chain with four emeralds with combined weight of eighty carats, and pairs of gold cuff links with a total of 192 diamonds and 20 emeralds. A watch drawer held thirty gold or platinum timepieces for which Jim had paid $500 to $2,000 each. He enhanced their value by having them studded with gems.

On hand in other drawers at one time for gifts to friends and houseguests were a gold chain with sixty-five pearls, a ring with eight diamonds and a pearl as big as a good-size marble, one pair of shirt studs containing four emeralds and eighty

Diamond Jim had thirty sets of jewelry, each with a theme. This is a portion of the diamond-studded Transportation Set. *Top:* tie clip. *Center:* cuff link (*left*), vest button (*right*). *Bottom:* pocketbook clasp.

diamonds, and a gold watch with forty-one diamonds that had belonged to the emperor Napoleon (given by Jim to his old friend and trusted tailor, Jules Weiss). For women, the cache of handouts included diamond and pearl collars, gold mesh hand-bags, brooches, bracelets, and rings. Friends who smoked could expect to be given silver or gold cigarette or cigar cases. Imbibers got silver or gold pocket flasks. And there were bejeweled eye-glass cases, pen knives, pencils, hat brushes, and small silver knives for buttering ears of corn.

FOUR YEARS BEFORE Diamond Jim Brady moved from the apartment on Fifty-seventh Street to the house on Eighty-sixth, lyricist Charles N. Lawlor put words to a tune by James W.

Blake that forever defined life on the island of Manhattan in geographic terms. Their song was titled "The Sidewalks of New York." But everyone who sang or whistled it believed the name was "East Side, West Side."

North of Washington Square Park, the line of demarcation between East and West was Fifth Avenue for no reason other than it ran up the middle of the island. But as the city spread northward, "East" and "West" also came to represent bifurcation in tastes in architecture, culture, fashion, and social standing, dictated by wealth. None of Mrs. Astor's 400 ever presented her butler a calling card with a West Side address.

Explaining how it came to be that living on the East Side was "better" than living on the West Side, social historian Stephen Birmingham wrote, "In the late nineteenth century, it had a lot to do with the West Side's physical distance from society's traditional epicenter on Fifth Avenue."

The difference in lifestyle was also evident in architecture. Except for the mansions of the millionaires that stood opposite Central Park on Fifth Avenue, the East Side streets were lined with high-stooped houses with brownstone facades, flat roofs, and symmetrical windows. West Side houses had fronts made of a variety of materials. Roofs were gabled, dormered, peaked, or pyramid. The architectural style was "American basement plan." Front doors were usually street level and opened onto a large reception hall. The parlors and sitting rooms were on the second floor. As in Jim's house, the kitchen was ground level and connected to the second-floor dining room by a dumbwaiter. This architectural individuality gave the West Side a sense of variety and fun that the East Side lacked.

"Going up to the West Side in 1890," wrote Birmingham, "felt like entering an entirely different city, one with its own special mores, customs, usages and social tone."

The East Side was a culture of afternoon teas, formal-dress dinners served by butlers with white gloves, evenings of chamber music in drawing rooms, shopping in the finest Fifth Avenue stores, traveling by coach, leaving calling cards, having debutante balls, sitting in the dress circle at the Metropolitan Opera and Carnegie Hall, attending the Presbyterian Church, and voting the Republican ticket. The Democratic West Side was everything common. Its connection to the rest of the city was not by Fifth Avenue but Broadway. If one went out to dinner, the chances were excellent that one could at any time have an encounter with a brash, overweight, overdressed, and overly adorned salesman of Irish lineage who socialized with the theatrical crowd, spent a great deal of his leisure time carousing in the city's drinking establishments, was living "in sin" with a woman who was many years younger, and openly aspired to be accepted as an equal by the East Siders—simply because he had money.

Although he was not invited to leave his new house and travel "crosstown" to enter the homes of the grandees of wealth in their East Side mansions, when Diamond Jim went out on business during the day and "on the town" at night, he discovered that he was viewed as the personification of the era. All eyes turned to him. He found himself emulated in how he dressed and what he did. If a tailor told a well-heeled client, "Diamond Jim Brady owns two hundred of my suits," he could count on selling the customer a dozen outfits, instead of the three or four that the man had intended to order. Hat dealers and shirt and shoemakers pulled the same trick. As one writer observed, "Jim was the studded decoy duck that filled the coffers of New York's merchants."

Waiters discovered that if they told patrons that Mr. Brady was having a particular dish, or that he was sipping a certain wine, even though Jim was quaffing orange juice, the customers would usually respond, "I'll have the same, please."

As a result, when Jim walked into a lobster palace, headwaiters bowed low.

When a new restaurant opened its doors, the proprietor vied to induce him to try the fare and prayed that he would like it well enough to come back regularly.

In the last year of the Gay Nineties, there were many such places, but none was welcomed more heartily by Diamond Jim Brady than a lobster palace that opened on Broadway between Forty-third and Forty-fourth on September 23, 1899.

Jim had met its proprietor while attending the Chicago World's Fair and had begged him to open a restaurant in New York. His name was Charles Rector.

13

"Have You Got the Sauce?"

❧☙❧

W HEN RECTOR'S OPENED at what was then Longacre
Square (it would not become Times Square until 1904),
the crossing of Broadway and Seventh Avenue at Forty-second
Street (three blocks west of Commodore Vanderbilt's Grand
Central Terminal, which New Yorkers had ridiculed as a white
elephant that was too far away), was well on its way to becoming the city's center of nightlife. As the section became the hub
of theaters, restaurants were needed to feed the people who
came to enjoy the new-style musicals. Pioneers among these
eateries were Shanley's and nearby Churchill's, run by an ex-
policeman. They were specifically designed with ornate lobbies
and a stairway for the stars of shows to be seen and applauded
when they came in. This practice led to such places being
known as entrance restaurants.

Learning in Chicago of the availability of a two-story building in Longacre Square that was ideal for use as a restaurant,
Charles Rector went to New York, inspected the property, and
bought it. To give it unchallenged title to the best of the entrance restaurants, he spent more than $200,000 to renovate
it. The facade was Greco-Roman with a green griffon above a
revolving door–the first in America. Over it, RECTOR'S blazed in
white electric *lights*. The interior had mirrors and furnishings
done in paradise green and gold. Its main ground-floor dining

room had a hundred tables covered in Irish linen. The second floor had seventy-five tables and four private dining rooms.

To guarantee the finest menu and service, Charles Rector raided the staff of Delmonico's. Lured away with greatly increased wages were *saucier* Charles Parranin, maître d'hotel Paul Perett, and business manager Andrew Mehler. Waiters (165 of them) were graduates of professional schools in Switzerland. To encourage them to entice customers to order extra dishes and the best of the wines on the list, they were paid bonuses in the form of a percentage of the cost of the "extras" and half a dollar for each cork they persuaded a patron to let them pop.

The opening night menu was prepared by head chef Emil Hederer. It offered two first nighters named Jim—Diamond Jim Brady and boxing champion Gentleman Jim Corbett—Egyptian quail, English pheasant, African peaches, and Southern European strawberries.

Rector's also went into the history of New York restaurants by providing an orchestra not only for accompaniment while eating but for dancing between courses.

For the next quarter century Rector's reigned as the place, as the owner boasted, where no personal triumph was complete "unless validated by an evening at Rector's, in much the same way that the conqueror exhibited the conquered in a procession through the arches of ancient and imperial Rome." Champions, challengers, opera stars, explorers, captains of industry, gamblers, authors, and adventurers celebrated and were celebrated there. Through the years and revolving door came O. Henry; Stephen Crane; Richard Harding Davis; painter Frederic Remington; and the man they'd worked for in covering the Spanish-American War, William Randolph Hearst. King of the dudes Berry Wall sported a pearl derby, white vest, cutaway coat, and spats with a flower in his lapel and a cane in hand. Rector welcomed politicians, generals, the greatest actors and actresses of the era, and, more regularly than anyone else, "the best twenty-

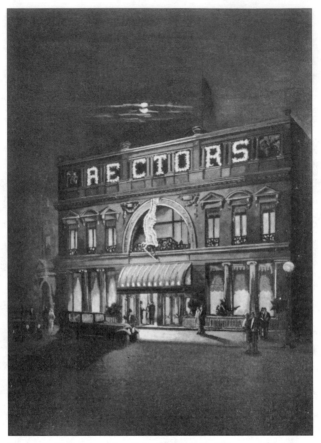

Rector's "lobster palace" on Broadway. Owner Charles
Rector considered Diamond Jim Brady "the best twenty-
five customers I ever had."

five customers" he ever had. He considered Diamond Jim Brady
a gentleman, "even though he did wear his napkin around his
neck."

Conceding that a napkin placed on the Brady knee would
have been as "inadequate as a doily under a bass drum," Rector wrote, "Diamond Jim's stomach started at his neck and
swelled out in majestic proportions, gaining power and curve as
it proceeded southward. Therefore, the only place where a napkin would have done him any good was around his neck. And
there he wore it. It looked like a bookmark in a tome of chins."

When Diamond Jim extolled the virtues of the *Sole Marguery* that he'd had in Paris, Rector pulled his son out of college and sent him as an emissary to France (bankrolled by Jim) to purloin the recipe for the sauce. The espionage and efforts to duplicate the sauce in Paris took three weeks. Satisfied that he had mastered how to replicate the sauce, he cabled his father that he was leaving for New York on the next boat.

Jim was at the dock to greet him with a bellowed, "Have you got the sauce?"

That evening, George Rector recalled, "a group of *bon vivants* sat down at one big table and prepared for the feast that followed."

Jim's guests included Victor Herbert, Adolphus Busch, Sam Shubert, Marshall Field, and theatrical producers Klaw and Erlanger.

After nine servings, Jim told Rector, "If you poured some of that sauce over a Turkish towel, I believe I could eat it all."

(For Rector's recipe for *Sole Marguery,* see "Notes and Sources.")

In quickly gaining and retaining a reputation for attracting outrageous, self-promoting, style-setting, and indelible characters, Rector's of the "naughty naughts" would not be equaled in the pageant of New York nightlife until the dawn of the disco music craze of the 1970s and the opening of Studio 54.

While Diamond Jim felt secure in his role as the champion of flash and flamboyance, he had a few contenders. The most mysterious character among the exhibitionists who breezed into New York City was a handsome, suntanned youth named Walter Scott. No relation to the famed and knighted Scottish poet of that name, he'd been born in Kentucky in 1875 but left home at nine. He wound up in Humboldt Wells, Nevada, at age ten as a wrangler on a horse ranch. Two years later he was driving twenty-mule teams pulling borax wagons across the California desert from Mojave to Death Valley. At age thirteen he arrived in New York for a visit. After going to Staten Island to take in William F. Cody's Wild West (the extravaganza that wowed them on the Midway at the Columbian Exposition), he made disparaging remarks about the abilities of riders in a display of "Cossack horsemanship" and was overheard by Buffalo Bill himself. Challenged to show he could do better than the Cossacks, the cocky boy so impressed Cody that he was added to the show. Listed in the program as "cowboy," he named himself "Death Valley Scotty." He became an instant hit and darling of the Broadway lobster palace set. They listened with fascination to his tales of the wild and woolly West as Scotty ate and drank his fill at their expense.

When Buffalo Bill's outdoor show closed for winter months, Scotty headed west with the avowed purpose of prospecting for gold and silver. These seasonal expeditions would go on throughout the 1890s, with Scotty coming back to Buffalo Bill with nothing to show for digs in the desert than sand in his boots. But at the turn of the century, after being fired by Cody for a cause that went unrecorded, Scotty persuaded a wealthy New Yorker named Julius Gerard to stake him to another venture into Death Valley. He claimed to know just the spot for striking it rich. He announced that he'd found the mother lode near Barstow, California, but he would not say where it was located. In fact, there was no mine. The source of money that Scotty flashed in the lobster palaces, gambling dens, and bordellos was a Chicago millionaire who was promised a fifty-fifty share in the proceeds of Scotty's nonexistent mine. Scotty's charade as struck-it-rich prospector continued well into the twentieth century as generations of tourists in love with the stories of the West went to Death Valley to meet him. He died in 1954, never admitting that his mine had existed only in the imaginations of himself and the gullible romantics of New York's Gilded Age.

The source of the wealth of another figure out of the West who captured fancies in the lobster palaces was never in doubt. Leader of the pack of Diamond Jim's rivals in flamboyance was a prospector who had truly struck it rich in copper in Montana. His name was Jim Murray, and he used his wealth to indulge a passion for pearls.

"God never made nothin' more beautiful than a pearl," he averred. "No diamonds or no emeralds or rubies ever had the life and color of pearls."

Like Jim Brady with diamonds, he wore jewelry made from pearls and carried them loose in pockets. He never toted fewer than two hundred and claimed that they were worth not a dollar less than a million bucks. His passion for the stones got him the nickname "Pearl Jim." But with all his pearly decoration, he never attained Diamond Jim's popularity in the lobster palaces, primarily because he did not have Diamond Jim's mastery of what was required to be a standout personality and remain one in a rough-and-tumble city that quickly recognized flash-in-the-pan celebrities, chewed them up, and spit them out. Nor was Pearl Jim willing to copy Jim Brady by throwing around his money, as Diamond Jim liked to say, "just for the hell of it."

No one connected with the new Broadway lobster palaces offered Jim Brady an opportunity to demonstrate his largesse better than a pair of wine salesmen who saw in the big spenders a chance to peddle their firms' top-of-the-line champagne. They were "wine agents." Representing Moet et Chandon, George Kessler was a tall and slender figure with a vaguely Oriental look. Hoping to sell restaurateurs on the virtues of Mumm's was dapper, white-haired Mannie Chappelle. If either entered a palace such as Rector's, customers found themselves recipients of a complimentary bottle, in the hope they would find it so good that they would demand that the proprietor stock it regularly. If Kessler and Chappelle happened to be in a restaurant at the same time, customers found themselves treated to both brands.

Should the wine agents discover Diamond Jim Brady seated at his usual table, they did not have to send complimentary bottles. Jim bought as many as the salesmen had and sent them to friends and even strangers with his card on which he wrote, "With the compliments of James Buchanan Brady."

Among Rector's patrons regularly receiving chilled bottles was Charles Gates. The son of John W. "Bet-a-Million" Gates, Charlie was young, good looking, and slow-witted. When he let his father down by dropping out of college, John bought him a brokerage firm in the hope that he would settle down. Charlie had as much trouble grasping the intricacies of Wall Street as he had in his studies and was quickly replaced in the firm. Because John worried about Charlie being on his own whenever John had to leave the city on business, he asked Diamond Jim to keep an eye on the youth. Jim did so gladly, inviting Charlie to parties at Eighty-sixth Street and taking him to the theater, prizefights, and the racetracks. Most important, Jim kept him under his wing late at night in the lobster palaces, lest Charlie get carried away by the soft lights and certain alluring women on the lookout for easy pickings in the form of indiscreet boys with wealthy fathers.

Like Diamond Jim, Bet-a-Million Gates had started out as a salesman and made money in steel and stock speculation. In 1896 he'd turned his attention to gaining control of a product that had become essential in the America in which vast regions were being made into farms—barbed wire fencing. Backed by friends and early employers, he bought and combined seven factories into the Consolidated Steel and Wire Company. After adding other steel plants, he changed the name to the American Steel and Wire Company of Illinois. Less than a year later he established the American Steel and Wire Company of New Jersey. He then merged them with eleven more mills and factories with a capitalization of $90 million.

Gates's purpose in taking control of the wire-making business was to attract the attention of another tycoon who was actively consolidating steel companies and looking forward to pulling off the biggest industrial deal in history. If all went as J. P. Morgan planned, Andrew Carnegie would agree to co-operate with Morgan in creating the world's first billion-dollar corporation.

Gates hoped to be cut in on the Morgan-Carnegie deal. When Morgan rejected the price Gates wanted in order to be bought out, a struggle of wills ensued. Gates eventually surrendered. But in so doing he gained $110 million in stock in a new goliath company that controlled 90 percent of the national output of iron and steel. Morgan named it United States Steel.

Thirty others who benefited from the coup became known as Pittsburgh Millionaires. They immediately became familiar faces in the theater crowds that sustained the lobster palaces of Longacre Square. Although Rector's and other restaurants served before-theater dinners, they prided themselves on serving "late supper." With the theaters letting out, Broadway and the side streets were cluttered by carriages and hansom cabs to take most people home. But others made their way to the restaurants for feasts that began with cocktails. Drinks were followed by oysters, a steak, salad, and dessert.

At midnight all eyes turned toward the front in eager anticipation of the grand entrance of the Broadway theater's leading ladies and the wealthy men who escorted them. Many of these gentlemen sought to outdo Diamond Jim. None succeeded.

ALTHOUGH LAW had wedded Brooklyn, Queens, the Bronx, and Staten Island to the island between the Hudson and East rivers, everyone who thought, wrote, and spoke of New York City meant Manhattan. To go and succeed there would ever be the dreams of countless people born elsewhere. One of them was Theodore Dreiser. From Terre Haute, Indiana, he had held a succession of newspaper jobs in Chicago, St. Louis, and Pittsburgh before settling in Manhattan in 1894. Twenty-nine years later in *The Color of a Great City* he would say that the thing that interested him about New York was "the sharp, and at the same time immense, contrast it showed between the dull and the shrewd, the strong and the weak, the rich and the poor, the wise and the ignorant."

A female character in the novel asserts, "I would rather live in my hall-bedroom in New York than in any fifteen-room house in the country that I ever saw."

Another writer who would come to New York and take up the subject of Manhattan was Alexander Woollcott. Fourteen years younger than Dreiser, the future drama critic and founding member of the circle of 1920s wits known as the Algonquin Round Table, and the inspiration for the George S. Kaufman–Moss Hart comedy *The Man Who Came to Dinner,* arrived in 1909 and settled into a rooming house on West Twelfth Street.

In 1928 he would write in an essay titled *No Yesterdays,* "Since God lifted this continent above the waters and so clad its plains and valleys that it could be a homestead for a numberless multitude, it must fill Him at times with mingled surprise, amusement and exasperation to note how many of us are perversely scrounged together in a monstrous determination to live crowded on Manhattan Island and there only—there or not at all."

Theodore Dreiser wrote of Broadway at Forty-second Street on spring evenings at the turn of the century when doors of shops were open and windows of nearly all restaurants were wide to the gaze of the passersby, very few of whom could afford to dine in them.

"At Rector's temple of pleasure and perdition," wrote New York historian Lloyd Morris, "any patron willing to spend twenty dollars on a supper party for five was able to include in his hospitality two bottles of champagne and a round of cigars."

For Manhattanites living between the poverty of Jacob Riis's "other half" and the plush of Tony Pastor's Upper Ten Thousand, with dreams of one day qualifying as one of Mrs. Astor's 400, a new form of dining out was available in nine restaurants owned by brothers William and Samuel Childs. Having learned the restaurant business by working in a nationwide chain of low-priced eateries and with $1,600 between them, they struck out on their own with an idea for a restaurant that could serve thousands of people a day.

In doing so, they invented the cafeteria.

After assessing the Childs' establishment at 130 Broadway in February 1898, a writer for *The Caterer's Monthly* reported that when you entered you would find "a large lunch counter on your left, filled with piles of sandwiches." Opposite the counter, and about four feet from it, "is a metal, ornamental open partition three feet high, extending the full length of the counter. Before stepping into the passageway you notice a big pile of empty trays from which each guest takes one. Now as you pass along the lunch counter, you take off whatever you want and place it on your tray, not, however, forgetting to take a cup of coffee from the big urns."

Decades before the cafeteria and lunch counter juke box, the Childs' restaurant provided music to eat by from a five-piece orchestra.

Three years after the first Childs' opened its door, a pair of Philadelphia entrepreneurs named Horn and Hardart introduced New Yorkers to a cafeteria that they called "an automat" on Broadway at Thirteenth Street.

Although there is no record of Diamond Jim standing in line with a tray in hand to help himself in one of the Childs' restaurants or a Horn and Hardart Automat, it's reasonable to say that when he ventured even farther uptown for sporting events at the Polo Grounds, he sampled and joyfully devoured several steaming sausages in buns sold by Harry M. Stevens, called "red hots." After a newspaper cartoonist depicted the innovation as a dachshund in two slices of bread, Stevens's red hots got a name—the hot dog.

HAND IN HAND with the shifting of the theater district from Broadway in the 1930s to the new houses around Long-acre Square came a splurge in hotel-building, further realizing

Cornelius Vanderbilt's vision of a thriving Forty-second Street. Erected on the corner of Forty-second and Broadway, the Hotel Knickerbocker was called "the country club on Forty-second Street." It offered Diamond Jim Brady a sumptuous new venue. Bellied up to the longest bar in the world, graced by a Maxfield Parrish mural of Old King Cole, Jim could sip root beer or lemonade while treating prospective customers to all they wanted of beer, champagne, wine, and the hard stuff.

Not long after the debut of the Knickerbocker, seven blocks north and two to the west of Broadway and Forty-second, another hotel announced its existence with a grand opening that was attended by the cream of high society. The lavish new hostelry at Fifth Avenue and Fifty-ninth Street was named the Plaza. To its inauguration came Vanderbilts, Harrimans, and Goulds; the big names in business, commerce, and politics; and theatrical celebrities whose attendance was considerably more interesting to readers of the newspapers covering the event than nabobs of society and industry.

They were led by Diamond Jim with glittering gems that outshone everything worn by the social elite. He escorted Lillian Russell in a huge feathered hat and ruffled gown adorned by jewelry from him and Jesse Lewisohn. It was stunning, but no match for her escort's display.

The Plaza's debut also inaugurated an amenity that surprised even the man who seven years earlier had introduced New Yorkers to the automobile. Lined up along Fifth Avenue were green and red "taxicabs." The brainstorm of Harry N. Allen, the motorized vehicles contained devices that registered distance traveled and the fee to be paid by the passenger. The drivers—they were called chauffeurs—wore uniforms and were described by a newspaper reporter as looking like "Hussars." A year after creating a sensation with his taxis, Allen had seven hundred of them on "taxi lines" at all the important hotels and train stations and at Hudson River docks when an ocean liner was due.

The Plaza of 1900 lasted only two years. Sold in 1902 for $3 million, it was replaced by an even grander one in 1907. When it opened on October 1, Diamond Jim was there again, if only to congratulate his friends in the Fuller Company, which owned it and the first skyscraper in the city. At the crisscrossing of Fifth Avenue and Broadway at Twenty-third Street, it was formally named the Fuller Building. Because it was in the shape of heavy triangular irons used for pressing clothing, New Yorkers called it the Flatiron.

An unexpected feature of the site and the building's shape was swirling winds. As men who passed by held onto their hats, women found to their horror that the strong gusts caused their skirts to fly up. In order to dissuade males from loitering by the building to gawk, policemen were assigned to order them to move on. Lecherous loungers told to scram got the "twenty-three skidoo."

Of all the structures that made Madison Square the pulse beat of Gilded Age Manhattan, the Flatiron Building (now its official name) is the only one still standing. Long-since gone are the Fifth Avenue Hotel where Diamond Jim picked up the election returns that allowed him to win wagers on the outcomes of races, the Brunswick, the Hoffman House, and the old St. James where John Toucey had detected promise in a chubby bellboy named Jim Brady.

"For above all we have no yesterdays," Alexander Woollcott noted in his 1928 essay on the transitory nature of residing on "an enchanted isle" named Manhattan, "no reminders from one day's dawn to next that ever folk have walked before in the streets where now we walk."

Like the city of his birth, Jim Brady had been constantly remaking himself while moving uptown. He'd been born above a saloon on West Street. He'd escaped by working as a bellhop in a hotel at Twenty-sixth and Broadway. He learned the business of running the railroads in John Toucey's office in Commodore Vanderbilt's Grand Central and on the road for Charles

Moore. He'd returned from countless sojourns as a salesman to reign at the Hoffman House bar as the character he had invented and another salesman had named Diamond Jim. In that guise he accumulated more than enough wealth to become the constant companion of the beautiful Lillian Russell. He was Mr. First Nighter, gentleman sportsman, pacesetter in dress and behavior in the lobster palaces, and owner of an Upper West Side townhouse furnished with all the trappings expected of a man of accomplishment at the dawn of the twentieth century.

Along the way he had become friends with many of the richest men in the nation as they congregated for drinks and card games in New York's plushest hotels. They liked him because of his flamboyance and easygoing manner. As they were in the stock market, they expressed their fondness by giving him tips that fattened his bank accounts. If a situation arose in which they needed someone to front for them by letting them buy shares in his name and hold on to them until a chance came to make a killing, they could count on Jim to reply "Why the hell not?"

Consequently, when Jim's pal John Gates asked him to a meeting to talk over a way to make "a nice bit of money" at the expense of "that bastard J. P. Morgan," Jim grinned, rubbed his hands together, and said, "Just tell me where and when."

The place was a private dining room at the Hoffman House. As Jim walked in, already seated around a table were Gates; George Crocker, a California millionaire; an up-and-coming young financier named Bernard Baruch; Edwin Hawley, president of the Minneapolis & St. Louis Railroad; Wall Street player Thomas Sully; and Jesse Lewisohn. The one thing these men had in common, besides wealth, was a dislike of J. P. Morgan.

In the case of John W. Gates, the emotion was downright hatred. Seething at having been bettered by Morgan in the U.S. Steel deal, Gates had been quietly plotting his revenge.

For more than a year he had built a cadre of spies to keep him informed of the activities of the House of Morgan. Analyzing snippets of fact and gossip in the office of his own firm, Harris, Gates & Company, in a suite in the Waldorf-Astoria, Gates discerned that Morgan was plotting to end competition against the Morgan-controlled Southern Railway Company by taking over the rival Louisville and Nashville Railroad. The company had issued $5 million worth of new stock. Morgan intended quietly to obtain enough shares to control the line, putting him in position to be the dominant power in rail transportation below the Mason-Dixon line.

After explaining this history to the men he'd called to the Hoffman House, Gates proposed that they beat Morgan to the punch by buying L and N shares, then selling them to Morgan at a greatly inflated price. With the blessing and backing of the seven men at the meeting, Gates stealthily launched his campaign.

When Morgan realized what was going on, he commenced a stiff fight by ordering the chairman of the L and N, August Belmont, to dump a block of fifty thousand shares. This was illegal, but J. P. Morgan had never been a man who felt restrained by inconvenient laws. Undaunted by the move and with the ardent support of the Hoffman House seven, Gates bought the shares and let Morgan and Wall Street know that he and his "associates" could have paid quadruple the price for the shares.

This now-public battle over the Louisville and Nashville triggered a buy-and-sell frenzy over a single railroad's stock that was unprecedented in Wall Street history. In the first hour of one day's trading more than 350,000 L and N shares were bought and sold. By noon the figure stood at half a million.

Late in the afternoon, as the fevered trading continued, Gates informed Wall Street and the House of Morgan that the war could end easily. He said, "Let Morgan settle."

As Wall Streeters gasped at Gates's audacity and J. P. Morgan fumed, Diamond Jim and Bet-a-Million's other allies chortled with delight.

Diamond Jim eagerly enlisted in a plot by his friend John W. "Bet-a-Million" Gates (shown here on the left with his son Charles, right, and their wives) to buy up stocks of a railroad that financier J. P. Morgan planned to buy. Gates's "Hoffman House seven" were then in a position to sell their shares to Morgan at a huge profit.

Rather than deal with Gates face to face, Morgan dispatched an emissary to the Waldorf-Astoria with orders to do nothing that might cause the cocky copper millionaire from Montana to demand an even higher price for the stock. Morgan's delegate, George W. Perkins, was told what Gates was willing to accept: sale of Gates's holdings in blocks of one-third at a time at an increasing rate, beginning at $125 a share and ending at $150. Otherwise, Gates warned, he would exercise his right to call the shares Morgan had bought short. No one had to tell Perkins or Morgan that the result of such a demand would be stock market panic.

A few hours after Gates's threat, the House of Morgan issued a statement announcing "At the request of Messrs. Harris, Gates and Company who, on their own independent account have recently made large purchases of Louisville and Nashville Railroad stock, Messrs. J. P. Morgan and Company have consented to take control of the stock so purchased and to receive the same on deposit, and they have so consented solely to relieve the general financial condition and not for the benefit of any railroad company."

As Gates and the Hoffman House seven celebrated their victory, Gates offered a toast, which Jim joined by lifting a stein of root beer. Gates declared, "Here's to us who have taught J. Pierpont Morgan that what's sauce for the goose is sauce for the gander."

When the deal was closed and Gates handed Jim a check for his share of the deal in the amount of $1,250,000, Jim slapped his friend on the back and said, "I consent to receive this money solely for the purpose of relieving my general financial condition, and not for the benefit of any railroad company."

14

Farmer Jim

❦❧❦

A MONG THE TEAM of reporters laboring on behalf of
James Gordon Bennett's *Herald* was Albert Stevens Crockett. He spent years reporting the doings of people of the lobster
palace set, especially the activities of the phenomenon named
James Buchanan Brady. In a memoir of the era, *Peacocks on Parade,*
published in 1931, he wrote:

> In strictly private life, Diamond Jim acted as a getter-up of
> parties where the Big Fellows, aided by a lavish application of
> liquors and by pleasant attentions from light but passably
> pretty ladies, might coax gentlemen from The Sticks into
> business commitments from which day light and sober sense
> might have made them revolt. Jim had a wide acquaintance
> along Broadway, and his particular blonde [Edna McCauley]
> knew others. Besides, if the preference of the gentlemen was
> for brunettes, his address book was filled with telephone num-
> bers, each indicating a young woman willing to "go as far as
> you like," provided assurance was given that a hundred-
> dollar bill would be found under her plate at table, or would
> be deposited in what was called her "national bank" in a
> method acceptable to the donor. More than once the male
> guests corralled by Jim for the Big Fellows consisted largely
> of legislators whose good opinion—or otherwise—of certain
> measures then under consideration was desirable.

Jim sometimes got the result he desired by inviting a potential customer to a dinner and insisting that he "bring along the wife." The dinner would be elaborate and the wine abundant. But it was not food and drink, or even the Brady charm, that beguiled the lady. Once she spied the jewels that illuminated Jim's shirtfront, she would invariably express admiration. Should she single out a diamond, emerald, or other sparkler, Jim would pluck it off and present it to her as a "little remembrance of this delightful evening." He did so knowing that the commission from the sale that followed in the morning would more than cover the cost of replacing the bauble.

Another journalistic observer of Diamond Jim Brady at this time was Irwin S. Cobb. Then a young cub reporter for the *World* he became a celebrated humorist in the 1930s and 1940s. At a late Sunday breakfast with friends at Café Martin on lower Madison Avenue, Cobb watched as "tip-hungry waiters converged like gulls" around Jim's table. In an autobiography published in 1941, *Exit Laughing,* Cobb described the object of attention of everyone in the restaurant:

> His gross displacement was awe-inspiring. He had a huge frame to start with and fat was draped upon it in creases and folds. He had three distinct chins and the nethermost one ran all the way around his neck as though, being fearful of punctures, he was carrying an extra spare on behind. His coat was of a shrieking checked pattern, needing only the name of a stable across the rear to be a blanket for some racing filly—and about the right dimensions, too. It being the Sabbath day he was content to wear his comparatively inobtrusive star sapphire set: matched stones, the size of plover eggs in his cuff-links, on his watch fob, upon two of his dropsical-looking fingers, down his shirt front, in his vest buttons and, if rumor had it right, mounted also in his front and rear collar studs, his suspender buckles, his gold penknife and his sock supporters.

Cobb's recollection moved on to the "manful way" the object of his discreet observations "tackled" his breakfast. It began with a waiter bringing a "silver platter suitable for a large roast turkey" but that held "a quadruple portion of corned-beef hash, mounded like an igloo and shingled over with at least eight poached eggs."

With this order came "a towering edifice" of hotcakes that Diamond Jim piled atop the hash and eggs "like a fast work-man double-tiling a bathroom." He then "sluiced the ensemble with large quantities of melted butter and maple syrup, using a carving knife and fork—no ordinary table tools would have served—he chopped the whole thing into chaos. Using a dessert spoon he ate it to the last bite and the last lick."

The restaurant in which Cobb watched Diamond Jim at breakfast, Café Martin, had been opened in 1899 by Louis Martin, who had successfully operated a small hotel on Ninth Street that was a favorite of French visitors. When he learned that Delmonico's was vacating its site on Twenty-sixth Street to move uptown, he leased the building and created an intimate restaurant that introduced side-by-side seating known as a banquette. This cozy atmosphere proved very attractive to men who wished to entertain young women who were not their wives. Among them were Stanford White, whose studio and apartment with their velvet swings were nearby, and the man who had been Mrs. Langtry's protector while she was in New York, Freddie Gebhard. Café Martin became an immediate success as a rendezvous of the smart set for luncheons and dinners.

One of Louis Martin's employees was Jacques Bustanoby. Wanting to strike out on his own, and recognizing opportunities for a restaurant close to the Longacre Square theater district, he left Café Martin and with two brothers opened a place at Forty-second and Sixth Avenue called Café des Beaux Arts. The place caught on immediately not only with theatergoers but the headliners of the shows.

Part of the attraction for these luminaries were *soirees artistiques* at which Jacques cajoled the stars into performing. (Not a lot of coaxing was needed.) Among the first to do so was Lillian Russell. She invariably entered the restaurant to applause and in the company of Jesse Lewisohn, Diamond Jim and Edna, and producer Florenz Ziegfeld and his wife, the tiny singer Anna Held, whom "Flo" had brought from France and made a star in the United States.

Many years later Bustanoby told a columnist of the *New York Mirror,* "I will never forget how Anna Held and Lillian Russell would come in with Diamond Jim and Flo and Lillian and Anna would compete with each other. Anna would sing 'I Cannot Make My Eyes Behave,' and how her great eyes would roll and sparkle. And then, when everybody was applauding Anna, Lillian would get up to sing her famous 'Come Down, My Evenin' Star.'"

As decades later "Over the Rainbow" would become associated with Judy Garland, "People (Who Need People)" with Barbra Streisand, "Cabaret" with Liza Minnelli, and "The Sound of Music" with Julie Andrews, Lillian Russell claimed as "my song" a number written by John "Honey" Stromberg. The lyrics by Robert Smith were in the style of a Negro spiritual and written in the cotton-fields English that white Americans attributed to all blacks in an era when comedians routinely donned "darky" makeup and bushy wigs and actresses played roles as men:

When from out de shades ob night
Come de stars a shinin' bright,
I spy de one I do love,
I recognize ma true love
Amid de tiny orbs ob light.

Search de sky from east to west
She's de brightest and de best,
But she's so far above me,

I knows she cannot love me,
Still I loves her, an' more dan all de rest.

   REFRAIN
Ma evenin' star,
I wonder who you are,
Set up so high like a diamond in de sky.
No matter what I do,
I can't go up to you.
So come down from dar, ma evenin' star.
Come down! Come down!
Come down from dar, ma evenin' star.

The proprietor of Café des Beaux Arts also recounted in the *Mirror* interview a contest of a different kind involving Lillian. Instead of competing with Anna Held, she'd vied with her old friend Jim Brady in eating. If she could match him course for course, Jim promised, he'd give her a huge diamond ring the next day.

"Lillian slipped out to the ladies' room," the restaurateur's account continued, "and came out with a heavy bundle under her arm, wrapped up in a tablecloth. She told me to keep it for her until the next day. 'But don't look,' she told me."

Lillian went back to the table, said Bustanoby, "and ate plate-for-plate, and beat Jim fair and square."

The bundle she had handed to him contained her corset.

What Edna, Jesse, Flo, and Anna thought of the spectacle was not recorded. Others in the restaurant were probably not astonished that Lillian Russell could hold her own in the gustatorial combat but were surprised that the American Beauty was in the city. The first lady of operettas and Weber and Fields burlesques had leased a mansion at Far Rockaway on Long Island that she had named Cedar Hill.

Withdrawing from the city did not mean she wished to be left alone. The seaside house had fourteen rooms reserved for guests, few of whom could resist her invitations to come and spend the weekend, or the whole summer. Frequent lodgers were other leading ladies of the stage whom Lillian called "farm flirts." Most often in attendance were Irene Perry, Isadora Rush, Blanche Bates, and old friend Marie Dressler. Of the getaway spot Marie warned, "Heaven help the tired actress, actor, playwright or director who comes out here with the idea of spending a quiet visit!"

Guests were expected to obey two rules. They had to be on time for meals, and everyone was to exercise at least an hour a day. For that purpose there was a tennis court, a croquet lawn, an outdoor gym with barbells, punching bag, and medicine balls. An array of bikes (not gold-plated) were available, along with several horses for riding.

Often counted among the weekenders was Edna McCauley. She was usually with Jim, but if business demanded that he remain in the city or make a business trip somewhere, she went alone.

On one of Jim's visits he surprised everyone by announcing that he had decided to emulate Lillian by getting a country place for himself. "It ain't gonna be something elaborate," he explained, "just a place for weekends and the like."

AFTER MUCH SEARCHING, he found just the spot halfway between New York and Phildadelphia, where he did a lot of business with the Pennsylvania and the Reading railroads. He paid the president of the Consolidated Playing Card Company $68,000 for a three hundred–acre farm at Long Branch, New Jersey. It had "a simple little house" with thirty rooms.

Jim named the spread Ellesdale Manor Farm.

To "improve" it he again retained Collins Marsh. During months of consultations with Jim and Edna, Marsh scoured the country and much of Europe for ideas as to what a well-dressed farmhouse should wear. Everything had to be of the finest material and most expensive design, from linens, furniture, and decorative items to statuary. When the job was done, Marsh presented Jim a bill of over $100,000 for his services.

While Marsh was tending to the house, Jim took charge of everything outside. One wag quipped that he spent so much on farm equipment that International Harvester Company declared an extra stock dividend. One newspaper went to press with a story that Diamond Jim Brady's cows were milked into solid gold buckets trimmed with diamonds, sapphires, and rubies. The buckets were merely gold plated and were brought out only if Jim wanted to impress a visiting prospective customer. The bovine herd was made up of twenty-five prime Guernseys. The other livestock consisted of pigs, chickens, and horses.

Claiming the farm was a business tool, he billed much of it to his many expense accounts and justified it by declaring "I'm gonna use this place to entertain my customers in the summer, so why the hell shouldn't I spend my expense account money fixing it up?" Companies that were beneficiaries of Jim's salesmanship voiced no objections.

Just as he'd tried to outdo the dudes in style, outflash everyone with jewelry, and match the East Side homes of the 400 in lavishly furnishing his Eighty-sixth Street house, he set mind, heart, and bankroll on making Ellesdale Manor Farm not only an agricultural showplace but one that produced better crops than any other in the state of New Jersey. The result was produce that cost five times as much to raise, but it was also very tasty. The farm's output proved so abundant that Jim, Edna, and the farmworkers and their families had more than they could eat.

Finding the idea of marketing his farm's wares demeaning, and not wanting to compete with farmers who relied on selling their crops to make a living, Diamond Jim Brady chose to give it to customers and the needy. In his definition "needy" meant theater folk. Hardly any struggling actors or actresses declined an invitation to spend a few days at the farm with all expenses paid by the host. These outings became known around New York's theater district as "going down to Brady's."

When the time came to return to the city, a visitor was given a huge hamper made from zinc and insulated to prevent melting of shaved ice that was layered around two-pound bars of butter wrapped in fern leaves, cleaned and dressed poultry, eggs, red beets, carrots, cauliflower heads, cabbages, string beans, tomatoes, and ears of corn. As the guests departed in a convoy of Jim's cars, a truck brought up the rear, loaded with the hampers.

"What the hell, we got so damn much food down here that I gotta do somethin' with it," said Jim. "It's a case of feedin' it to the pigs, or give it to my friends—and the damn pigs get too much to eat as it is."

While in temporary residence at Ellesdale Manor the pampered men and women had at their disposal anything they might desire in forms of recreation to while away the hours. Grounds around the house offered ample room for tennis, badminton, croquet, horseshoes, and a putting green for golfers. Most felt the need for some kind of exercise to offset the amount of food they ate for breakfast, lunch, midafternoon snacking, dinner, and near-midnight suppers.

One day not long after Jim became a New Jersey farmer, going down to Brady's for one group of city dwellers proved more exciting than living in New York. They found themselves ducking for cover under tables and behind chairs to avoid being shot.

The gunfire was the culmination of Jim's coachman having a love affair with the wife of one of Jim's farmhands. When the husband discovered what was going on while he was in the fields, he grabbed his double-barreled shotgun and strode up the hill to the manor house just as Jim and his guests were sitting down to dinner. As they were about to dip silver spoons into their soup, they heard two explosions in the kitchen.

Neither blast of the shotgun proved effective, and by the time Diamond Jim rushed into the kitchen to see what had happened, the coachman was gone. He'd spotted the gunman as he'd entered the room and managed to dive through an open window a second before a double load of pellets shattered the glass, splintered the frame and sill, and raked the surrounding wall.

The coachman who fled the farm was not the expert mechanic Jim had hired to drive the automobile he'd bought at the Chicago World's Fair. William Johnson was still on the payroll, but now he was in charge of cars that were considerably more complicated to operate than the battery-powered carriage that had been the first to scare horses on Fifth Avenue. In Jim's garage at Ellesdale Manor Farm were German-built, gasoline-powered cars—two Mercedes and a Benz. Johnson was in charge of two teams of chauffeurs and footmen as the owner of the autos kept them running between New York and the farm and back again and to and from the railway station. Johnson eventually grew so fat that he could no longer fit behind a steering wheel. Jim was forced to get him a job as a night watchman in a garage in New York.

For some of Jim's visitors a weekend meant trysts in the company of ladies, provided their presence would not be embarrassing to any of the other guests. They arrived late Saturday night and stayed until Tuesday or Wednesday. To be certain that none of the men showed up with a woman who might be objectionable, Jim sent each invitee a list of guests. Should a man be thinking of escorting a woman who was not his wife, it was his obligation to contact the other guests to determine if the lady was acceptable. Sometimes it was not a mistress to whom others objected but a missus.

"I've found it to be true about a lot of the rich men I know who came to New York," Jim was fond of saying, "that they're married to gals they fell in love with when they were young and in the sticks. When the men got money, they changed. The gals didn't."

Describing these "newcomers to wealth" who rushed New York during the Gilded Age, historian Albert Crockett noted that more than one such devoted woman "developed heartache when her consort began to let his eyes dwell on sights practically foreign to the small town in which most of his early life had been spent."

In *Peacocks on Parade* Crockett observed:

Unless the wife of his bosom was particularly attractive, or else wonderfully wise, she was apt to have a hard time holding her husband's attention and interest when he began to realize that the possession of money had brought him power of sorts.

Coming to New York with what often seemed unlimited wealth, they not infrequently exhibited a preference for the flesh pots. Here swarmed flocks of pretty women—on the streets, in the restaurants, or in hotels, particularly in the lobbies of the big hotels. And my, how those women did dress! Why, it was Sunday best with them all the time. And what an eyeful the girls made! If a fellow could get away from his wife for an evening, and knew somebody who knew the ropes, somebody who could produce a bunch of "beauts" with swell frocks and dainty lace underthings and so on and, mind you, wearing silk stockings all the time! And gosh! They weren't shy at all. Why, some of them, if you offered to buy them a pair of garters, might even let you put 'em on them.

Many such men could attest that no man in New York knew "the ropes" any better than Diamond Jim Brady, whether he was conducting business by entertaining in hotels and lobster palaces in New York or down on his farm. They were newly minted millionaires such as John Gates whose riches were copper colored, silver-rich men from Denver, cattle barons of Texas, lumber tycoons from the Northwest, monarchs of the meat business from Chicago and Kansas City, and the men who'd built and profited from America's romance with and dependence on the railroads.

All knew that when they came to town Diamond Jim would be there to ensure they had a good time, and no one would leave without signing a Brady contract or having given the genial host a tip on what stock to snap up. He entertained and courted their business separately or in groups, sometimes throwing five parties at once in neighboring hotels so that he could go back and forth between them. If the men wanted chorus girls, Jim replied, "Easiest thing in the world. I'll call up Flo Ziegfeld and he'll have half a dozen snappy numbers over here after the show."

The prince of flash and the showman who promised audiences "the most beautiful girls in the world" had taken the measure of each other on the Midway during the Columbian Exposition, where Ziegfeld had promoted his only attraction, Sandow the strongman, by feeding reporters a phony story of a romance between the muscle man and Lillian Russell.

Two years later Jim provided Ziegfeld $10,000 to go to England to sign up a beautiful young singer who was playing to sold-out audiences at the Palace Theater in London. Returning to New York, Ziegfeld not only had Anna Held under contract, he was head over heels in love with her. When they married at the Hotel Netherland on March 28, 1896, Jim and Lillian Russell were among ten witnesses to one of the strangest weddings New York had ever seen. Instead of exchanging vows in a religious or civil ceremony, the couple signed an agreement "to be known as husband and wife henceforth."

On September 21, 1896, Flo Ziegfeld presented her in *The Parlor Match,* a new musical with a song that left audiences pleased but shocked. In "Won't You Come and Play with Me," for the first time in Broadway history, words were blatantly sexual:

I have such a nice little way with me,
 A way with me,
 A way with me,
I have such a nice little way with me,
I should like to have you play with me,
Play with me all the day long.

Should Anna Held's husband's bevy of chorus line beauties not be available to enlist in entertaining customers at parties, Jim felt free to call on two of the most famous men in America to spellbind guests with either tales of the boxing ring or adventures in the wild and woolly West. The former were presented by Jim's buddy from Harry Hill's saloon, John L. Sullivan. Yarns about cowboys and Indians were related by Colonel William F. "Buffalo Bill" Cody. Sullivan, who was more than down on his luck, was paid $100. The white-hatted, buckskin-clad impresario of rodeos took his pay in the form of a bottle of Hennessey's "Three Star" whiskey. For an extra bottle or two he might also bring along one of his show's stars. Annie Oakley showed a talent for using his rifle to shoot out the room's light bulbs.

Yet no amount of carousing with Ziegfeld chorus girls could quench a thirst for thrills in Jim's newly rich customers quite like an evening of gambling. Again, Diamond Jim knew where and how to accommodate them.

ALTHOUGH JIM LIKED games of chance, he never wagered to the extent of Bet-a-Million Gates and others. He'd been in more than enough gambling dens to recognize that the odds were stacked against the player. "A man's a sucker to try to buck the dealers," he warned his guests. "He may for a while, but in the end he'll lose his shirt."

For the new millionaires with piles of money in banks and Wall Street shares, however, the possibility of losing a shirt, or an entire wardrobe, was immaterial. They had come to town for a good time, and that meant experiencing the exhilaration of placing big bets in the gambling rooms of Corey's and Frank Farrell's House of the Bronze Doors, whose portals were guarded by a pair of burly sentinels who could spot a raiding party of unbribed cops a block away, so as to sound the alarm to the players inside that a raid was in the offing. A further safeguard against suspicious characters acted as a greeter in the reception hall. Once inside, gamblers indulged in every kind of game in rooms on three floors.

As fancy as was Farrell's, it paled in comparison to the establishment belonging to the "Prince of Gamblers." Richard Albert Canfield was erudite, unobtrusive, tall, brown-haired, gray-eyed, clean-shaven, and always perfectly clad in black or gray suits. He owned a casino one block from Delmonico's at Fifth Avenue and Forty-fourth Street. In the four-story brownstone the guests of Diamond Jim found such elegant paraphernalia as hickory roulette wheels inlaid with ivory. The walls of the gaming rooms were hung with paintings that Canfield bought on yearly "art trips" to Europe. Should a customer find himself invited to Canfield's top-floor apartment to settle up for losses downstairs, he encountered another Canfield passion: one of the country's finest private libraries.

What James Buchanan Brady found fascinating about America's most famous gambler was that Richard Canfield had also attained wealth by coming up the hard way. Born in 1855 in the whaling port of New Bedford, Massachusetts, the fifth of six children, he'd also lost his father at a young age. He had then gone to work in the shipping department of a Boston store for $2 a week. Dissatisfied with his economic status at age fifteen, he'd partnered with another lad in running a ten-cent poker game in Providence, Rhode Island, until the enterprise was shut down by the police. After knocking around New England and Europe, he'd arrived in New York City at twenty-one and landed a job as a hotel night clerk in Union Square.

Studies of Richard Canfield

A newspaper artist's "studies" of Diamond Jim's friend, the "King of the Gamblers," Richard Canfield. When an antigambling, crusading district attorney closed down Canfield's opulent gaming house, Canfield fled the country until things cooled down.

This commonality with Jim took a different turn, however. Whereas John Toucey had spotted Jim as a future railroader, Canfield caught the attention of hotel guests whose interest was gambling. After two years he used these connections to become night clerk of the swanky Monmouth House, a New Jersey summer resort favored by gamblers. Subsequent ventures in gambling took him back to New England, but this time a police raid resulted in a sentence of six months in prison. It was in the lockup's library that he'd developed his passion for books.

Released from incarceration, he returned to New York and opened a poker room on the Lower East Side. Within a year his profits reached $300 a week. In 1888 he'd met and gone into business with another gambler, John Duff. The gaming club was convenient to Madison Square's hotels, including Diamond Jim Brady's favored Hoffman House. Play became so vigorous that Canfield quickly accumulated $1 million and gambling casinos in Newport, Rhode Island, and Saratoga Springs, New York.

Surprisingly, he was as candid about a man's chance of "beating the house" as Diamond Jim was in warning his guests. Interviewed by a *New York Herald* reporter Canfield said, "Every time a roulette wheel is spun the percentage on a thirty-six inch wheel is 5 5/19 per cent against the player. In business, if you or I can lend money enough at five per cent we think we are doing pretty well. Every time a roulette player loses on one of my wheels, if I have any patronage at all, you can imagine what interest I get on my money in any one night."

Canfield's nightmares were Bet-a-Million Gates and men like him whose fortunes were so immense that they had the wherewithall to dare the odds. For Gates gambling was business, and the higher the stakes the better. It didn't matter whether he put money on a Wall Street stock, the speed of a horse, the turn of a card, or a spin of a wheel.

Gates explained, "For me, there's no fun in betting just a few thousand. I want to lay down enough to hurt the other fellow if he loses, and enough to hurt me if I lose."

As the guardians posted at Frank Farrell's bronze doors attested, the patrons of gambling emporiums risked more than money. As they placed their bets, they were taking a chance on being interrupted by police conducting a raid. This was especially true when New York experienced periodic outbursts of public outrage against rampant vice and immorality in the form of drinking, prostitution, and gambling dens. In these fevered periods the New York Police Department took steps to show that the force that boasted that it was "the Finest" was not as corrupt as everyone appeared to believe. Even if places such as Farrell's had dutifully met their obligation to pay graft to the neighborhood precincts to be allowed to operate, their patrons might find cops bursting in and bellowing "Dis is a raid, and yiz is all pinched."

It happened to Diamond Jim one night at a den named Corey's in the Haymarket district on Sixth Avenue. He'd taken some guests to try their luck but had not himself ventured a dollar on the whims of "Lady Luck." As he consumed steak in a corner of the dining room, he heard the commotion of about a dozen cops announcing their presence and intention to pile everyone into waiting paddy wagons. Suddenly he felt hands gripping his coat. But it wasn't a policeman. The owner had grabbed hold of him. After struggling to yank Jim out of his chair, Corey pushed him toward a back window. Unfortunately, Jim got stuck. Corey gave him a mighty shove. When Jim landed with a thump, he first checked to see if he'd lost any of his diamonds, then looked to see if he'd been injured.

Unscathed, he went around to the front of the building, flagged down a hansom cab as unlucky Haymarket customers were being loaded into paddy wagons, and told the driver to take him to a place that was never raided. At Rector's, none the worse for the experience, he resumed his interrupted dining by ordering two steaks. When he was finished, he hailed another cab and told the driver to take him to the police station house to which the cops had taken his unfortunate guests. After a few minutes of good-natured bantering with the desk sergeant, a lieutenant, and the precinct captain, dollars changed hands, apologies were tendered by the police, and Jim's customers were freed.

Among the high rollers whom Jim regularly encountered at Corey's, Farrell's, and Canfield's casino were the Dwyers. Brothers from Brooklyn, Phil and Mike were horse fanciers with a stable of the most celebrated Thoroughbred racers of the period. In 1885 they had organized the Brooklyn Jockey Club and later opened Gravesend Race Track, where each spring the Brooklyn Handicap opened the racing season. A virtue of the

Brooklyn track discerned by Diamond Jim and Lillian Russell was reasonable proximity to Lillian's house in Far Rockaway.

Accompanied by Edna McCauley and Jesse Lewisohn, they went to the track in their finest carriages and dressed to the nines. They arrived, in the words of one observer, "in sheer impressive splendor rivaled only by the extravagances of royalty at England's famous Ascot Derby." Jim sported his Racing Set, the centerpiece of which was a stickpin in the shape of a huge horseshoe in diamonds.

As if he and his illuminations and Lillian and Edna's finery were not enough to grab the attention of "admirers of the breed," Jim decided to force eyes to pop and jaws to drop in wonder by outfitting two coach footmen in scarlet and gold liveries and seating them at the rear of the carriage. But ordinary footmen were not what he had in mind. He hired midgets. Unfortunately for Jim and them, the publicity-getting stunt turned into a farce. Whenever the coach hit a bump in the road, the pair bounced out of their seats and landed on the ground. Neither was seriously hurt, but due to their inability to stay on board and a fear that one or both might be killed, Jim paid them off and settled for full-size footmen.

A feature of the running of the Brooklyn Handicap was an opportunity for photographers to snap pictures of the winning horse, its jockey, and the stable owner gathered in the paddock to receive Lillian Russell's congratulations.

Had Phil and Mike Dwyer been satisfied with owning Gravesend, they might have been able to afford to lose heavily in Manhattan gambling parlors and survive, but the brothers also bet on horses and lost far more often than they won. They also speculated in stocks that fared no better in the win-lose category. Following one particularly bad Wall Street venture, they found themselves broke and forced by creditors to pawn or sell most of their belongings.

In the spring of 1901, desperately in need of cash, Phil went looking for Diamond Jim. He found him in the bar at the Waldorf-Astoria.

As Jim sipped a mug of foamy root beer, Phil asked, "How'd you like to start a stable of your own by buying a couple of my racehorses?"

15

Off to the Races

❧❧❧

IN WRITING A CHECK to Phil Dwyer in the amount of $10,000, Diamond Jim Brady became owner of two horses, one of which was one of the most successful racers in the nation. A dappled little two-year-old named Gold Heels, he had won five and placed in eighteen of twenty-four starts. The second horse, named Major Daingerfield, promised a bright turf future.

To prevent finding himself in a potentially difficult position with customers to whom a man who owned racehorses might be as unacceptable in business affairs as Lillian Russell had been to the society ladies of Chicago, Jim set up his racing venture under the name of an amenable friend. For taking on the role, F. C. McLewee would receive a fifth of winnings. He began work by obtaining the services of one of the racing world's best trainers.

Before going into racing, Matthew Allen had been a faro dealer in the gold fields of the West. Because he had protected his sensitive fingers by always wearing kidskin gloves, he got the nickname "Kid Gloves." He immediately justified McLewee's confidence in his abilities by getting Gold Heels into such good condition that he not only won Diamond Jim's first race as an owner, albeit a silent one, he captured the 1901 Woodlawn Cup in record time.

Thrilled by the triumph, Jim decided to plunge into racing wholeheartedly by purchasing a stable at Sheepshead Bay. Registered in Allen's name, the property had a house and four barns. After the buildings were repaired and spruced up with fresh paint, Jim expanded his stable by adding ten colts. In the 1902 season Gold Heels and Major Daingerfield won every race of the early spring season. But the true test for Gold Heels was to be the mile-and-a-quarter, nine-horse-entry Suburban Handicap. The odds on him were three to one. Informed by Allen that the horse had drawn an unfavorable position for the start (on the outside) and would be carrying the top weight of 124 pounds, Jim uncharacteristically got cold feet. Instead of betting $10,000 on his entry, he wagered only $5,000. Gold Heels instructed his owner on the cost of cut-rate loyalty by quickly moving from the outside to the rail. He held that position to come in first by three lengths.

By midsummer Jim's horses had won every important race for a total of $82,230 in prize money. Although McLewee was officially listed as the horses' owner, everyone knew the truth. When Gold Heels took the Brighton Handicap, the racing writer for the *Mail and Express* felt free to note that in Gold Heels and Major Daingerfield "McLewee and James Brady have the two greatest horses of the year, and in fact, many competent judges declare that they are the two greatest horses ever foaled in this country." The writer added to these hurrahs his opinion that Gold Heels in covering the distance in 2:03⅘ "stands out as the best performance from a time standpoint in the history of American turf."

By this time Jim cast aside all pretense that he was not a racehorse owner. He celebrated this win and all subsequent victories by his stable with big parties at Tappan's and at Villepigue's restaurant in Sheepshead Bay. There he found not only great food but a restaurateur who surpassed him in girth. Weighing more than three hundred pounds, Jim Villepigue prided himself on serving huge meals to hungry "admirers of the breed" and their jubilant host.

The revels at Villepigue's were often followed by visits to other establishments as the numbers of celebrants, many of whom Jim had never met, grew.

Still in a mood to hail his horses' victories the next day, Jim invited friends to partake of an English-style buffet breakfast. In the Eighty-sixth Street house's dining room a huge table and sideboard were laid with kidneys, scrambled eggs, meat pies, chops of all kinds, fish cakes, flapjacks and waffles, toast, marmalade, orange juice, coffee, and buckets of iced champagne.

As stories about Diamond Jim Brady's entry into the sport of kings made their way into newspapers and around town by word of mouth, some members of the Jockey Club wondered how a newcomer could win big races. Rumors floated that somehow he had rigged the outcome. Others openly expressed dislike of Jim's flamboyant personality. Whatever the motivation, at the conclusion of the 1902 season the club adopted new rules that outlawed silent ownerships of racing stables. This left Jim with a Hobson's choice: own up to ownership and perhaps draw the ire of customers in the form of the cold shoulder and loss of business, or get out of horse racing as an owner. He chose to put the stable and the prizewinning horses on the auction block. The sale was contingent on the buyer pledging them a good new home and a comfortable retirement when the time came.

One November night in 1902 Jim ended his brief career as horseman with a party at the Hoffman House. The guest of honor was Gold Heels (not in the flesh, but as a life-size plaster statue that looked so real that people touched it to be sure). The invited were fifty of the most prominent people of the theater, racetrack, and commerce. They sat at a horseshoe-shape table with the statue in the center. Around midnight, a tearful Jim rose to speak of the happiness and pleasure of watching his horses win. When he sat down, waiters came into the room carrying small velvet cushions. At the center of each was a gift. Every woman got a diamond brooch. The men received diamond-studded watches. The mementoes cost more than $60,000. The party lasted from four P.M. Sunday to nine Monday morning and cost $100,000.

It was a party Jim could well afford. In November 1902 he was worth $12 million, much of it garnered through stock market speculation. And in an age when there was no income tax, every cent he earned was his alone.

LONG BEFORE James Buchanan Brady took a fling at owning Thoroughbred racehorses, he had exhibited a passion of the Irish for horses that some detractors claimed was as inborn as overindulging in strong drink. As soon as his bank accounts grew large enough to allow him to get along without worrying about finances, he'd acquired the finest carriages money could buy and the best horses to draw them. When his doctor worried that his most portly patient was not getting enough exercise, Jim had bought three large saddle horses and took to riding them in Central Park. They were kept in elegant style in a private stable.

In an article in *Harper's* in 1901, Robert Wickliffe Woolley noted, "Rich men, and even those of moderate means, have few luxuries from which they derive more genuine pleasure than from their private stables. The townsman especially finds his horses and vehicles the source of much health and happiness, and the housing and care of them a deeply interesting occupation."

Some of the stables were equestrian palaces with tiled floors and marble walls. One was built at a cost of $200,000. A few that survived well into the century of the automobile were so grand and roomy that they were converted into houses for people.

In years of conspicuous consumption called the Gilded Age, the horse became a measure of one's success, whether by ownership for the purpose of transportation or in the peculiar institution known as "horse society" that convened for the month of August in an upstate New York resort on the breezy, cooling shores of Lake Saratoga.

SALINE SPRINGS, which local Indians called "Saratoga," meaning "place of swift water," lay 180 miles north of New York City on a plateau twelve miles west of the Hudson River. The first white man known to have benefited from the supposed therapeutic effects of the waters was Sir William Johnson. Taken there by his Mohawk friends in 1767, he claimed relief from his many ailments. That was enough to attract others, resulting in rapid development of the area as a spa and all-around resort for people who could afford to go there and had the time to do so.

In the summer of 1870 twenty-seven-year-old Henry James decided to have a look at the spa and report what he found in an article for *The Nation*. Of the men he'd observed, he wrote:

> They suggest to my fancy the swarming vastness—the multifarious possibilities and activities—of our young civilization. They come from the uttermost ends of the Union—from San Francisco, from New Orleans, from Alaska. As they sit with their white hats tilted forward, and their chairs tilted back, and their feet tilted up, and their cigars and toothpicks forming various angles with these various lines, I seem to see in their faces a tacit reference to the affairs of the continent. They are obviously persons of experience—of a somewhat narrow and monotonous experience certainly; an experience of which the diamonds and laces which their wives are exhibiting hard by are, perhaps, the most substantial and beautiful result; but, at any rate, they have *lived* in every fiber of the will. . . . They are not the mellow fruit of a society which has walked hand-in-hand with tradition and culture; they are hard nuts, which have grown and ripened as they could.

When they talk among themselves, I seem to hear the cracking of the shells.

If the men of Saratoga were remarkable to James, the ladies were wonderful. In Saratoga they were in "the place of all places in America where women adorn themselves most" and "the greatest amount of dressing may be seen by the greatest number of people."

Twenty years later little had changed in the manner in which men and women used Saratoga summers to advertise themselves.

"There is no more effective picture of the wealth of the United States," noted *Baedeker's United States* in its 1893 edition, "than at Saratoga during July or August."

Saratoga's reputation was that of a locale where the wealthy could escape city heat by gambling in Richard Canfield's luxurious Casino and bet on the racehorses at the most beautiful track in America, described as the "dowager queen of the American turf," the "proving ground of champions," and the "graveyard of favorites."

Plush hotels, streets, piazzas, dining rooms, and ballrooms were a stage on which paraded a remarkable cross section of the gilded life. The guests came from everywhere and infused the resort with the characteristically American diversity of speech, dress, manner, and provincialisms. While Newport, Rhode Island, opened its doors to high and fashionable society defined as Mrs. Astor's 400, but turned its back on those who ranked below on that rigid scale, such as Diamond Jim Brady and Lillian Russell, at Saratoga they were embraced as celebrities.

The democratic mood of Saratoga was the result of its being a public resort. Newport was private homes and mansions. (The owners called them "cottages.") Saratoga's accommodations were hotels, boardinghouses, and seasonal rentals. From the time visitors got up in the morning until they retired they were thrown together in communal pursuit of holiday diversions.

Lillian Russell with one of her racehorses. If she attended a race, she invariably found herself being asked to pose with the winning entry.

In *Saratoga: Saga of an Impious Era* historian George Waller wrote, "They trooped to the springs for a glass of mineral water before breakfast, gossiped on the piazzas and shopped along Broadway, sat elbow to elbow at mealtimes and lingered collectively over the leisurely midday dinner. They strolled together in the after dinner promenades and set out for the lake together in a coach parade. They attended the band concerts and the races together, and made each other's acquaintance all over again in the salons of casinos and in the ballrooms of the hotels."

One enthusiastic regular's diary received this season-ending notation:

> Another beautiful summer has gone and autumn, wrapped in her misty robes and haloed with a crimson and golden glory, comes over the distant hilltops. The time has come to say goodbye to Saratoga. The gay season is over, and only bright memories of all the brilliant scenes which have just passed come to take their place. But go where you will, in Europe or America, there is no other Saratoga, no other place which offers so much to the summer guest, whether he is in search of health, rest or pleasure; for Saratoga is all things to all men. It is a miniature world in itself; and here you may be grave or gay, wise or foolish, giddy or devout, as the mood seizes you. And the man or woman who cannot be charmed by Saratoga must indeed be hard to please, and would fail to be delighted anywhere on earth.

There were dissenting voices. Taking a disapproving view of the resort in 1888, New York newspaper magnate James Gordon Bennett thought he was condemning the spa with bitter irony when he wrote, "Beautiful Saratoga! Cradle of fashion and intrigue! Rendezvous of lackeys and jockeys! Seraglio of the prurient aristocracy."

The blast backfired. Rather than damaging Saratoga, it promoted the spa as the nation's most fashionable resort, even for some men and women whose social standing was acceptable in snobbish Newport. Two years after Bennett's carping editorial, the head usher at the plushest of the Saratoga hotels, Joseph Smith, noted in his diary, "The season of 1890 is especially replete with wealthy and conspicuous visitors. All the millionaires of the land seem to be in Saratoga, and there are thousands of men here with families who are spending hundreds of dollars a day."

The magnet for many of these wealthy men was betting on horse races and the gambling houses, especially Richard

Canfield's opulent Casino. But when it opened its doors for business in the summer of 1894, an outraged headline in Joseph Pulitzer's *New York World* blared:

OUR WICKEDEST SUMMER RESORT

Justification for this accusation was supplied by the *World's* (and the real world's) most famous woman reporter. Her name was Elizabeth Cochrane, but she wrote under the name Nellie Bly. She had recently achieved the status of national heroine by challenging the fictional hero of Jules Verne's novel *Around the World in Eighty Days* and beating Phineas Fogg by circling the globe in seventy-two days, six hours, ten minutes, and eleven seconds. Her orders from Pulitzer in going to Saratoga were to expose Saratoga's "evils."

She found, and headlines emphasized, a "wild vortex of gambling and betting," including "little children who play the horses."

A Bly/Pulitzer story entitled *The Monte Carlo of America* began, "This town has gone mad with the mania of gambling." Claiming that a health spa ("the Carlsbad of America") was a "Monte Carlo with the reckless law-breaking of Leadville combined with the vulgarity of the Bowery," the item continued:

> Gambling is in the atmosphere. Formerly men of wealth and social position, statesmen, philosophers, students and artists gathered here to drink the waters that nature forces through fissures and enjoy the crisp, invigorating air and the picturesque scenery which have united in making Saratoga America's most famous southern resort. They came to ride, to drive, to dress and to secure that freedom from business and domestic care that gives perfect rest and brings back bodily health and vigor.
>
> Now the great summer population of Saratoga is largely composed of those gathered here to gamble or to live off

those who gamble. From one of the most reputable and most exclusive of the American watering places, it has been transformed into the wickedest and wildest.

Although Saratoga's year-round residents exerted efforts to clean up the resort's image, by the end of the Gay Nineties little had changed. Money spent by visitors in hotels, restaurants, boardinghouses, and other amenities, including the springs, totaled $1 million a day, more than enough to keep the town's 13,000 inhabitants well fed and snug during the other ten months of the year. The gaming proprietors thrived to the tune of an estimated $2 million a day in bets, almost all of which were won by the house.

Because Diamond Jim Brady had never been what the professional gamblers called "a big plunger" in casinos, he indulged in wagering offered by the Saratoga Racing Association. At its head was a leader of New York City's horse society, William Collins Whitney. He'd originally taken up racing with the purpose of beating the horses of his Wall Street rival James R. Keene, "the Nevada Silver King." Bitten by the racing bug, Whitney soon had a stable second to none in the world. It was his imprimatur on horse racing, and his control of the Saratoga racing season, that went a long way to correcting Nellie Bly's sordid image of the resort.

Saratoga's attractions also proved to be a lure to political leaders and businessmen with responsibility to choose locations for conventions. With numerous large hotels, plenty of restaurants, casinos, and the track, Saratoga became the site of many such meetings.

As noted earlier, Diamond Jim Brady had ventured there in 1896 for the annual conclave of the Master Car Builders with a silver-plated Fox truck and twenty-seven Japanese houseboys. But even without the alluring prospect of doing business at a convention, each season the people at Saratoga could count on observing him at luncheon and dinner at the United States Hotel. A typical evening menu offered these courses and choices:

Soup: Gumbo Filet Braselienne
               Hot or Cold Consommé in Cup
               Noodle au Boullion
Olives, Radishes, Onions, Caviar
Anchovies a l'Italienne
Fish: Striped Bass, Genoise
               Filet of Sole, Margueri (the recipe had
                 made its way everywhere)
Potatoes Hollandaise, Cucumbers
Meat: Fresh Tongue, Sauce Piqauite
               York Ham with Spinach
               Veal Fricandeau, Turtle Club
               Lamb Sauté, Chasseure d'Afrique
               Frogs Legs, Cardinal
               Ribs of Prime Beef
               Saddle of Mutton, Currant Jelly
Vegetables: ("Fresh daily from United States Hotel Farm")
               Mashed Potatoes
               Boiled Potatoes
               Green Corn
               String Beans
               Onions, Bechamel
               Celery, Marrow Sauce
               Russian Turnips
Roman Punch
Salads: Watercress
               Chicken
               Escarole
               Chickory
               Lettuce and Tomato
               Romaine
Desserts: Tutti Fruiti Pudding, Kummel Sauce
               Apple Pie
               Custard Pie

Assorted Cake
Coffee Eclairs
Lady Fingers
Pound Cake
Coconut Drops
Chocolate Africaines
Genoise Glacé
Rhine Wine Jelly
Vanilla Ice Cream
Marble Ice Cream

Fruits: Oranges, Peaches, Plums, Bananas,
                  Watermelon, Pears, Figs, Layer Raisins
Assorted Nuts
Cheese: American, Pineapple, Cream, Roquefort,
                  Cottage, Edam
Crackers: Albert Crackers, Banquet Wafers,
                  Water Crackers
Coffee
Cigars

Although Diamond Jim's passage drew looks and briefly stopped traffic, he was not the only flashy personality to do so. Among the other exhibitionists was "White Hat" McCarty. After noting that a man ahead of him when checking into a hotel registered his name and added "with valet," McCarty inscribed "White Hat McCarty and valise."

Regularly in attendance were tobacco heir Peter Lorillard, financier and railway tycoon Jay Gould and family, and "King of the Dudes" Berry Wall, with his years-younger bride. The former Giulia Morosini and daughter of a banker, she drove a black-and-yellow Brester coach drawn by three spirited horses.

As resplendent as Berry Wall was, even he could be impressed by the sight of Diamond Jim with all his illumination. He also admired Jim's way with women. He noted in his memoirs, "And what ladies! None of us who knew him well will ever forget them. They were the pick of the Floradora Sextette and later the Follies. Blonde or brunette, they were the loveliest charmers on Broadway. Like his excessive jewelry, they were part of Jim Brady's game, part of his business, part of the endless advertising that he managed so cleverly, and, of course, they helped him entertain his friends. The idea that he was on intimate and tender terms with any of them, let alone all of them, is much exaggerated. He was much too fat for that."

Wall was one of those who went to Saratoga but also found welcome at Newport. When at Saratoga he could mingle with Diamond Jim, Lillian Russell, Flo Ziegfeld and Anna Held, and others from the New York lobster palace/Broadway theatrical circle. The gulf between society and "the stage" as existed in Newport and New York was summed up in a Berry Hall maxim: "Broadway only cuts across Fifth Avenue; it never parallels it."

Having become resigned to never being permitted to move from a West Side townhouse to one on the East Side, and realizing he could never be welcomed in Newport, Jim embraced Saratoga's alternative society as enthusiastically as it accepted him. Following his first visit to the resort for the Master Car Builders' convention, he became a Saratoga perennial in the company of a woman whose passing by never failed to make eyes pop and carriages slow.

Whether riding about town encased like a jewel in her smart little black Victoria drawn by its two matching black Thoroughbreds, pedaling her golden bicycle, taking a stroll with her Japanese spaniel with its $1,800 collar, resting on a hotel porch, or seated at a table in Canfield's Casino alternately placing bets and nibbling crêpes suzettes made just for her by chef Jean Columbin, Lillian Russell never failed to cause a sensation. She and Jim became the leaders of their own uninhibited social set in the hotels and casinos, at the track, and on Saratoga's main boulevard with a name that made Lillian feel at home—Broadway.

The custom was that after dinner, everyone strolled the wide avenue for music at Congress Spring Park or to one of the hotels that vied to book the most popular orchestras and singers. A frequent attraction was march king John Philip Sousa and his band. The Grand Union Hotel paid a huge fee to engage Victor Herbert to lead its fifty-four-piece orchestra in playing songs by the country's most popular composer. The manager of the Grand Union was W. Edgar Woolley. As a gesture of friendship to him at the end of each season, Herbert handed his baton to the manager's young son, Monty, and let the boy lead the orchestra in one number. After he became a star in the movies in the 1930s and 1940s, Monty told friends that the praise he'd received for his portrayal of Sheridan Whiteside in the film *The Man Who Came to Dinner* was not as thrilling as taking the baton from Victor Herbert on those languid summer evenings at Saratoga.

During one season at the Grand Union, Herbert finished an evening's program and went for a stroll with Tom Witt, the hotel's house detective. Of that "cool moonlit evening, one of those evenings generally advertised as being especially made for love," Witt recalled, "we walked in the garden, as we often did, since Mr. Herbert liked a few minutes of quiet before joining his friends. The lights were being dimmed. Off in the shadows we heard a soft voice say, 'Kiss me.' This was followed by silence, then, 'Kiss me again.' Mr. Herbert gripped my arm. 'By God, Tom,' he said. 'By God.' He was unusually quiet and busy for several days and I thought no more of it."

Herbert had been writing *Mlle Modiste*. When it opened in New York the following year, Diamond Jim and other first nighters heard the result of Victor Herbert's inspiration that had been sparked by the lovers in the garden in the enduringly popular "Kiss Me Again."

On another Saratoga evening kissing became a reason for a wager that involved Anna Held. At a supper party given by

Florenz Ziegfeld, one of the young male guests questioned how many kisses could be exchanged before the lips of the kissers went numb. He wagered he could kiss Anna two hundred times. His stamina and lips gave out at one hundred fifty-two. No one noted for posterity whether Anna was ready and able to continue.

Such a contest entered into at Newport would have been a scandal. In Saratoga it raised not a single eyebrow. In 1894 Nellie Bly had "exposed" Saratoga's wickedness as a place where "married men publicly flaunt their attentions to shameful women." A few years later, as Anna Held lent her lips for the sake of a bet, the publication *Everyone's* observed on the subject of the resort as a place where a woman could enjoy herself, "She may do with impunity in Saratoga those things which she may not approach even in thought elsewhere, and it is perhaps because of this temporary freedom that she loves her Saratoga as she loves no other resort."

Escorted representatives of the "fairer sex" were certainly welcome at the best-known, most luxurious, and most expensive gambling house in Saratoga (and the country). Owner Richard Canfield boasted that more money was won and lost across his green baize tables each August than Monte Carlo saw in a year.

Among the high rollers none was more ubiquitous during the season than Jesse Lewisohn. The great gambler on Wall Street, horses, and any other game in which percentages could be studied had been a patron of Canfield's Manhattan betting palace. When Canfield announced that he'd taken over a foundering Saratoga gaming establishment and planned to turn it into the resort's biggest and best, no one was more excited than Lewisohn. He was also delighted to learn that men would be required to wear evening clothes.

Concerned that some of them might feel that cash-stuffed wallets and pockets might mar the lines of exquisitely tailored tuxedos, Canfield shocked other Saratoga gambling house owners by declaring that guests could play on credit and remit their losses by check. In the event a player won big, a safe in Can-

Diamond Jim (left) dressed for the summer races in Saratoga.

field's office was stocked with $1 million, half in thousand-dollar notes and the rest in five hundreds, hundreds, and fifties. The daring policy resulted in a profit of $250,000 in the first two months, which was about the amount Canfield had paid for the club.

Following a night of gambling at Canfield's or competing houses, the men in tuxes and the ladies in their most elegant finery were welcome at several restaurants at the racetrack for breakfasts at tables that afforded views of the Thoroughbreds being put through their morning paces. The fare consisted of melon, berries, fried chicken, corn bread, preserves, and coffee. For the more daring there were frogs' legs and champagne.

When August ended, so did the racing. Overnight went the horses, jockeys, high rollers, and their stylish, liberated women.

Also gone with the first morning trains on the first of September were the bookies. Part of the Saratoga season almost from the town's beginning as a racing mecca, they were members of the Metropolitan Turf Association. They controlled betting at all New York state tracks and wore identifying buttons that were bought and sold like seats on the Stock Exchange, but with no risk of being suddenly wiped out by a reversal of fortune. Their leader was the dapper "Irish" John Cavanagh. With unchallenged authority, he settled all disputes between members who plied their trade using colorful monickers, such as the Boy Plunger, Big Store, Tiffany Wolfgang, and Fashion Plate. They were found in stalls with blackboards on which they'd chalked entries and odds. A bettor made his choice of horses, whether he expected it to win, place, or show, and got a ticket. If it was a winner, the money was collected at another stall from a "pay off man."

To help wagerers pick a sure winner, "tipsters" drifted through the merry crowds offering to share "inside knowledge" for a price. Of all the people engaged in the betting, they were the only ones who always went away winners.

"Goin' up to Saratoga," declared Diamond Jim as he, Edna, Lillian, and Jesse boarded a Manhattan-bound train at the conclusion of the 1903 season, "is a hell of a great way to spend a month in the summer."

LEWISOHN'S FATE was linked to a chain of events that dated back to a twenty-first birthday party held on December 19, 1901, at a New York restaurant, followed by several hours of gambling. Host and guest of honor at the affair was Reginald Vanderbilt, a Yale undergraduate and grandson of the Commodore. The gaming house to which they adjourned after dinner was not Canfield's. But that would not matter in the least to the recently elected district attorney, William Travers Jerome. An ambitious lawyer, he was an ardent antivice crusader and member of a group of reform-minded citizens, the Parkhurst Society.

When the word went like wildfire through the city that young Vanderbilt and frolicking friends of his had lost $70,000 gambling, the result was an explosion of outrage in newspaper editorials, from pulpits, and by most of the public. Because Richard Canfield was known as the most popular gambler in the city, everyone assumed Vanderbilt and pals had been in Canfield's gambling house. That this was not true mattered not in the least to District Attorney–elect Jerome. He vowed that when he took office on New Year's Day of 1902, he would see to it that Canfield's would be closed and that Canfield and other gambling-den operators would be run out of town.

After New Year's Eve play was completed, Canfield trumped Jerome's hand by closing the house on his own and keeping it shuttered for several months. Believing the storm had passed, he reopened it in the spring. But in November a private detective hired by yet another reform group gained admittance to the gaming rooms, found them in full use, and reported his findings to the D.A.'s office. Jerome acted on December 1 by personally leading a raiding party. But they found only Canfield and a few friends at dinner at 5 East Forty-fourth Street, possibly because Canfield had gotten a tip that uninvited visitors should be expected. Undaunted, Jerome ordered cops to arrest Canfield. He told Canfield that he would be let off with only a $25 fine if he would plead guilty to being "a common gambler."

Canfield refused, turned the matter over to his lawyers, and went to London.

The frustrated district attorney directed his ire to Canfield's friends in general and Jesse Lewisohn in particular. While he and the others refused to testify against Canfield, Jesse went one step further by ordering his attorney to challenge Jerome's authority to compel them to testify by taking the matter to the Appellate Division of the New York Supreme Court.

Meanwhile, Canfield was in London having his picture painted by James Abbott McNeill Whistler. Titled "His Reverence" by the artist, it would be the last portrait painted by the famous American expatriate and friend of Lillie Langtry and Oscar Wilde.

Asked by reporters in London to comment on continuing attacks on him by reformers at home, Canfield answered, "I do not care a rap what other people think about me. The only person whose respect I want is that of Richard Canfield. I have made it a rule to look at myself in the mirror every morning, and I feel that if I can look in my own eyes and be satisfied with the examination, then I have no reason to regret anything I have done."

It is safe to assume that if Diamond Jim Brady read these words in the bedroom of the house on Eighty-sixth Street with its mirror and barber chair, a big cheer went up. One may also reasonably assume that when Jim greeted Canfield at Saratoga that August, he gave him an approving slap on the back.

But Canfield's bravado did not end the efforts of his adversary in the New York district attorney's office. That winter Jerome won a major victory in his fight against gambling when the state legislature passed and Governor Benjamin B. Odell signed the Dowling Amendment to the state code of criminal procedure. It enabled a district attorney to compel obstinate witnesses, such as Jesse Lewisohn, to testify.

In May 1904 Lewisohn was subpoenaed and testified truthfully. Yes, he knew Richard Canfield. Yes, he'd been to his house. Yes, he had gambled there.

The testimony and that of others was sufficient to convict Canfield. He pleaded guilty to being a common gambler and paid a fine. The $1,000 penalty was 1 percent of what he'd paid in legal fees to fight the case.

Asked by a reporter as he left court to comment on the movement to outlaw gambling, Canfield offered an unrepentant but mystifying reply. "They gambled in the Garden of Eden," he said, "and they will again if there's another one."

Three years later, Canfield's wealth was estimated at $12 million, of which $5 million had been gained that year through gambling and Wall Street speculations. But half of that fortune was lost in that autumn's stock market panic, including $1.5 million on one day. Retiring from gambling early in 1911, he sold the Saratoga property to the town and disposed of the casino's furnishings at public auction. The house on Forty-fourth Street was also sold so that he could take up residence in a brownstone in the fashionable East Fifties. He then traveled frequently, collecting art, and was elected to membership in the Walpole Society, a select group of fine art connoisseurs. He died after a fall down the steps of a Brooklyn subway station in 1914.

THE SECOND EVENT in May 1904 that set Diamond Jim Brady worrying concerned the fate of two men who had taken Lillian Russell out of operettas and into musical comedy. On the twenty-ninth of the month on the stage of the New Amsterdam Theater on Forty-second Street, the team of Weber and Fields was dissolved. They appeared in a final performance of *Whoop-dee-doo,* a show in which Lillian had once starred. Official demise of the partnership had been long in coming. It fell victim to steady decline in business, loss of many of their top stars, condemnation of their Music Hall as a firetrap, and years of professional jealousy. Broadway had been rife with tales of their battles, and the two comics hadn't spoken to one another off stage for more than a year.

The historic theatrical alliance that had pioneered a new kind of entertainment might have ended while they were appearing in Boston, but sad friends, including Lillian Russell, had begged them to end the partnership where they won their first success—in a Broadway theater.

Front row and center as the final curtain came down were Diamond Jim and Lillian, both in tears and wildly applauding. The moment was recorded the next day in the *New York Herald* in these words:

> An audience which filled the new theater, and composed of representatives of society, clubdom, the world of the first night, the theater and every walk of life, called for the curtain to rise again. Then, in response to demands, speeches were made by members of the stock company in which the two men who had made Weber and Fields a household word were told that they were committing business suicide, were told that they were making a grievous mistake, amid cries of "Right! Right!"
>
> A Broadway audience is not particularly sentimental, but the tears that streaked the painted and powdered faces of the stage were multiplied many times in the audience as "Auld Lang Syne" became the final musical number.

The departure of Weber and Fields meant, of course, that Lillian Russell, if she were to continue her career, needed a new impresario. She found one in three brothers. Newcomers to the Broadway scene, they were Sam, Lee, and J. J. Shubert. Sons of a ne'er-do-well and an alcoholic peddler from Lithuania, David Szemanski, they claimed to have been born in Syracuse, but were probably born in Lithuania and had birth certificates altered to show they were Americans. They had come to New York after achieving success as upstate theater operators and had leased the Herald Square Theater in 1900.

The property for which they signed Lillian Russell was a musical, *Lady Teazle,* with her in the title role. It opened at the Casino on Christmas Eve 1904 with Lillian supported by W. T. Carleton, Clarence Handyside, and Van Rensselaer. Lillian's main song began with the words "I am ze dainty milliner." This first production for which a marquee announced that "The Messrs. Shubert present" would run only fifty-seven performances.

In keeping with the current style of musicals, the production featured eighty-six chorus girls. When interviewed for the *New York World,* some said they did not mind that they were paid small salaries. They had "independent means." Seventy-eight of the leggy lovelies boasted that they owned jewelry and furs, and seven bragged about being driven to the theater each night in private carriages. The reporter felt no need to translate. His readers understood that the girls were being "kept" by rich men.

To promote the fact that the Messrs. Shubert had Lillian Russell under contract, the "press agent" for the brothers, Channing Pollock, handed out an announcement accompanied by photos of Lillian's new home at 161 West Fifty-seventh Street, which had been decorated by the era's most fashionable, and expensive, decorator. Henry Duveen had created a Louis XVI music room, Marie Antoinette drawing room, an Old English supper room, Dutch dining room, Turkish Den, and a pink-and-gold American bedroom for the American Beauty with an enormous brass bed and adjoining tiled bathroom.

"My new home," said Lillian, "is rather like a journey down the Pike at the world's fair."

As the Columbian Exposition of 1893 in Chicago had its Midway, "the Pike" was the entertainment area of the 1904 "Louisiana Purchase Exposition" in St. Louis.

For months in advance of the opening of the extravaganza on the shore of the Mississippi River, the event had been heralded by a popular ditty by Tin Pan Alley songsmiths Kerry

Lillian Russell in a costume for her title role in *Lady Teazle* in 1904 at age forty-three.

Mills (music) and Andrew B. Sterling (words) that had almost everyone in the country going around singing:

Meet me in Saint Louie, Louie,
Meet me at the fair;
Don't tell me the lights are shining any place but there.
We will dance the hoochie koochie;
I will be your tootsie-wootsie,
If you will meet me in Saint Louie, Louie;
Meet me at the fair.

Because St. Louis had been a gateway to the West since President Thomas Jefferson sent Meriwether Lewis and William Clark to explore the vast Louisiana Territory he had purchased from France in 1803 for 60 million francs (about $15 million), the city had become vital to the westward extension of railroads. In 1904 it was an important rail-shipping point for the produce of the Great Plains (wheat, corn, flour), 30 million pounds of Liggett and Myers' tobacco a year, shoes and boots, stoves, and beer (15 million gallons a year brewed by Anheuser-Busch).

For many years prior to the exposition, the city's attraction to Diamond Jim Brady had been its manufacturing of railway and tram cars. Consequently, when the train pulling his private car arrived at the Main Street Station in early September, he was a familiar and welcome figure to porters helping him with his baggage. As they profited from his generous tips, so did clerks and bellhops of the Planters hotel and waiters at the city's best restaurants (Delmonico's, Faust, and Moser) and in Schneider's beer garden, where he feasted on German-style dishes.

As in Chicago in 1893, he found the host city of the exposition bustling with excited fair-goers and many of his associates in the railroad and steel businesses. Like the Columbian Exposition, the St. Louis extravaganza was a celebration of American industry. It had officially opened at 1:06 P.M., April 30, 1904, with President Theodore Roosevelt using the same telegraph key in the White House with which President Cleveland had signaled the start of the Chicago fair.

At that exposition electricity had been a fascinating novelty to the people who jammed into the exhibition halls. Without it in St. Louis in 1904 the fair could not have been held. To provide lights and energize machinery and displays in eleven exhibition "palaces," the Union Light and Power Company, in collaboration with the Westinghouse Company, spent $2 million to create the largest generating plant in the world.

Writing in the May 14, 1904, edition of *The American Inventor,* Charles Alma Buers noted in enthusiastic but florid prose,

"Were it not for this mysterious power, which man has brought down, as if from the sky, the greatest World's Fair ever held on the globe would lie inert; for not a wheel would turn nor a light be seen. It would repose in quietness and darkness like that which envelopes some isolated tomb. And why should not this exposition receive its 'vital spark' from electricity? Why should not this be an electrical fair? This is an age of things electrical, and to keep abreast with progress, naturally, a display of that, in science, is now most important."

Aglow and humming with this wonder, inside and out, were "The Palaces" of Electricity and Machinery, Agriculture, Education and Social Economy, Festival, Horticulture, Liberal Arts, Manufacturers, Mines and Minerology, Varied Industries, and, of most interest to Diamond Jim Brady, of Transportation.

Built to evoke the style of the nation's great railway terminals, it covered fifteen acres and measured 525 by 1,300 feet. Behind three huge arches and beneath its expansive roof was a display of old locomotives representing the long struggle for speedy transportation from stagecoaches to the Pullman Palace car. An old horsecar and the modern "trolley" stood side by side. Visitors inspected a dazzling array of automobiles, descendants of the battery-powered one Jim had ordered eleven years earlier.

Centrally displayed in the hall was an exhibit of the Cleveland, Cincinnati, Chicago & St. Louis Railway (known as the Big Four Route) of a locomotive and tender mounted on a turntable. It was an innovation in railroading that solved the problem of turning around an engine by driving it onto a revolving platform. In this example the turntable measured seventy-five feet across. It was built by the Chicago Bridge and Iron Works and supported the 162 tons of the American Locomotive Company engine and tender, capable of pulling ten freight cars at sixty miles an hour.

Second only to the turntable in the interest of visitors was the private railway coach that had been used by Abraham Lincoln during the Civil War. It was housed in a separate building devoted to a museum displaying other Lincoln relics, including a log cabin advertised as being the actual one in which the president had been born. Constructed by the government in a workshop in Alexandria, Virginia, the coach was furnished in rich tapestries and plushly upholstered chairs and sofas. It had made its first runs over the lines of the Pennsylvania and the Baltimore & Ohio. Lincoln had used it during his second campaign in 1864 and had addressed trackside crowds from the platform at the end of the car.

Should a visitor want to experience a train ride without leaving St. Louis, the fair offered "The Scenic Railway." The climax of the ride was a precursor to the roller coaster in which passengers found themselves screaming and holding on for dear life as the track took three dips in quick succession at a swift speed. As with future roller coasters, most people immediately lined up to do it again.

The Scenic Railway pavilion from which the trains came and went stood at the western end of a mile-long boulevard called The Pike. As in the Chicago fair's Midway, it was solidly lined with amusements, starting at the main entrance at the eastern end with a group of life-size statues done by painter and sculptor Frederic Remington to show "Cowboys Shooting Up a Western Town." By the time visitors reached the Scenic Railway pavilion at the far end of The Pike, they would have been exhorted by men with megaphones to experience the delights of the more than fifty Midway-style diversions.

Although the people who went to the fair were not diverted by the belly dancing of Little Egypt and the dulcet tones and ample figure of Lillian Russell, they found these notable features of the St. Louis Exposition:

- The Liberty Bell, brought to the fair at the request of 75,000 schoolchildren and exhibited from June 8 to November 16

- John Philip Sousa and his band in the month of May, during which he introduced the official world's fair march, "Louisiana"
- A performance of Handel's "Messiah" on July 9
- Newsboys' Day (August 16)
- World's Press Week (May 16–21), hosting seventy-five foreign journalists
- An eighteen-foot lighthouse built of pure salt
- A low-temperature exhibit that attained a temperature of minus 259 degrees F
- A "corn temple" supplied by the state of Missouri
- A Brazilian display featuring artificial flowers made from bird feathers
- The Poultry Show with 10,000 entries
- Model Playground Day (on Thanksgiving Day, November 24)
- President Theodore Roosevelt, basking in his election to the presidency he had assumed upon the assassination of McKinley in 1901, sharing the stage with former President Grover Cleveland (November 26)

From July 1 to November 23 the fair was also the site of the games of the third Olympiad. Unfortunately, the Olympic competitors were almost entirely Americans. Because of the great distances foreign athletes would have to travel, and because of the Russo-Japanese War, only thirteen countries sent teams or individuals. As a result, of the 625 participants, 533 were from the United States. They won 238 of the 282 medals.

The first runner to cross the finish line in the marathon on August 30 was Fred Lorz of the Mohawk Athletic Club of New York. But of the thirty-two starters, eighteen failed to complete the course, largely because of the heat (in the nineties), stultifying humidity, and thick dust kicked up from the dirt roads. One runner managed an extra burst of speed, however, when he was chased for a mile by an angry dog. An entrant from Cuba, Feliz Carvajal, ran in cutoff trousers, but he didn't finish because he stopped in an orchard to eat a green apple and got too sick to continue.

Waiting to present the gold medal to Fred Lorz was President Roosevelt's daughter, Alice. As she was about to place a laurel wreath on his brow, Lorz was stricken with a case of guilty conscience. He blurted that he was not the real winner because he had traveled eleven of the twenty-five-mile course in an automobile.

The real victor was Thomas Hicks of Cambridge, Massachusetts, a circus clown by profession. He completed the run in three hours, twenty-eight minutes, and fifty-three seconds, fueled by brandy and doses of strychnine, which he ingested to keep himself going.

The month of August had been brutally hot. But if Pike strollers felt the need to cool off and quench their thirsts, they could stand in line to sample the wares of one Richardson Blechyden. A young Englishman, he proved the axiom that necessity is the mother of invention. Representing the tea growers of India and Ceylon, who were desirous of carving out a market for tea among America's coffee drinkers, he had looked with despair as sweltering fair-goers passed him by in favor of stands offering chilled juices and lemonade. In desperation, he bought a large supply of chopped ice, filled glasses with it, poured his hot tea over it, and then shouted to the crowd, "Iced tea here! Get your iced tea here!"

For ice cream seller Charles Menchen the problem needing an inventive solution one hot August afternoon was a sudden lack of dishes into which he scooped his very popular treat. His answer to the crisis was found at the stand where Ernest Hamwi, a Syrian, was selling Zalabia, a Middle Eastern snack of syrup served in a pastry. Menchen took as many of the Zalabias that Hamwi was willing to share, rolled them up, scooped his ice cream on top, and entered history and the gratitude of hundreds of millions of people by inventing ice cream cones.

There is no account of Diamond Jim strolling The Pike while licking a cone and sipping iced tea, but that he did, and with great delight again and again, would not be a far-fetched assumption.

16

Peacocks Parade

❧❦❧

BY 1905 the pace of life in New York had been increased to such a gait, one who had not seen it in a dozen years must have rubbed his eyes," recalled journalist Albert Stevens Crockett in his 1931 memoir. "Gaiety, high living and chorus girls were coming into their own. Automobiles had begun to jam traffic on Fifth Avenue. There was now a great deal of wealth in New York. But there was a tremendous amount of poverty as well, and public opinion was keen and quick to censure lavish expenditures for pleasure, and to scan, with minute attention, the source of the wealth that made such performances possible."

In 1896 a shocked public had read press reports of the Herbert Seeley party at which a police captain hoped to nab Police Commissioner Roosevelt ogling the gyrations of Little Egypt. There had been outrage expressed when a Vanderbilt scion and his Yale friends had blithely lost $70,000 at Richard Canfield's luxurious gambling den. Readers of Nellie Bly's "exposé" of the scandalous goings-on among New York City's rich at Saratoga had sold a lot of copies of Joseph Pulitzer's *World*. But these and other self-indulgences were to pale in comparison to a party to be held at Sherry's restaurant in January 1905.

The name of the host on Diamond Jim's invitation was familiar. James Hazen Hyde was the son of the founder of the

Equitable Assurance Society. James seemed to be quite person-
able whenever Jim observed him at Sherry's and other lobster
palaces. Tall, with a lithe figure and a neatly trimmed dark
beard, he spent a good deal of time in France, and was a patron
of French art and a member of the Legion of Honor. The fortune he stood to inherit, together with his winning personality
and charming manners, made him one of the most popular and
sought-after bachelors.

Jim's invitation was to a "Versailles Ball."

When he arrived at Sherry's, he found the ballroom transformed to represent a portion of the Palace of Versailles, with
frescoes, mirrors, and period furniture copies to the last detail.
Hyde greeted guests in white satin breeches, long silken hose,
coat, and blouse of the era of Louis XVI. His sister, Mrs. Sid-
ney Dillon Repley, was dressed as Marie Antoinette.

"The *piece de resistance* of the occasion," noted Crockett in his
account of the ball, "was the appearance of Mme. Réjane, the
great French actress, who was, in effect, a guest of honor as
well as the chief performer. Her arrival provided a real sensation, for she was borne into the ballroom seated in a sedan
chair, the bearers being four husky men in the uniform of the
Swiss Papal Guards. Guests were seated during her act, which
consisted mainly of recitations. There was nothing in the slight-
est degree immoral or suggestive, at least to ears accustomed to
English, and certainly eyes could not have detected anything
that need offend the tenderest susceptibilities of even mid-
Victorian morality. As a matter of fact, the whole entertainment
was highly artistic."

Mme. Réjane was no Little Egypt, but it was not her presence that resulted in a storm of press and public outrage. People were appalled that the affair was reported to have cost
$100,000. How dare anyone spend such an amount on pleas-
ure, even if he was an heir to a fortune? Some people whispered that the party had been paid for out of Equitable Assurance Society coffers.

In the face of the intense heat of such criticism, Hyde dashed off to France and made it his permanent home. The newspapers duly reported his self-imposed exile, then waited for the next affair staged by one of the rich and/or famous in hope of whipping it into a scandal. The term for this sensationalism was "yellow journalism." The sobriquet was inspired by the first comic strip. Drawn by R. F. Outcault for Pulitzer's *World,* "The Yellow Kid" pictured the adventures of an engaging slum urchin. To compete with the popular cartoon, William Randolph Hearst hired his own artist, George Luks, to entertain readers of the *Journal* with its version of the yellow kid. This contest of comic strips and fierce competition to print ever more sensational stories and outbursts of outrage against the wealthy symbolized the titanic struggle between New York City papers to boost circulations. But it drew the ire of such leading Americans as the man who had been the object of the raid on the Seeley dinner. Theodore Roosevelt growled, "Of all the forces that tend for evil in a great city like New York, probably none are so potent as the sensational papers. Until one had experienced them it is difficult to realize the reckless indifference to truth and decency displayed by papers such as the two that have the largest circulation in New York."

After leaving the presidency, Roosevelt recalled unpleasant treatment by such portions of the press with this denunciation:

> Yellow journalism deifies the cult of the mendacious, the sensational, and the inane, and throughout its wide but vapid field, does much to vulgarize and degrade the popular taste, to weaken the popular character, and to dull the edge of popular conscience, as any influence under which the country can suffer. These men sneer at the very idea of paying heed to the dictates of a sound morality; as one of their number has cynically put it, they are concerned merely with selling the public whatever the public will buy.

There was truth in this, but had someone asked James Buchanan Brady what he thought of the yellow press in particular and of the institution of journalism in general in the Gilded Age, he would have admitted that without the attention paid to him by the newspapers, he could never have sustained the character named Diamond Jim Brady. Had there been no reporters around to observe and relate his antics to the public, he would have been just a rich, ridiculous-looking fat man wearing too much jewelry, eating alone.

In true Horatio Alger fashion he had pulled himself up by his bootstraps to strut upon a stage known as New York as a self-created character who needed no footlights. He carried his own limelight. For more than twenty years he'd been an original. In a parade of peacocks, wrote Crockett, "no male fowl, however decorative nature had made him, succeeded in rivaling the effect upon optic nerves or in stopping traffic so effectually and repeatedly."

If Diamond Jim was correctly defined as a peacock, Lillian Russell was a peahen. Like him, she could not have sustained her remarkable stage career and the real-life operetta that was her private life without unrelenting press attention. Although the papers could not be relied on to be continually adoring, they were constant in their amazement at her resiliency. When she opened for the Messrs. Shubert in *Lady Teazle* on Christmas Eve 1904, an astonished reviewer for the *Evening Sun* wrote, "Somehow, she had summoned the freshness and charm of youth to melt the ripeness of maturity."

Another newspaper's critic gushed, "Miss Russell was all that her audience expected. Her reappearance in each act in gowns that hourly grew more resplendent was the signal for applause, genuine hearty applause, applause that came right from the eye, for Miss Russell as a spectacle certainly outshone the remainder of the show weighted against her *en masse,* and that is saying a great deal."

Delighted with the success of the show, Lillian let reporters into her dressing room and told them, "If *Lady Teazle* had proved

The Peacock and the Peahen:
Diamond Jim (*left*) and the
American Beauty (*above*).

a failure, I would never have set foot on the stage again. I would
have taken in washing first."

Not an ink-stained wretch believed a word of it.

EIGHTEEN DAYS after the Shuberts presented their first Broadway show, a crowd gathered in bitter cold at the intersection
of Broadway, Seventh Avenue, and Forty-second Street at three
in the afternoon to witness the dedication of the second tallest
building in New York. Highest was the Park Row building
downtown (thirty-two floors). For the new home of the *New
York Times,* architect Cyrus L. W. Eidlitz had constructed on the
triangle of land formed by the three streets a twenty-five-story,

terra-cotta and cream-colored brick structure in Italian Renaissance style.

In recognition of the new dominant feature of the crossroads, the city's board of aldermen had officially changed the name of the area to Times Square.

The former horse market continued to experience an explosive growth in restaurants and hotels. Arguably the most dramatic was the Astor. Built by William Waldorf Astor in 1904 on the west side of Broadway between Forty-fourth and Forty-fifth, it was breathtaking in size and opulence. When it opened its rooftop restaurant in the spring of 1905, dinner and supper patrons found themselves in a lush garden of geraniums, lilies, mossy grottoes, fountains, and trees in an area equal to seventy city lots. Gazebos dripped with honeysuckle and moonflowers; whole huge vases held rhododendrons, hydrangeas, and eucalyptus. Wire baskets of flowers and ferns dangled from beams supported by white columns. Through all of this flora tiny electric bulbs glowed like a swarm of fireflies.

Similar aeries had become the current rage, drawing the rich, famous, and "cosmopolitan" New Yorkers to them, as authors Michael and Ariane Batterberry wrote in *On the Town in New York,* "like homing pigeons."

Five blocks uptown and two east of the Astor, at Fifth Avenue and Fifty-fifth Street, yet another Astor-owned hotel had opened its doors in the autumn of 1904. In doing so the St. Regis Hotel realized John Jacob Astor's plan to offer a hostelry that would rank as the world's finest. He wanted a "skyscraper" with a small lobby, handsome dining rooms, large private rooms, and great suites, all as lavishly furnished as current fashion would accept. To assure guests the best-run hotel in town he brought in R. M. Haan as manager. A Hungarian who had run successful restaurants in the city, he immediately imported one of the finest chefs in Paris, Edmond Bailly.

"He was an artist," wrote Crockett. "Whenever a dinner was ordered in advance, he demanded an opportunity to study the host or hostess; if so permitted, the result was a perfect composition in the way of a meal."

In the first of the flock of curious, rich New Yorkers rushing to sample his menu was, of course, Diamond Jim Brady. While continuing to sell and manufacture railroad equipment, he was fattening his bank accounts with earnings of stocks in railway-car roofing companies, door manufacturing firms, and the Morgan Steam Laundry Company, a company that did all the laundry work for the Pullman Company, which paid a 48 percent cash dividend every year. Among his stock holdings were large blocks of the Reading Car Wheel Company, the Buffalo Car Wheel Company, and Magnus Steel, which manufactured parts for trucks.

His conduct of his selling business still required travel to towns and cities to see people he had known since his first sales ventures for Manning, Maxwell and Moore. But now little of the old salesmanship was required. He arrived knowing what the client needed, and the matter was settled in minutes. Then it was off to the best restaurant in town and, after dinner, to Jim's hotel suite for a night of card playing.

On one such excursion to Boston he finished his meal, as usual, by asking for a box of chocolates. In New York he was accustomed to being served a five-pound box of Maillard's, an array of Allegretti, or Huyler's chocolate-covered nuts and coconut creams. He also saw to it that a supply of sweets was on hand in his Cortlandt Street offices for munching during the day. And during an evening at the theater he nibbled from a box or two of chocolate peppermints. The candy a waiter brought to his table in Boston was from a local candy maker, Page and Shaw.

Jim liked it so much that he bought twenty one-pound boxes to take back to New York. He devoured half of them on the train and the rest the next day. After swallowing the last tidbit, he announced to Edna McCauley, "This is the best damned candy I ever put in my mouth. From now on, it's the only kind I'm gonna buy."

His demand for the chocolate morsels on Page and Shaw became so great so fast that the company informed him that it was a small firm with limited production capacity and could not keep up with his consumption. Jim asked how much money would be needed to expand the facilities. Page and Shaw proposed $75,000. Jim replied, "Hell, the whole world ought to be eatin' this candy. I'll lend you a hundred and fifty thousand without interest so that you can make your factory twice as big."

In the same manner in which he bought candy, he continued accumulating the symbols of his public persona, paying for both with the proceeds of his salesmanship and a booming stock market. A decade after the Reading Railroad and the National Cordage Company went belly up, the Panic of 1893 and Cleveland Depression seemed like a bad dream. That something like that could happen again was unthinkable. There was a new order. Formation of great and powerful trusts had crushed competition and kept organized labor at bay. Production and marketing costs were being cut, resulting in more, better, and cheaper goods. Europe was clamoring for American products. The gold drain was a nightmare of the past. On Wall Street, the mood and the direction of the values of shares was up.

There were burps of outrage from Teddy Roosevelt in the White House on the subject of trust busting, but the people who had money for speculating in stocks seemed not to care as they watched the value of their investments climb. Impressed (and instructed) by the ease with which he had gleaned over $1 million, and his friend John W. Gates had made several million, in the contest with J. P. Morgan, Jim saw no reason to not join in the fun.

During one of his railroad inspection trips into the South, he traveled on a little one-track line that ran down the middle of Georgia to Savannah. Looking through the window at the pretty countryside, he noticed several blooming peach orchards. When he mentioned to the owner of the railroad, Daniel Egan, that he loved peaches, Egan replied that the Georgia peach crop was growing at such a pace that his tiny line, Central Railroad of Georgia, would probably have to expand rapidly to be able to handle it.

The day Jim returned to New York, he bought $70,000 worth of first-, second-, and third-income bonds of the line. Within five years he was able to sell them for a profit of $500,000.

Having tasted the sweetness of one commodity's stock, he turned his attention to cotton. When Peacock Alley friend James Keene whispered one day, "Go long on July cotton," Jim took the advice the next morning by placing an order with his broker for 100,000 bales. He then held it for two months and sold it (at the Waldorf bar) for a profit of nearly $1 million.

Not every Brady brainstorm and friendly tip had paid off. In association with another of his friends, Edward Hawley, in an attempt to inflate the stock of the Minneapolis & St. Louis Railroad and sell it to railway tycoon E. H. Harriman, they came a cropper. They managed to jack up the stock to $96, but Harriman balked at buying their shares. Jim and Hawley were forced to liquidate at a huge loss.

With a shrug of massive shoulders, Jim said to Edna McCauley, "Hell! Ya can't always win, can you, darlin'?"

No one benefited more from Jim's financial successes than Edna. She was the recipient of more than $1 million worth of presents, most of them jewels. But she was not alone in experiencing his largesse. Besides Lillian Russell, hardly a well-known actress did not at one time or another get a glittering gift. On opening nights, closing nights, birthdays, for Christmas, or on any occasion that struck his whim or fancy, he sent, or presented himself, a dazzling gift to be worn in the hair, upon the breast, around a wrist, or on a finger or two or three.

Rare was the evening in Times Square theaters, lobster palaces, the Astor Roof, and hotel dining rooms that Diamond Jim Brady was not glimpsed with Edna, Lillian, and Jesse Lewisohn as they tripped the light fantastic to syncopated piano music called ragtime.

Developed out of the popular dance known as the cakewalk, the form had been much in evidence at the 1904 World's Fair. Its most famous practitioner was a black pianist and composer named Scott Joplin, performing mostly in and around St. Louis. Credit for introducing ragtime to New York was claimed by Benjamin Robertson Harney. He'd performed it at Tony Pastor's in 1897, published *Rag Time Instructor* the same year, and wrote several ragtime songs. But the biggest hits of the ragtime songs were "Under the Bamboo Tree," "Good Bye My Lady Love," and "Bill Bailey, Won't You Please Come Home?"

Although Diamond Jim's friend Victor Herbert was the nation's most popular composer, on November 7, 1904 (a month before Lillian opened in *Lady Teazle*), Jim and the usual crowd of Broadway first nighters found themselves tapping their feet in the Liberty Theater to a couple of sprightly tunes performed by the writer, producer, and star of *Little Johnny Jones*. Regarded by Broadway historians as creator of the first true musical comedy, George M. Cohan captured the essence of "horse society" with a yarn about an American jockey who had gone to England to ride a horse named "Yankee Doodle" in the British derby. When he lost, he found himself falsely accused of throwing the race. The two songs that set Jim and Edna and the rest of the audience applauding were "Yankee Doodle Dandy" and "Give My Regards to Broadway."

Cohan's show did not fare well with critics. They faulted him for writing slangy dialogue and assailed the "flag waving" and the provision of more musical melodrama than musical comedy. *Little Johnny Jones* lasted only fifty-two performances, but

Cohan brought it back in May of 1905 for four months and again for the month of November.

Starring in the production were Cohan's parents (a hallmark of George M. Cohan shows) and his wife, Ethel Levey, playing Johnny Jones's girlfriend, "Goldie Gates." The choice of the name was in keeping with the theatrical vogue in such plays: a girl with a golden heart redeems the hero.

In a number titled "Life's a Very Funny Proposition After All" that has not endured as a Cohan classic, Johnny takes time to ponder his troubles in a musical soliloquy in which he asks, "Did you ever sit and ponder, sit and think, why we're here and what this life is all about?"

It was a question to which Diamond Jim Brady would have replied then and at any time in his life, "My life is about makin' as much money as I can and usin' it to have as much fun as possible and sharin' what I've got with my friends."

To assist him in the effort he employed a clerk whose sole duty was to keep track of the largesse. On the roster of the Brady Beneficent Society were more than twelve hundred names of people of every stripe and from every walk of life, from railroad "gandy dancers" to officials in the city, state, and federal governments. Over three hundred people on an "active" list received a box of candy in the first week of every month, a basket of fruit in the second, another five-pound box of candy in the third, and flowers and plants in the fourth.

Should a recipient tell Jim he did not have to send gifts to assure a friendship, he replied, "Hell, I make a million a year and I like to spend it on my friends. If it gives me pleasure to send you little presents, I'm gonna go right on doin' it, whether you like it or not."

Some men who regarded Diamond Jim Brady as their friend reciprocated by cutting him in on deals that added considerably more to his wealth than he gave away. No one had been more generous than Bet-a-Million Gates in making Jim part of the Hoffman House cabal that beat J. P. Morgan at his own game. Grateful for having been included in the fun, Jim found a way to return the favor by passing on to Gates a bit of tightly held information concerning the future of the Pennsylvania Railroad.

In the course of conducting his basic business of selling railroad equipment, Jim learned that the Pennsy intended to challenge the New York Central's monopoly on train service in and out of Manhattan. The secret plan of the men who ran the PRR involved buying the Long Island Railroad and extending its service to the island with a tunnel under the East River. The plan also envisioned a Hudson River tunnel, ending the need for the PRR's "New York" trains to dead-end on the New Jersey side of the river. Accommodating both LIRR and Pennsy trains, a West Side terminal would be built near Herald Square. To work toward this goal, directors of the line in 1900 had authorized an increase of $100 million in PRR stock. Their agents then began to quietly buy several parcels of property between Seventh and Eighth avenues and Thirty-first and Thirty-third streets. The land to be acquired for the monumental Pennsylvania Station covered eight acres and held more than five hundred buildings, most of them little more than shacks.

When Diamond Jim passed along this information to Gates, Bet-a-Million's eyes popped with amazement and his smile stretched wide with delight. "Holy cow, Jim," he exclaimed. "I guess I'd better hurry up and buy everything on Seventh Avenue all the way from Twenty-third Street to Fifty-ninth!"

His idea was to clear the existing buildings, widen the avenue, and turn it into "one of those fine boulevards in Paris." He saw Seventh Avenue becoming "the finest street in the whole world, with big shops and all the merchants who aim to cater to a fashionable trade flocking to get on that street." If they couldn't afford to put up their own stores, he said, "we'll build them and sell them, or rent them."

Beaming at Jim, he continued enthusiastically, "There's money in it—big money. Why, in twenty-five years we could clean up from five hundred million to a billion dollars."

It was a prescient dream and grand scheme, but not even Bet-a-Million and friends with whom he discussed the idea could match the Pennsylvania Railroad's fortunes or bring to bear the political influence at the PRR's disposal. The company persuaded New York's legislature to pass and Governor Benjamin Odell to sign a 1902 law giving New York City authority to grant the company a franchise for construction of the tunnels and the terminal. When the first Pennsy trains roared under the Hudson on September 8, 1910, they arrived at a railway terminal without equal in the world, including Grand Central.

Designed by Stanford White, who found inspiration in the baths built by the third-century Roman Emperor Caracalla, the building had an exterior of granite and tavertine, Doric columns (eighty-four of them) each thirty-five feet high, and a Seventh Avenue entrance topped by six stone eagles that weighed 5,700 pounds each. The waiting room consisted of a skylighted concourse with ceilings that soared 150 feet high. From its triangular building at the intersection of Broadway and Forty-second that was already claiming to be "crossroads of the world," the *Times* declared, "This new terminal sets the stamp of excellence on the city.

With his dream of owning Seventh Avenue unrealized, John W. "Bet-a-Million" Gates died one year after the opening of Penn Station.

"So it was a great dream," wrote Albert Stevens Crockett. "That was one striking characteristic of the Golden Peacocks—or many of them. They, as they might have phrased it, 'dreamed big.' Almost equally important, they had the ingenuity, the enterprise, the force, the power of persuasion, the confidence of the born gambler in his own good luck to translate big dreams into tremendous realities."

However loud or uncouth they may have been, however repugnant they might have made themselves to those who considered good manners the first essential, they'd managed to do big things, as Diamond Jim Brady would put it, "in mighty damn big ways."

17

"Oh, My Poor Jim"

❦❦❦

O N JUNE 25, 1906, Diamond Jim Brady donned white tie
and tails and adorned it with his Transportation Set to
take Edna to see a bit of theatrical fluff titled *Mamzelle Champagne* at the city's newest and reportedly fanciest rooftop restaurant. This one was at Madison Square Garden and had been
designed by Stanford White.

Regarded as one of New York City's most visionary citizens, the architect whose firm, McKim, White and Meade, had
been chosen to build Pennsylvania Station had already given
the city the Metropolitan and Brooklyn museums; the Washington Memorial Arch at the foot of Fifth Avenue in Greenwich
Village; the Century, Metropolitan, and University clubs; Low
Memorial Library at Columbia; the *Herald* building; Sherry's;
the Tiffany residence; J. P. Morgan's private library; the townhouse of William Collins Whitney; and splendid homes for
other rich and powerful in New York and Newport. Far more
gregarious than his partners, "Stanny" White had become as
familiar in high society circles as his clients. Yet this fifty-two-
year-old, elegant, and handsome married man was also the subject of lurid stories about sexual trysts with chorus girls.

One of the lovely young chorus girls who had caught
White's eye was Evelyn Nesbit. She was such a beauty at the
age of fourteen that she had modeled for the best illustrators,

including Charles Dana Gibson. In 1900 she made her debut in the Broadway hit *Floradora*. The highlight of the lavish production, set on a fictional island in the Philippines named Floradora (because of its fragrant flowers), was a song titled "Tell Me, Pretty Maiden." It was an unusual number in that it was a hit that was not performed by one of the show's stars but rather rendered by a double sextette of men and women. The gorgeous females were immediately named "Floradora Girls" and were chased by stage-door Johnnies, playboys, and the newly minted millionaires who had flocked to New York to give the first decade of the twentieth century the name "Naughty Aughts."

Not long after sixteen-year-old Evelyn became a Floradora Girl, she found that she was the apple of Stanford White's eye. This meant receiving all the benefits the distinction brought with it, from flowers to diamond forget-me-nots. Soon she was spending many evenings in his mirrored studio, nude and swaying on the red-velvet swing. While being Stanford White's mistress (one of several) had its rewards in expensive and beautiful gifts, fine clothes, a very nice apartment, and lessons in how to appreciate the finer things in life, Evelyn understood that she could never become Mrs. Stanford White.

Consequently, when another wealthy man but half White's age expressed interest in her, she saw no reason why she should not indulge his obvious obsession. She had dinner with him at times when White was out of town, out of the country, or otherwise engaged with the duties of being a husband. Her twenty-year-old swain was Harry Kendall Thaw.

Born in 1872 in Pittsburgh, he was beneficiary of a multimillion-dollar trust fund based on his late father's holdings in Pennsylvania Railroad stocks and coal mines. Although Thaw's father's will had left Harry an allowance of $2,000 a year, Harry's doting mother controlled the trust and let him have $80,000 a year. Finding Pittsburgh limiting, Harry headed to New York in order to indulge in the good life available to a wealthy bachelor. He also wanted to partake of the city's endless supplies of cocaine and young women who would not object to his rough kind of sex.

Although Evelyn heard stories that Harry Thaw had a penchant for mistreating women in a way that was downright sadistic, she believed that she could control him because he was so obsessed with her. She also detected a masochistic side to Harry. Therefore, when he invited her to accompany him on a trip to Europe, she accepted, but only if her mother could go along as chaperone. Unfortunately, Mrs. Nesbit and Harry did not get along, and Mrs. Nesbit soon returned to New York. In the relationship that developed, Evelyn found pleasure in taunting Harry with details of her relationship with Stanford White. Thaw was at the same time aroused by her stories and enraged at White, calling him "that beast."

This strange arrangement culminated in Thaw proposing marriage. Their wedding took place on April 4, 1905, and they settled in Pittsburgh. Although they were far from Stanford White, they could not escape the architect's shadow in the form of Evelyn's increasingly embellished, lurid tales of White forcing her to participate in his debaucheries, including being naked as she rode a red-velvet swing.

Fourteen months after Evelyn became Mrs. Thaw, the couple returned to New York for several days of the kind of fun Harry could not find in Pittsburgh. For Evelyn it was a chance to see her theatrical friends and flaunt the fact that the former Floradora Girl was now the wife of the heir to a fortune.

For Harry the sojourn provided a way to stock up on his supply of cocaine, strut with the peacocks, and show off his beautiful wife.

On the evening of June 25, the Thaws dined with two of Harry's friends and then joined the crowd that gathered to celebrate the opening of the Madison Square Garden "roof" and to hail the brilliant architect who had designed it. When Stanford White arrived at the theater alone, Evelyn did her best to ignore him. Harry glared at him icily.

About halfway through the second act of *Mamzelle Champagne,* Evelyn declared that the play did not interest her and said she wished to leave. Thaw agreed and the party of four made its way toward an exit. But as Evelyn and the others went out, Thaw turned back, calmly walked to White's table, drew a pistol from a pocket, and fired three bullets into White's head.

As the horrified crowd turned to see what had happened, they found Thaw standing over the slumped body. He held the pistol by the muzzle, indicating that he had finished what he'd intended and posed no threat to anyone else.

Someone took away the gun.

The police came and escorted Harry out.

He had killed White, Thaw explained, because White had ruined Evelyn by making her a "love slave," drugging her, seducing her, and making her perform nude on a swing.

As press and public engaged in an orgy of interest in the killing, most of Stanford White's friends ducked for cover. Of all the men who had been proud to be seen strutting their riches at the Waldorf-Astoria, Plaza, St. Regis, and other hotels; the lobster palaces; Broadway opening nights; and the annual horse show at Madison Square Garden; only Diamond Jim Brady attended White's funeral.

The funeral might also have been attended by Jesse Lewisohn, but Lillian Russell's love had been taken out of circulation by a puzzling illness. In the spring of 1906 his already slender frame had become alarmingly thinner. Along with this dramatic loss of weight, his skin looked waxen. His hands trembled constantly. Courses of recommended treatments ranged from electric shocks to a long stay at a costly European spa. But Diamond Jim's physician told Lewisohn that the cause of his malady was a dissipated lifestyle. The copper magnate was advised to give up theatergoing, drinking, gambling, staying up all night, and overindulging in wine.

This prescription came when Lillian Russell was preparing to go on the road with a show called *Barbara's Millions*. Lewisohn had promised to accompany her and declared to Jim that he intended to keep the promise. Jim retorted, "She's old enough to take care of herself. She was looking after herself for thirty years before you came along. I'll tell you what you're goin' to do. You're headin' down to my farm. Since I'm goin' to be travelin' on business for a few weeks, Edna will go down there with you to look after you."

Lewisohn grudgingly agreed, Lillian departed for the hinterlands with her show, and Jim proceeded with calls on customers. From time to time he and Lillian were relieved to hear from Ellesdale Manor that the patient was coming along just fine.

Lillian's new show was not a musical but a straight play with a comic theme. To prepare for it she hired Mrs. Scott Siddons, the best drama coach in the city. The show opened at the New Power's Theater in Grand Rapids, Michigan, to chilly reviews. While critics agreed that Lillian had done a fair job, the play itself was described as an inept and meretricious piece of work.

When it was taken to Chicago three days later, reviews of the play and of Lillian were brutal. They contended that the role she played called for someone "young, vivacious, ingenuous, impetuous and girlish," but despite Russell's numerous charms, "she lacks all five attributes."

Stung by the criticism, Lillian said the Chicago reviewers didn't know what they were talking about and looked forward to a triumph in New York. Again, critics lambasted the play.

The critic for the *Sun* couldn't resist noting that when a character asked whether Lillian's character ever thought of marrying, an audience well aware of Lillian's numerous marriages roared with laughter. A year earlier the same reviewer, Acton

Davies, had written of her, "Songs may come and songs may go, but age cannot wither nor variety stale Miss Russell. She is the same old Lillian, and her voice is the same old voice."

Lillian had winced at the use of the words "age" and "old."

WHILE LILLIAN had been feeling the sting of reviewers in Michigan and Chicago and Jesse was under Edna's care on the farm, Jim took care of business by calling on customers up and down the East Coast. At each stop he found railroad executives expressing alarm concerning an act of Congress expanding the Interstate Commerce Commission from five to seven members. The Hepburn Act also gave them authority to fix "just and reasonable" maximum railroad rates and to prescribe uniform accounting methods. The commission's jurisdiction was also broadened to include express and sleeping car companies and power to restrict granting free passes. This was a potential blow to Jim, who traveled free. The commission also wanted to ban railroads from carrying commodities they produced or that were made by firms in which they held an interest (another threat to Jim's way of doing business). President Theodore Roosevelt signed the law and pronounced it "a fine piece of constructive legislation."

Other disconcerting action in the federal capital, in Diamond Jim Brady's view, was the commencement of conspiracy proceedings on orders from Attorney General William H. Moody against trusts. The targets were Standard Oil; American Tobacco; meatpackers Armor, Cudahy, and Swift; and the Chicago Alton Railway line.

Other events contributed to a sense of unease in James Buchanan Brady's assessment of the national economy at this time. With McKinley's election in 1896, the gold standard had been secured, but three wars (Spanish-American, Boer, and Russo-Japanese) and the devastation of the San Francisco earthquake in April had set off a global demand for capital. Commodity prices had risen sharply. Continued outpourings of new security issues in the United States and abroad was fostering a scarcity of money available for investment, driving up interest rates. As a result, the man who didn't mind gambling a little money, but shied away from higher-stakes games, decided to safeguard his financial position by vastly improving his liquidity.

Still regarding himself as a gentleman sportsman, Jim spent $40,000 for a racehorse by the name of Accountant from another admirer of the breed, Harry Brown. The colt proved to be the sensation of the season whose earnings more than repaid his price.

Between conducting his business and spending time at races in which Accountant was an entry, and an August visit to Saratoga, Jim passed the summer without going to Long Branch to see Edna and to find out how Jesse Lewisohn's recovery was progressing. He did not go to the farm until early September, arriving on a Friday evening with old friend Jules Weiss and intending to stay only for the weekend.

Immediately upon entering the manor house, he sensed something was amiss. Instead of a kiss on the lips, Edna gave him a mere peck on the cheek. The atmosphere at dinner, he thought, seemed strained. When the meal was over and a game of cards begun in the parlor, he turned to Edna and demanded, "All right, what the hell's the matter?"

With a glance at Edna, Jesse Lewisohn blurted, "Edna and I are in love. We're going to be married."

After a long silence in which his face went from the paleness of shock to the bright red of fury, Jim lurched to his feet. Gazing with disbelief at Edna, he pleaded, "How can you do this to me?" As she averted her eyes, he blared at Jesse, "You, Sir, are a cad and a cur. How can you do this to Nell?"

Lewisohn smiled and replied, "Nell will be fine. You said it yourself, Nell can take care of herself. She was taking care of herself long before she met me."

Jules Weiss, the loyal friend who had known Jim Brady longer than anyone outside Jim's family, and who had outfitted Jim Brady as he transformed himself into Diamond Jim Brady and then had turned that character into a legend in his own time, said of what followed, "He flew into the worst rage of his life. He cursed Edna and Jesse furiously, and at length. I guess it helped relieve the hurt and the bitterness."

The tirade over, Weiss and Jim returned immediately to New York.

The next morning Weiss found Jim at his office, working as usual. Hoping that his friend had cooled down, he said, "You know you didn't mean all those things you said to Edna last night. Why don't you go down to the farm and see her? Talk it over when you're calm and quiet. After all, she's been with you for ten years."

The huge head twisted slowly as Jim replied, "What's done is done. I asked her plenty of times to marry me and she always refused. Do you know why? It's because there ain't a woman in the world who'd marry a fat, ugly guy like me."

For the first time in his life Jules Weiss watched Jim Brady cry like a baby.

The painful task of telling Lillian Russell what had happened fell to Jim a few days later when Lillian stepped off a train at Grand Central.

"Oh, my poor Jim," she said consolingly as she hugged him, "to think that Edna would run off with another man after you've been so good to her."

18

"Why Ruin a Beautiful Friendship?"

❧❦❧❦

ASSESSING THE STATE of the nation from the "bully pulpit" of the White House in the closing months of 1906, Theodore Roosevelt said, "We still continue to enjoy a literally unprecedented prosperity." But the president's annual message to Congress warned that "reckless speculation and disregard of legitimate business methods on the part of the business world can materially mar this prosperity."

Inhabitants of that world viewed the remarks as further evidence that Roosevelt had no intention of relenting in his policy of trust busting. To them, if the chief executive was not an outright revolutionist, he was certainly "the most effective planter of the seeds on uninformed socialist propaganda."

Consequently, when the stock market was jolted by a wave of selling in March 1907, with values dropping by $2 billion, E. H. Harriman of the Union Pacific Railroad, whose stock plummeted 25 points in one day, placed the blame on Roosevelt. TR retorted, "I cannot condone wrong, but I certainly do not intend to do aught save what is beneficial to the man of means who acts squarely and fairly."

As finger-pointing went on between Washington and Wall Street throughout the spring, Diamond Jim Brady paid little attention. The free-wheeling, jovial character who had been such a delightful and constant amusement to the denizens of a world centered on Broadway was clearly a man with a wounded heart who needed cheering up. In an attempt to buck up his sagging spirits, his theatrical friends gave parties in his honor and did their best to persuade him that all broken hearts eventually mend. Attesting to this were two veterans of the battle of the sexes who had often lost, Nat Goodwin and De Wolf Hopper. What Jim needed to do, they counseled, was get on with his life. Take a long vacation. Go to Europe. Redecorate his house!

Jim chose to do the latter. Everything in it, from cellar to attic, was taken out and given to friends and customers. The replacements were to be the best of the current vogue that money could buy. Along with this new look for the rooms of the Eighty-sixth Street house would come a freshly outfitted owner. Contents of seven closets were to be ruthlessly winnowed and replaced by a wardrobe in keeping with the fashions of the new century. The only aspect of his life that would not be altered was the one that he had adopted as his emblem and that had served him well since a salesman advised him that nothing a salesman could do to attract attention to himself, and to be remembered, was as effective as sporting diamonds.

The plain truth about James Buchanan Brady was that had he not created "Diamond Jim," his career as salesman would not have been as successful and life not so much fun. Because he'd become his nickname, he was everyone's friend. He went to all the best places, entertained and was entertained by the stars of the stage, hobnobbed with the high rollers of Wall Street at the Waldorf-Astoria and the Union Hotel in Saratoga, caroused with chorus girls, bought what he wanted and gave away what he wished to give away, and all in all did whatever it might be that tickled his fancy, day and night.

He'd been jilted by Edna McCauley. But he could still enjoy the friendship of that other remarkable, self-invented character of the Gilded Age of whom Acton Davies rightly observed that age could not wither nor variety stale.

While Jim was salving his wounds by remaking his house and his wardrobe, Lillian was on the road again, but in magnificent style. For a fifty-two-town tour through the West and South in Joseph Brooks's production of *The Butterfly,* she had enlisted Jim's assistance in arranging her use of a private Pullman car. The eighty-foot *Iolanthe* had a drawing room, three bedrooms, two servants' bedrooms, bath, kitchen, dining room, and a small conservatory. The drawing room had a baby grand piano, writing desk, and several lounge chairs.

After thirty-two weeks on tour, Lillian returned to New York in July in order to spend the month of August in Saratoga. In the plush comforts of the *Iolanthe* she had covered about 27,000 miles while being paid a salary and a percentage of profits of *The Butterfly,* for an average pay of about $2,000 a week.

"From this time on you may count me as one of the most enthusiastic laudators of the one-night stands," she told reporters as she stepped from her Pullman at Grand Central. "Leaving the kegs of money that we made out the question, I really enjoyed my tour hugely."

She then startled New Yorkers by announcing that she intended to dispose of her house. Her income from *The Butterfly* notwithstanding, everyone jumped to the conclusion that she was broke. Concerned that this might be true, Jim rushed to offer her money. She shook her head and replied, "It isn't that I'm poor. I just don't need the place."

Reporters were told, "I shall be traveling a large part of the next three seasons, and in the summer I go either to Europe or to my house on Long Island. If I did keep the Fifty-seventh Street house, I should be obliged to rent it, and I can't fancy myself receiving telegrams while on tour asking me to have the kitchen range mended, or to paint the bathroom. I shall reserve a few of my books, all of my Chinese porcelains, and a few other pieces, but the bulk of my things will go under the auctioneer's hammer."

On October 10, 1907, at the Fifth Avenue Galleries, the fabulous Russell furnishings were put up for bids. Throngs of curious New Yorkers crowded the place. The sale ran three days. New York would not witness anything like the buying frenzy until the week of October 22 to 30, 1917, and an auction of possessions on behalf of the estate of James Buchanan Brady.

FOURTEEN DAYS AFTER Lillian Russell's property went on the block, she had a bank balance of $75,000 with the Knickerbocker Trust Company. The institution had been recommended as the soundest in the city by Lillian's sister, Mrs. Westford. She was president of the Professional Women's League, which had $3,500 on deposit in its vault.

At the corner of Fifth Avenue and Thirty-fourth Street, opposite the Waldorf-Astoria, the bank opened its doors at nine in the morning to a large crowd. Within seconds the marble main room was flooded with depositors demanding withdrawal of all their money. By closing time at three o'clock the crush was just as great. The situation was repeated the next day, forcing suspension of all transactions. The bank was broke. Lillian lost her $75,000. Suddenly a loan from Jim did not seem so far-fetched an idea.

As news of the collapse triggered panic on Wall Street, stock prices tumbled to new lows, and interest on short-term loans rocketed to 125 percent, Jim came through relatively unscathed. His decision in 1906 to drastically cut back on his holdings had rendered him impervious to the stock market crash, and the safe in his house contained plenty of cash, along with a treasure in glittering objects whose value never went down. While Theodore Roosevelt bargained with J. P. Morgan to save the American economy, Jim Brady remained calm in his refurbished house and confident that this panic, like the one of 1893, would pass and the country would get back on track.

This rosy outlook was justified. The financier and the hero of the San Juan Heights struck a deal that nipped the panic through banks buying government bonds on credit and authorizing them to issue currency with the bonds as collateral. The "Morgan interests" prevented a further panic by getting the trust buster to let them save an embattled bank, the Trust Company of America, by taking over its shares of the Tennessee Coal and Iron Company, a move that worked to the benefit of U.S. Steel.

As if nothing had happened to the economy, and fully recovered from being abandoned by Edna McCauley, Diamond Jim Brady thrilled Charles Rector by returning to his old ways. As Jim pushed through the revolving door one evening in November 1907 and descended the grand entrance staircase with Lillian Russell on his arm, the restaurateur's eyes brimmed with tears of joy. It was a month with an "r" in it, and that meant oysters.

Diamond Jim's favorites were giant Lynnhavens from Chesapeake Bay. Rector had them shipped from Maryland in a barrel with "For Mr. Brady" painted on the side. "Even way down in Maryland," Rector recalled, "the seafood dealers knew about Diamond Jim."

The city's most famous lobster palace owner's recollection of the Brady passion for the dish continued:

> I used to like to watch him eat those Lynnhavens. Nearly all of them had extra large oyster crabs in them, and Diamond Jim considered these a delicacy, as they really are. Of course as soon as the oysters were opened and served the crabs took a new interest in life, and started exploring. Jim would be talking to the pretty lady who happened to be with him at the moment and the crabs would slip out of the shells and start crawling about on the table. Then, without even stopping his

conversation, Diamond Jim would strike out with his fork and impale those crabs so fast that the eye couldn't follow his hand. And he'd pop them into his mouth one by one, still talking all the while.

When he'd eaten about four portions of the oysters—some nights it varied a portion or two either way—it would be time for his *Lobster Americain*. I always made this myself for him, in the largest chafing dish we had in the place. Where the recipe called for one lobster, for Diamond Jim I used two—it was always two of everything for him.

After the lobster he'd have a dozen or so hard-shelled crabs, and when he finished with these he was ready to settle down to the regular dinner.

Rector remembered one night when his best twenty-five customers came in alone and invited his host to sit with him while he ate. "I never made a practice of doing this unless a patron particularly asked me to," Rector related, "and as I sat there with him I was amazed to note that more than a dozen people came up to the table to borrow money from him."

Every time someone asked, Jim reached into his wallet and brought out dollars.

"Naturally, I was very much embarrassed, for I didn't like that things like this could go on in my restaurant," Rector continued. "I said to him, 'Mr. Brady, if you'll pardon me for speaking, I think you're letting most of these people take advantage of you.'"

Jim replied, "George, I know they're all pullin' my leg, but did you ever stop to think that it's fun to be a sucker—if you can afford it?"

People did not reach out "to put the arm" on him only in Rector's. They sent letters. One was from a showgirl who claimed she and her touring company had been stranded by a manager who'd absconded with the proceeds of the box office. She asked, "Would you be so kind as to send me the fare for a train ticket back to New York?"

Jim instructed his bank to telegraph an Indiana bank to give her the money, and the rest of the troupe.

Many letters were from cranks and from obvious frauds. These were usually caught by his secretary. But hundreds of others asking for money that were deemed genuine were answered.

Nor did appeals from charitable organizations go unheeded.

Generosity also extended to theater tickets. His custom was to attend every opening of a new show. Occasionally two shows scheduled their debuts on the same date. When that occurred Jim bought front row seats for both, flipped a coin to see which one's opening he would attend, and sent the tickets he couldn't use to a friend. He then bought seats for that show's second night.

Producers of new productions knew that the fat man in the front row was not just another customer. Having attended the theater regularly for three decades, he'd become quite discerning regarding quality in performers and in the shows in which they appeared.

Florenz Ziegfeld said, "If Diamond Jim went to sleep before the first act was over, the managers knew it was a sure bet that the show would be a flop. If he stayed awake for two acts, they knew that the chances were the show would have a fair run. And if he stayed awake for all three acts and was still interested at the fall of the curtain, the managers knew they could go out front and hang up the 'Seats Reserved Six Weeks in Advance' sign. The show was a success."

When Lillian Russell told Jim about her next choice in material, he became as excited as she seemed to be. A comedy written just for her by George Broadhurst and George V. Hobart, *Wildfire* was about horse racing. Her role was that of a widow left with an estate consisting of little more than a racing stable. As she tries to bring home a few winners, she is courted by an automobile fancier (a concession by the writers to the popularity of cars, just as composers of the Gay Nineties had seized on the bicycle craze). The auto enthusiast's competition for the lady's heart is a villainous bookmaker.

Painfully mindful of the snide comments by critics regarding her age and avoirdupois, Lillian prepared for the role by dieting and exercising. As she starved and sweated, she knew that her future career depended on how she was accepted not only by audiences but critics. With her most ardent admirer front row center at the Liberty, *Wildfire* opened on September 7, 1908.

The next day's review by Charles Darnton of the *World* was couched in the lingo of the racetrack:

> Miss Russell last night made the biggest "killing" of her career. She was in her very best form, and with little Willie Archer taking second money as a stable boy, and Frank Sheridan a close third in the role of a trainer, *Wildfire* scored a red-hot hit. Miss Russell excelled her past performances. Her animation and charm seemed as new as her beautiful frocks. She acted so well that you only remembered she hadn't sung when you got home. If she had stepped upon the stage for the first time last night, she would have won in a walk.

The show ran for 566 performances and went on a successful tour.

WHEN THE DECADE known as the Naughty Naughts ended, Lillian Russell was forty-eight and Diamond Jim Brady had turned fifty. In the years since Edna McCauley and Jesse Lewisohn left them in the lurch, they had again become the duet in diamonds whose glamorous lives and antics had fascinated New Yorkers and the entire nation for two decades. They had embodied the Gay Nineties and become living legends. The woman who still laid claim to the title American Beauty might be reported in newspapers as being courted by a number of gallants, but the items noted that the constant man in her life was Diamond Jim Brady. He seemed perfectly content to bask in her light, confident that it would reflect off his jewelry and leave onlookers bedazzled.

No one was prouder of the grown-up corn-fed girl from Iowa than the elephantine jewel-bedecked former Irish kid from the Hudson waterfront when the Hawkeye State's Historical Department announced that she had been named to the Iowa Hall of Fame. In tribute to the native of the town of Clinton, the group declared, "France gave Sarah Bernhardt the Cross of the Legion of Honor, and the State of Iowa has officially decided to hang the portrait of Lillian Russell in the State Historical Society Building as a representative daughter of the Commonwealth."

The decision did not sit well with many people, including the Reverend Hubert D. Knickerbocker of Fort Worth, Texas. He expressed a widespread American opinion of actresses. "They spend their time after the play," he asserted, perhaps picturing Lillian's hand on Diamond Jim's arm as she made a grand entrance, "in low-down resorts, drinking, gambling, singing, carousing and carrying on in an indecent way."

Lillian dismissed the Texas clergyman with a New York name as a fanatic, then pointed out that she was respectable enough for John D. Rockefeller, who had given $500 to the Ossining Hospital with a request that at a hospital benefit Lillian would do him "the personal favor" of singing "Come Down, My Evenin' Star." Although the oil tycoon "had never had the pleasure" of seeing Miss Russell on stage, he had heard her present the song "on my gramophone."

Lillian sang the song and then showed up in Iowa to unveil her portrait.

While some members of the clergy expressed disdain for her, women across the nation in 1910 eagerly took note of the fact that she was outspoken on the issue of women's suffrage. In an interview in the *New York Morning Telegraph* she placed tongue in cheek and asked, "Why not take the real step of suffrage for women and abolish the male vote?"

She continued, "Absolute suffrage for women and the withdrawal of the power and the reins of government from men's hands will give men themselves a fuller opportunity to play the games in which they have been most successful—in business and on the battlefields."

In another interview she was asked what she'd learned on the subject of catching a man. She advised women: Maintain a little mystery; "Don't show too much brain, men think they're superior to women"; have other interests in life; don't run to your husband for help over every little thing; don't be jealous; keep a sense of humor; and, "By all means, don't let on you are trying to find a husband, but keep on the job every minute."

Her views so impressed William Handy, Sunday editor of the *Chicago Tribune,* that he suggested she contribute regularly to its Woman's Page. After initial reluctance, she signed a contract to do a column, "Care of Beauty of Face and Form," for $12,000 a year. She was aided in the writing by journalist Ida McGlone Gibson. Before long, the column was syndicated and appeared in newspapers all over the country.

She and Diamond Jim found pleasure in the idea that being in a Chicago newspaper was a kind of payback to the "ladies" who had her kicked out of the "notables" box at the racetrack during the Columbian Exposition in 1893. But no such snobbery tainted the society women of Philadelphia in 1910. When Lillian took a summer cottage at Ventnor, New Jersey, the ladies made a point of "dropping by" on their way to Atlantic City. Lillian received them graciously.

At this time a new man entered her life. A huge figure (but not as big as Jim Brady) with a long white face and a manner that some observers likened to a larcenous archbishop, Wilson Mizner was the black sheep of a respectable California family.

He had prospected for gold in the Klondike, managed middle-weight champion Stanley Ketchel, run a Broadway hotel where opium was openly used, and been the consort of the ex-wife of streetcar magnate Charles Yerkes. With an acerbic wit, he was regarded as the Voltaire of Broadway. When he stepped into Lillian's life, he was collaborating with playwright Paul Armstrong on a drama, *The Deep Purple*. It would be a hit of the 1911 season and hailed as "the first effective drama about city-bred criminals."

While Lillian was spellbound by Mizner's sharp-tongued banter, Diamond Jim viewed him as "a sharpshooter" who could do no good regarding Lillian's emotional and professional life. Because of this dim view of the new suitor, Jim exhibited an almost fatherly concern and made sure that he accompanied them when they went out on the town. Mizner bridled at being chaperoned. Lillian laughed it off with "Don't be silly. Jim and I are old friends."

The whirl with Mizner quickly ended.

Not long after the charming wit had moved on to other pursuits, Diamond Jim showed up at Lillian's house on Long Island unexpectedly. He was greeted at the door by Lillian's daughter Dorothy, now a twenty-year-old who was as beautiful as her mother had been when she'd sung a song for Tony Pastor and got a new name with lots of "l's" and a career as a musical comedy star.

When Lillian came into the parlor, according to Dorothy's later account of that day, Jim blurted, "Lillian, I want you to marry me. And this is going to be your wedding present."

The gift was $1 million.

Exactly how he presented it, Dorothy did not say. It's unlikely the million was in cash. Even in bundles of ten-thousand-dollar notes it would have been a lot to carry around. It was probably a check. However Jim proffered the fortune is immaterial. Lillian refused it.

She thanked Jim for the compliment but asked, "Why ruin a beautiful friendship?"

He offered to build a theater, "Broadway's biggest and most expensive showplace," to be called "The Lillian Russell."

She said there were too many poor people who could use the money. She said she would feel better if he gave some of the million to them.

"They can name a theater after me," she said, "when I'm dead."

Two years later she announced she was retiring from the stage to marry the Pittsburgh newspaper millionaire Alexander P. Moore.

Jim sighed forlornly as he thought about what might have been and said, "She could have done a lot worse than to take me."

SO MUCH MONEY was flowing into James Buchanan Brady's several bank accounts that some of his night-owl pals suggested he change his nickname to Croesus. The incoming tide provided more money in a day than the pudgy, ambitious bellhop of the St. James Hotel could ever have imagined earning in a lifetime. He had more than enough to buy anything but already owned all the things he'd ever wanted. Money brought him plenty of friends to keep him company through fourteen-course dinners, in hotel barrooms, at the racetrack, and during after-theater suppers. Money could finance lots of fun. But what he did not claim, and could not buy, was someone waiting for him when he went home to Eighty-sixth Street—someone to love him only for himself.

On one of his nightly forays to Broadway in the autumn of 1911 he heard talk that Weber and Fields had reconciled and were planning to return to the stage in a revue called *Hokey Pokey*. According to the rumor, the production would be a sentimental reunion of Weber and Fields with their stars Fay Templeton, Frankie Bailey, Willie Collier, John T. Kelly, and Lillian Russell.

Thrilled that Lillian was coming back to Broadway, her most loyal admirer bought a box in the Broadway Theater and took his seat on February 8, 1912. He wore his Number One Set, reserved for the most special occasions.

Only Lillian came close to matching his glitter as she took the stage wearing $150,000 worth of jewelry and draped in a sequined gown studded with opals and diamond chips. Her huge hat was plumed with pink ostrich feathers. The buckles of her gold shoes were diamond studded. Her role required carrying a shepherd's crook; the ebony stick had a diamond-crusted handle.

As she sang "Come Down, My Evenin' Star," there was not a dry eye in the house, and no cheeks were wetter than those of the fattest man in the house.

19

"Big, Genial Diamond Jim Brady"

❧❦❧

A S DIAMOND JIM BRADY had a late supper at Rector's early in April of 1912, the odds calculated by men who were willing to bet on anything were fifty-fifty that the new White Star Line's Royal Mail Steamer *Titanic*'s maiden voyage to New York would beat the maiden voyage speed of the *Olympic,* set on June 14, 1911. Wagerers who put their money on the *Titanic* were confident she would dock on Tuesday evening, April 16, a day ahead of schedule.

According to White Star publicity, the ship offered first-class passengers a magnificent Grand Staircase for making dramatic entrances, a Café Parisian, a fine à la carte restaurant, gym, Turkish Bath, heated swimming pool, elevators (an oceangoing first), smoking and game rooms, and staterooms rivaling deluxe continental and New York hotels.

Since the launching of the ship on March 31, 1911, with the claim that she would be the world's most luxurious ocean liner (built so well that she was unsinkable), Jim had been thinking of one day booking her best stateroom for a trip to England to see Sampson Fox and then a jump across the channel for a shopping spree in Paris. Just how sumptuous the *Titanic* proved to be he intended to find out from his friend

Charles Hays, president of the Grand Trunk Railroad, whom he knew was booked to sail on the liner on her initial crossing. He'd also heard that John Jacob Astor and his eighteen-year-old second wife, Madeline, would be aboard, along with the colorful Colorado mining millionairess Mrs. J.J. "Molly" Brown, Benjamin Guggenheim, Mr. and Mrs. George Widener and son Harry, Washington Roebling of Brooklyn Bridge–building fame, and President Taft's military aide, Major Archibald Butt.

When Jim went home well after midnight he felt sharp pains in his belly. Dismissing it as a bout of indigestion, he prepared for bed and had difficulty urinating. Experiencing the stomach pain in the morning, he went to see his doctor, expecting to be reminded that he had diabetes and get a lecture about consuming too much sugar. Other doctors with whom he consulted about his occasional cases of upset stomach and heartburn attributed them to his grotesque eating habits finally catching up with him. He'd weathered these attacks and continued living as he always had. But in this instance the pain was worse than ever.

That night it became so bad that he believed he was going to die. At some point in his agony he summoned his valet, gave him the combination to the safe, and ordered him to take out specified papers and burn them. Promissory notes totaling about $200,000 and a few letters that might prove embarrassing to those who'd written them went up in flames.

Surviving the crisis, he went to see his doctor and listened attentively as he was advised to get to Baltimore as fast as possible to be examined by gastrointestinal specialists at Johns Hopkins Hospital. Arrangements were made for an ambulance to convey him to the brand-new Pennsylvania Station where a special train waited to take him to Baltimore.

While he was en route, the hospital hastily prepared for their patient by reinforcing a bed and an operating table to cope with at least three hundred pounds. They also readied a fluoroscope to peek into a stomach that was so famous stories of its capacity had spanned the country. When the assembled doctors got a look at it, they were astonished to find that it was six times bigger than normal. They also discovered the cause of his discomfort. He had a kidney stone of spectacular dimensions, located in such a way that it would be difficult for them to deal with. However, on the staff of the hospital was a specialist who had developed a new technique for just such cases.

His name was Hugh H. Young, but he was about to leave for a medical conference to be held in Europe. Presented with the diagnosis, Dr. Young balked at performing the operation because he always saw his patients through the first stages of recovery. His trip to Europe would make that impossible. But he did agree to see the patient.

Moments later, wearing a neat, well-fitting morning coat with a tie and vest sparkling with diamonds, Jim was brought in. "I have with me," said the doctor accompanying him, "Mr. James Buchanan Brady."

Young's expression conveyed no recognition of the name.

Fingering the giant stickpin in his tie, Jim said, "*Diamond Jim* Brady."

Young's examination revealed what he termed in his account of the case in his memoirs "a formidable series of complications." They included diabetes, Bright's disease, a generalized urinary infection causing difficulty and frequency of urination, inflammation and obstruction of the prostate gland, high blood pressure, and long-existing coronary artery disease that resulted in severe angina pectoris. The cause of the urinary problem, he said, was chronic inflammation of the prostate, which formed an obstruction at the neck of the bladder. He advised surgery.

Jim reported that doctors in New York and Boston had told him that because of diabetes and heart disease, he could not stand an operation. Young agreed, but he informed Jim that he'd recently invented an instrument with which the operation could be done through the urethra and without an external incision. He also would not have to have general anesthesia, which was the greatest danger to a patient with heart disease.

The device he showed to Jim consisted of a tube with a short, curved inner end. On the under surface of the straight segment of the tube was a large hole into which the prostate blockage would drop as the instrument was withdrawn. A cutting tube would then be pushed in to cut through and remove the blocking tissue.

Jim asked, "What do you call that thing?"

"Prostatic incisor," Young answered. "Or punch."

Jim grinned. "Well, let's use the thing right away."

Young explained that he was preparing to leave for London to present a paper to a medical congress, that he planned to leave in four days, and that he did not wish to operate and then leave a recovering patient to the care of others.

"I appreciate that, Doc," said Jim, "but I'm the patient and I'm willin' to trust 'em."

Young agreed to perform the operation. With Jim's urethra anesthetized with a shot of cocaine, it took place on April 7. Jim was off the table in a few minutes, pleased that it went well and without pain. Kidney and gallstones were also treated successfully. But recovery did not go as well as Dr. Young hoped.

In an account of the surgery and its aftereffects in his autobiography, published in 1940, Dr. Young wrote, "Owing to the infection present, his convalescence was stormy. He had a chill and fever, his temperature increased each day, and when I went over to tell him goodbye on the morning of the fourth day, his fever was high and I was not sure but that a severe sepsis would develop, or even blood poisoning."

Young told Jim how much he hated to leave.

"You go ahead to your meetin'," said Jim. "And I hope you enjoy the crossin'."

The doctor went reluctantly, but when he and his wife, three children, a maid, and a nurse for the children arrived at Penn Station, he was astonished to be met by Jim's secretary. They found themselves escorted to the Vanderbilt Hotel and were met there by the manager, who took them to a suite with a drawing room, sitting room, and bedrooms for everyone. The secretary then handed Dr. Young eight front-row tickets for an all-star performance of *Robin Hood* that night at the Lambs club. So the Young children could see lights of "the Great White Way," Jim had also arranged a car and guide for a nighttime tour.

The car met them in the morning to take them to their ship. When they boarded expecting to be shown to the cabins indicated on their tickets, they discovered they had been moved, "with compliments of Mr. Brady," to individual staterooms. Mrs. Young's was crammed with flowers and candy. The doctor found in his a case of champagne, bottles of scotch, rye, and Irish whiskey, red and white wines, various liqueurs, Havana cigars, cartons of cigarettes, books, magazines, and the New York newspapers.

"All this from a man I had known for only a few days," Dr. Young wrote, "and who in Baltimore was so sick that I was not sure he would recover."

As Dr. Young and his family were sailing to Europe on the night of April 14 and Jim was growing impatient with being kept in the hospital, a lookout in the crow's nest of RMS *Titanic,* Frederick Fleet, peered into the blackness of the cold North Atlantic. He frantically yanked on the warning bell three times and yelled, "Iceberg right ahead."

The next morning when a nurse brought Jim a newspaper along with breakfast, he read that the *Titanic* had sunk, taking down most, if not all, of her 2,227 passengers. Later that day extra editions of the city's papers held out a hope that some had managed to get off the ship. A nearby ship was racing to pick up survivors.

When the *Carpathia* docked at a lower Hudson pier on Thursday night, April 18, Mrs. Brown, thereafter to be known as "Unsinkable Molly," and others who had been plucked from the freezing sea told of the final hours as the *Titanic* broke in two and slipped beneath the waves. To the bottom with her went Isadore Straus. He'd declined a seat in lifeboat #8, vowing "I will not go before the others." His wife refused to leave his side. Also lost were the Astors, Benjamin Guggenheim, Mr. Roebling, Major Butt, George and Harry Widener (Mrs. Widener escaped), Charles Hays, and 1,495 other souls.

Safely arrived in Europe, Dr. Young was glad to receive cables announcing the continued improvement of the most generous patient he would ever know.

"All this thought and care and generosity were the work of a man whom the doctors had given twenty-four hours to live," he wrote twenty-eight years after he'd operated on Diamond Jim. "He had thought of these little things for the comfort of someone else while he was on what he considered his death bed."

Jim also gave each nurse in the hospital a two-carat diamond ring, fifty in all.

While recuperating, he found he didn't like hospital food and had meals sent in from the exclusive Hotel Belvedere.

When he returned to New York in August, the occasion received more publicity in the newspapers than the arrival of any other person since Admiral Dewey had returned from the Philippines after defeating the Spanish fleet in Manila Bay in 1898.

The *World* gave its readers this front-page headline:

HIS GOLD LINED STOMACH MAKES
LIFE A JOY AGAIN
Diamond Jim Brady, as he Puts in a Lively and Lovely Day
at the Table, Says His Gastronomic Delight Is Worth
the $220,000 He Paid for Cure.
Out, Pepsin! In, Pullet! Cantaloupe, Bacon, Broiled Bass,
Turtle Soup, and Guinea Hens Among Things He
Eats—Coffee and Cigars, Too!

The accompanying story quoted Jim: "They certainly handed me back a newly lined, high-powered, pliant, and pleasantly dispositioned stomach. Why, if you roasted a full size bull moose and just put me in front of it, I guess I could eat the whole thing, and you'd probably find me gnawing at the hoofs and antlers. And no pepsin powders, either."

One rumor went around that Jim had asked doctors to transplant an elephant's stomach. Another story held that he'd paid a Baltimore widow $200,000 for her dead husband's stomach. A newspaper reported as fact that he'd been given a pig's stomach. Jim listened to these tales with a boyish grin, then explained that it was a kidney stone they'd removed, not his stomach.

The ever-attentive *World* sent another reporter to interview Jim at home who advised the paper's readers:

> His eyes were shining as brightly as his seventy-four horse-power diamond stick pin, or his incandescent cuff buttons, or his glittering waistcoat buttons, or his gem encrusted fingers as he said, "Two hundred and twenty thousand dollars isn't much to give for a new stomach when you need one. I do not feel at liberty to go into details of the treatment through which I have come out of the hospital a fully restored man, though I went in there a wreck."

Upon Dr. Young's return to New York, he found himself the guest of honor at a banquet at the Vanderbilt Hotel. Jim had invited a number of railroad presidents and other prominent businessmen. The toastmaster was the famous actor Raymond Hitchcock. Of the festivities Dr. Young wrote, "It was a rollicking evening. They poked a lot of good-natured fun at Diamond Jim, and he enjoyed it immensely."

Jim plunged back into his daily routines. He told doctors he'd follow their orders, with one exception. He refused to cut back on eating. When a friend of Dr. Young, another doctor, sat next to Jim at a dinner given by Young, he said to Jim, "I have always heard that you are a great 'sport,' but this evening you have refused a cocktail, sherry, Sauterne, champagne and cognac, and took neither cigarettes nor cigars."

"No, I don't drink or smoke," Jim replied, "but there's one thing I am very fond of." He patted his huge belly. "I love food and there's no such thing as too much of it."

Keenly aware that his most famous patient had spent hundreds of thousands of dollars on friends and had showered actresses with jewels, Dr. Young thought about all the money Jim had "squandered" and hoped that he might be persuaded "to build a monument" to himself. What he had in mind was a urological hospital.

Young had been contemplating the project for several years but had been unable to find financial backing. When Jim returned to Baltimore for a checkup, Young raised the subject, pointing out "the great need for an institute devoted to urology that would contain not only wards for public and private patients but laboratories for clinical and research work."

Noting that such a facility would carry James Buchanan Brady's name forever, he contrasted this with "the ephemeral character of the fame and pleasure" Jim got from the plays he'd backed, the actors and actresses he'd supported, and the sportsmen he'd banqueted. Here was an opportunity for him to hand his name down to posterity as Rockefeller's was by the institute in New York that bore his name.

Jim said he'd think it over.

As it happened, a friend and business associate of Jim's, George M. Stephens, president of the Chesapeake & Ohio Railroad, was also in the Johns Hopkins Hospital because of pain in the bladder. Dr. Young found a stone, crushed it, and removed it. As Stephens was recuperating, Young told him about the proposition he'd made to his friend Diamond Jim. He asked Stephens to lend a hand in persuading Jim to fund the institute.

James Buchanan "Diamond Jim" Brady sat for this portrait by George B. Shepherd in 1915 at age fifty-nine.

The next day, after Jim had visited Stephens in his room, Stephens told Young, "I think he is going to do it."

When Young next saw Jim, he announced his decision to give Dr. Young $200,000. He later pledged $15,000 a year for maintenance and altered his last will and testament to bequeath the institute $300,000.

Ground was broken on November 15, 1913, and on January 21, 1915, the first patients were admitted to the James Buchanan Brady Urological Institute. The date for formal dedication was set for May 4, 1915. Diamond Jim went down from New York on a special train filled with friends. That evening in the ballroom of the Hotel Belvedere, which had catered Jim's meals in the hospital, Jim sat between Young and the governor of Maryland. Master of ceremonies was again Raymond Hitchcock. When he called on the guest of honor to speak, Jim said only, "The sky was never so blue and the grass never so green as they are this day for me."

SIX MONTHS BEFORE the groundbreaking for the institute, on March 24, 1913, Diamond Jim showed up in full regalia for the opening of a new theater at Broadway and Forty-seventh. A vaudeville house with 1,736 seats, it was the gemstone of a chain of showplaces run by Keith and Albee and named the Palace. In a very short time it earned the title "Valhalla of Vaudeville." For the next seventeen years its audiences would applaud Elsie Janis, Pat Rooney, Houdini, W. C. Fields, Will Rogers, Jack Benny, Fred Astaire, Sophie Tucker, and even Sarah Bernhardt. But a year after the Palace opened its doors, a portent of the future of show business (and demise of the Palace as a live theater in 1930) could be found a block away.

The first true "motion picture palace" in New York, the Strand Theater, built at a cost of more than $1 million, opened in April 1914 with a film version of a Rex Beach play, *The Spoilers*. Soon stars of the Broadway theater such as De Wolf Hopper, Herbert Beerbohm Tree, Billie Burke, and even Weber and Fields were seen on Great White Way silver screens.

A year after "movies" arrived on Broadway, a pudgy, gregarious young woman from Iowa who had worked in vaudeville theaters as a piano accompanist returned from a long stint in her line of employment in Europe. She discovered a changed city.

"The New York I remembered," said Elsa Maxwell, "was a raucous, provincial town trying too eagerly and self-consciously to assume the air and attitude of a metropolis."

Two performers who embodied this new sophistication were a brother-and-sister dance team, Vernon and Irene Castle. He had been born in England. She had been a socialite. Together they gave the fashionable and faddish pacesetters of Elsa Maxwell's transformed New York a dance, "the Castle Walk." As bicycles had become a craze of the 1890s, lively dancing had taken the city by storm. New styles such as the turkey trot were all the rage.

At Louis Martin's café a suave dancer from Paris named only Maurice had demonstrated the adagio and the tango. An observer noted for posterity, "All New York flocked to see him, waiting breathlessly for the climactic moment when his pretty blonde partner leaped astride his hips and, clinging to his waist with her bent knees, swung outward and away from his whirling body like a floating sash."

It was rumored that during a dance called "the Apache" in Paris, the gracefully athletic Maurice had broken one female partner's neck. Undaunted by this story, and interested in learning the turkey trot and other new dances, Diamond Jim paid Maurice thousands of dollars for lessons. In taking to the dance floor, Jim showed more earnestness than grace. He abandoned the Frenchman and sought lessons from the considerably gentler Castles.

He had seen them in a bit of musical fluff, *The Hen Pecks,* in which a new star, Blossom Seeley, did a number titled "Toddlin' the Todolo." The elegant couple instructed Jim in the way to move when dancing the Castle Walk, the Grizzly Bear, the Lame Duck, the Half-and-Half, and the Innovation. Their reward for their patience was thousands of dollars.

Irene Castle remembered, "Diamond Jim was a gay dancer. He handled himself very well for so big a man and whistled the tune he was dancing to as he propelled his young charmer on the floor. When he danced with me he was very silent and his *joie de vivre* evaporated. I think he was either concentrating on his feet or felt conspicuous."

The dance craze of the twentieth century's mid-teen years was celebrated in a song by a popular new songwriter, Irving Berlin, in the jumpy "Everybody's Doin' It." Diamond Jim kicked up his heels to that ditty and others at the Castles' club Sans Souci and at the Casino de Paree, Maxim's, Bustanoby's, the Moulin Rouge, and Reisenwebers at Columbus Circle where there were four dance floors. He also became a regular tripper-of-the-light-fantastic at Lee Shubert's Palais de Dance atop the New York Theater and on the dance floor of Florenz Ziegfeld's New Amsterdam Theater roof on Forty-second Street.

Always young and pretty partners in these tireless nightly terpsichorean outings would be arranged in teams of half a dozen, with each paid $25 and given all they wanted to eat and drink. When the feet of one gave out, the next took her place in his arms. And each was allowed to wear an article of jewelry from the Brady trove, but just for the night.

Irene Castle found this diamond "lending library" amusing but wondered how Jim got them back. She asked, "Did he just pull up the ermine wrap off their shoulders as they departed from his car at their front door?"

The auto in which he went on these forays was one of two limousines, each with a crew of chauffeur and footman. It was one of them who saw to it, very politely, that the jewelry was returned to its owner.

At this time the former constant companion of Miss Lillian Russell found two beautiful dancers to squire about town. They were the Dolly Sisters, Jennie and Rosie. Because both were married, he invited them and their husbands to join him at the theater and at the table. To show his gratitude for their company, he bought each of the sisters an automobile and presented each with a diamond chain and a six-carat diamond ring.

When the Dollys went to California to make movies at a place called Hollywood, Jim followed them, establishing himself at the Alexandria Hotel. While ensconced there in luxury, he renewed his friendship with Charlie Chaplin. Not long after arriving in Los Angeles, Jim gave a party at the hotel for Chaplin, the Dollys and their husbands, actress Carlotta Monterey, film star Lou Tellegen, comedy-producer Max Sennett, and the silver-screen darlings Blanche Sweet and Mabel Normand. Chaplin was intrigued by the quintet of Brady, Dollys, and husbands. He found their relationship "puzzling." But Chaplin did not know Jim Brady very well. Had he, he would have understood that Diamond Jim Brady was not happy unless he was in the company of such vivacious people. Chaplin also admitted being surprised by the number of diamonds festooning Jim's figure. "That first night I could not believe my eyes," he wrote in his autobiography, "for he wore diamond cufflinks and studs in his shirtfront, each stone larger than a shilling."

A few nights later at Nat Goodwin's café on the Santa Monica pier, Chaplin gawked at the Emerald Set, each piece of which had a stone "the size of a small matchbox."

Chaplin exclaimed, "They're fabulous."

"If you want to see beautiful emeralds, look at these," said Jim as he lifted the bottom of his vest and displayed a belt "the size of the Marquis of Queensberry's champion belt," covered with the largest emeralds Chaplin had ever seen.

In April 1916 the New York Society of Restaurateurs made Jim guest of honor at their annual banquet (one of the rare instances when he did not pick up the tab). Called upon to speak, he offered a sentimental tribute, not to the places where he dined nor to the source of his money but to the part of his city that he loved even more than lobster palaces and Wall Street stock brokerages. He offered this poem:

Ah, boys—it's the same old Broadway
With its gayly glowing lights

That the bards have sung, since New York was young,
With the same old seductive sights.
It's the same White Way your daddies knew,
In their callow, youthful flights,
It's the same old Broadway for me and you,
That keeps us out at night.

It's the same old Broadway where the world parades
The same old circus and clowns.
The same Broadway where jays and jades
Come searching for gold and renown.
It's the same old Broadway where the nations play
On the Street of the Midnight Sun.
So, here's a toast—and let me say,
Old Broadway—there's only one.

At one point in the festivities, as part of the entertainment, the lights were turned down low, but, as reported by the *New York Times,* "still a great illumination came from the rear of the room in the middle of the speaker's table. The light came from Brady's blazing diamonds."

Watching over Dr. Hugh Young's most famous patient at this time was a Young protégé, Dr. Oswald Lowsley, of New York's Bellevue Hospital. He gave Jim a weekly checkup and a sermon on the "eleventh" commandment, "Thou shalt not eat so much."

Jim answered, "You ain't goin' to stop me eatin'. Hell, I've got to have some fun. I ain't got much longer to live."

Neither did he cut back on a work schedule that had become busier than ever after the outbreak of war in Europe in 1914. Allies arrayed against Germany, whose kaiser's jeweler had once insulted Lillian Russell with inferior diamonds, suddenly needed munitions. Although Jim was Irish and sympathized with Ireland's struggle for freedom from England, he had affection for the English people in general and Sampson Fox in particular. And like Lillian Russell, he was not fond of Germans he'd met in Europe and in the course of business.

When the United States government adopted a policy of supplying Britain and France, Jim directed activities of his Standard Steel Car Company toward production of freight cars to carry transport munitions and other war materials to Atlantic coast ports. When the French government placed an order for 38,000 freight cars, the company built a factory in France. The cars were made in Pittsburgh and shipped in sections to be assembled in the French plant by captured German soldiers. That his company and he were profiting from what amounted to slave labor did not bother Jim in the least.

SIX MONTHS AFTER New York's restaurateurs listened to Charles Rector's twenty-five best customers wax poetic about their city, they heard with dismay that Diamond Jim Brady had had a severe attack of gastric ulcers. What they did not know was that Dr. Young and other doctors had consulted and concluded that surgery was not an option because of their patient's diabetes and worsened coronary artery disease. They informed Jim that he had little time left to live and that he should be hospitalized at Johns Hopkins.

Jim declared, "I ain't goin' to die in no hospital. When I meet my maker I'm goin' to be wearin' a bright nightgown."

Not wanting to face a constant parade of well-wishers streaming to Eighty-sixth Street, he decided to go to one of his favorite seaside resorts.

In Atlantic City he settled into a $1,000-a-week apartment in the Shelburne Hotel on the Boardwalk. To look after him he engaged round-the-clock nurses. Local physicians kept watch on him between visits from Dr. Lowsley and periodic calls by Dr. Young and others from Johns Hopkins.

Put on a strict diet, and adhering to limitations on eating for the first time in his life, he sunned himself while sitting in a steamer chair in a glassed-in veranda overlooking the ocean.

Because of cold, driving rain on April 13, 1917, he stayed inside.

That night he went to sleep and did not wake up.

A special train carried his body back to New York.

On April 16 the funeral was held at St. Agnes's Roman Catholic Church on Forty-third Street in the shadow of Grand Central Terminal.

Arriving in a light rain to say farewell to the flamboyant character who'd made millions from trains were tycoons of the rails, industry, and finance; stage stars; newspaper reporters who had long ago recognized good copy in Diamond Jim; workers; cops; restaurateurs; waiters; taxi drivers; gamblers; jockeys; lawyers; and so many other supposedly steel-hearted New Yorkers with tears mixing on their grim faces with the drizzle that police reserves had to be called out for crowd control.

Among the mourners was Lillian Russell. As his coffin was placed in an ornate mausoleum at Greenwood Cemetery in Brooklyn, she sobbed as she said, "Big, genial Diamond Jim Brady. We're all going to miss you."

The bulk of his estate went to various philanthropic enterprises, including the $300,000 promised to Dr. Young for the Brady Institute.

The furnishings of the house he had hoped to leave to his widow, had Edna McCauley or Lillian Russell married him, were put up for auction.

Pieces of jewelry that had not been specifically bequeathed in his will were sold in one lot to a jewelry manufacturer for less than half their appraised value. The purchaser broke up many of the pieces and remounted the stones.

They are being worn today by women and men who have no way of knowing they once adorned the prince of the Gilded Age.

"When he did pass on," wrote Albert Stevens Crockett, "many a chorus girl out of a job or a needy actress who had

Catalog cover and admission ticket for the auction sale of Diamond Jim's house furnishings by lawyers for his estate. For sale were thousands of items in 1,748 groupings ranging from porcelain bric-a-brac and china to complete rooms of furniture.

496—GOLD CHATELAINE WATCH
In form of a swinging guitar, instrument and chains thickly studded with jewels. By Breguet, Paris.

Length, 4¾ inches.

497—FRENCH ENAMEL CHATELAINE WATCH
Setting thickly studded with seed pearls, and includes miniatures of amorini.

Length, 5¼ inches.

498—FRENCH TIMEPIECE
Antique gold watch studded with jewel chips; on the back a painted medallion half-length ideal portrait.

499—ANTIQUE FRENCH GOLD REPEATING WATCH
Open face, with three figures under the glass, which strike the bells. Back engine-turned. By Breguet & Fils.

For sale on the third afternoon of the estate sale were four watches from scores that Diamond Jim bought for himself and as gifts to his friends and customers.

known where to make a 'touch' for a 'five-spot' or even a twenty, lost a 'meal ticket.' Broadway and the night life of New York mourned a luminary whose place neither sun nor moon, nor even stars, could quite usurp. As Jim checked out, the last iridescent rays from the vanishing parade of the peacocks gave way to the night."

Notes and Sources

❦❧

Alas, James Buchanan Brady did not employ the chirography he had learned at Paine's Business College to pen memoirs. Fortunately, Lillian Russell did provide posterity her version of her extraordinarily long runs as queen of Gilded Age theater and Diamond Jim's ever-platonic consort and half of the duet in diamonds whom observers sometimes ridiculed as Beauty and the Beast. She wrote a series of colorful "reminiscences," published serially in *Cosmopolitan* from February to September 1922.

Their biographies were first written by Parker Morell, *Diamond Jim, The Life and Times of James Buchanan Brady* (1934) and *Lillian Russell, The Era of Plush* (1940). Because he wrote when some of Jim's and Lillian's contemporaries were still alive, Morell's books are touchstones for anyone who might set out to re-create the years when Diamond Jim strutted his stuff in lobster palaces, hotels, saloons, and gambling dens and at racetracks as the American Beauty graced the stages of America's theaters from coast to coast. Indispensable in learning about the manners and mores of the Gilded Age is Albert Stevens Crockett's *Peacocks on Parade: A Narrative of a Unique Period in American Social History and Its Most Colorful Figures* (1931).

New York City's fiercely competitive newspapers found rich pickings in the doings of Diamond Jim and Lillian Russell, neither of whom showed reluctance in being exhaustively covered. Another trove of fact and gossip was a cleverly written precursor to current celebrity-oriented magazines. Published by

"Colonel" William D'Alton Mann, *Town Topics* was a chatty periodical promising "the low down" on the leading lights of Broadway and the plush parlors of high society. "Lots of people, in society and out," noted Crockett, "gave evidence of familiarity with its text, so often did they make its disclosures a topic for conversation."

Insights into Diamond Jim, Lillian Russell, and others in their circle of friends were found in the memoirs of their contemporaries, including Irene Castle, Charles Chaplin, Irwin Cobb, Clarence Day, Marie Dressler, De Wolf Hopper, and George Rector. Especially helpful volumes on the era and its two most sparkling personalities are listed in the bibliography. When references to sources would not impede this book's narrative, they have been included in the text. Origins of other sources are cited below.

Introduction   Table for One, Dinner for Twenty-five

Details of Diamond Jim Brady's funeral were provided by the next day's editions of the *New York Times, World,* and *Tribune* and *Literary Digest* of April 28, 1917. George Rector's memories of Diamond Jim's illuminations and eating habits were found in Rector's introduction to a book of his restaurant's recipes.

1. Make Them *Like* You

The early life and rise of James Buchanan Brady are traced by Morell and in articles in *Fortune* magazine ("The Greatest Capital Goods Salesman of Them All," October 1954); *The Big Spenders* by Lucius Beebe (1961); *Horizon* magazine (Summer 1964), and *Esquire* (December 1967). The stories of Commodore Cornelius Vanderbilt's building of a railroad empire and Grand Central Terminal are recounted in numerous histories of America's railroads. Particularly useful was William D. Middleton's *Grand Central: The World's Greatest Railway Terminal* (1977).

2. The American Beauty

Colorful pictures of Harry Hill's concert saloon are in Ed Van Every's *Sins of New York* (1891) and Herbert Asbury's *The Gangs of New York: An Informal History of the Underworld* (1927). Details of the career of Tony Pastor are found in many volumes on the New York entertainment world and Robert V. Snyder's *The Voice of the City: Vaudeville and Popular Culture in New York* (1989). Accounts of Lillian Russell's early years are presented by Morell's biography and by the American Beauty herself in "Lillian Russell's Reminiscences" published serially in *Cosmopolitan* magazine, February to September 1922.

3. Mr. First Nighter

Diamond Jim's romance with the theater is detailed by Morell, in newspaper coverage of his life and death, the *Fortune* article, and show business and New York social histories by Beebe, Cleveland Amory's *The Last Resorts* (1952), Michael and Ariane Batterberry's *On the Town in New York: From 1776 to the Present* (1973), and Allen Churchill's *The Great White Way* (1962). The "dudes" fashion phenomenon and the contest for title "King of the Dudes" is described in numerous histories of the Gilded Age but with particular style in George Waller's *Saratoga: Saga of an Impious Era* (1966). The arrival of Lillie Langtry and Oscar Wilde and the swaths they cut through New York and America were noted breathlessly by the press at the time and are recounted in detail in several Wilde biographies as well as in Morell's biography of Diamond Jim.

4. "Nell, I'm Rich!"

Expansion of railroads westward is detailed in numerous histories of railways and of the West, along with accounts of how the railroads unilaterally imposed a standardized time system on the United States. Lillian Russell's marriage problems are found in Morell, the contemporary press, pages in Marie

Dressler's memoir devoted to her friendship with Lillian, and various editions of *Town Topics*. Jim's association with Sampson Fox is found in Morell and in the *Fortune* retrospective on his life.

5. Ain't It Grand?

New York City at the start of the 1890s is described in several histories, including *Exit Laughing* (1942) by Irvin Cobb; Allen Churchill's *The Great White Way*; Lucius Beebe's *The Big Spenders* (1961); the Batterberrys' volume; Walter Lord's *The Good Years* (1960); Edward Marks's *They All Had Glamour,* (1944); Morell's volumes; Joseph Wechsburg's *Red Plush and Black Velvet* (1961); and Larzer Ziff's *The American 1890s* (1966). The Panic of 1893 is told in many histories, including this author's *An Honest President: The Life and Presidencies of Grover Cleveland* (2000).

6. The Earth for Fifty Cents

Diamond Jim's foray to the Columbian Exposition to see Lillian Russell may be found in Morell and the contemporary press. Lillian's "romance" with strongman Sandoz was gossiped about in *Town Topics* and dismissed by her in the press at the time and in her later *Cosmopolitan* "Reminiscences." Detailed portraits of the 1893 World's Fair are contained in a number of books. Fascinating tidbits about the exposition may also be found on several Internet sites.

7. Sidewalks of New York

Diamond Jim Brady's historic automobile trip down Fifth Avenue and around Madison Square received wide coverage in the press and was retrospectively related in Lloyd Morris's 1951 *Incredible New York* as well as Parker Morell's Brady biography. The blossoming of new hotels and the creation of the Waldorf-Astoria are related by Crockett and the Batterberrys. Lillian's continuing romantic travails are found in Morell and her reminiscences. The story of corruption in the New York Police Department, led by Chief of Police Thomas Byrnes and Inspector Alexander "Clubber" Williams, and Theodore Roosevelt's campaign to clean up the department are described in this author's *Commissioner Roosevelt: The Story of Theodore Roosevelt and the New York City Police, 1895–1897* (1994); in TR's autobiography, and in the memoirs of Roosevelt's two journalistic allies, Jacob Riis and Lincoln Steffens. Roosevelt's calling upon Diamond Jim to control John L. Sullivan are found in Morell's biography.

8. Big Wheeler-Dealer

The bicycle craze was well documented by the press. Diamond Jim and Lillian Russell's traffic-halting sojourns were also reported in detail and recounted in Morell's Brady book. The Pullman strike, Coxey's Army, and other upheavals as a result of the 1894 depression are noted in numerous histories. Jim's activities during this time are found in Morell and the *Fortune* article.

9. I Can Always Start Over

My principal source concerning the role of J. P. Morgan in the fortunes of the New Haven Railroad and Diamond Jim's relationship with Charles Mellen was John L. Weller's 1969 book, *The New Haven Railroad: Its Rise and Fall*. The 1894 to 1896 political climate has been recorded in numerous histories of the Cleveland presidency. Diamond Jim's support of the Republican candidate, William McKinley, and his desire to keep it a secret from his friends in Tammany Hall, are told in Morell's biography. Workings of his gift-giving system (later called the Brady Beneficent Society) may be found in Morell and Amory.

10. Rogues, Rascals, and Railroaders

Oscar Hammerstein's troubles with the Olympic Theater were given extensive coverage in the press and described in several histories of Broadway. Portraits of many of Diamond Jim's associates were provided by Morell and in Crockett's *Peacocks on Parade*. Stanford White's rise to architectural prominence has been told in several books, including Gerald Langford's *The Murder of Stanford White* (1962). Diamond Jim's parties are detailed in Morell and in Beebe's *The Big Spenders*. The infamous Seeley party at the Gilsey Hotel is recounted in several histories of New York in the Gay Nineties. The introduction of all-steel railway cars and Diamond Jim's role in selling them to reluctant railroads are related in Morell and *Fortune*.

11. The Girl's a Lady

The chief source for Diamond Jim's relationship with Edna McCauley is Parker Morell. The portrait of Bet-a-Million Gates is found primarily in Morell and in Crockett's *Peacocks on Parade*. The Lillian Russell odyssey in Germany and her relationship with Jesse Lewisohn are recounted in her "Reminiscences" and in her biography by Morell. The main source for Diamond Jim's trip to Europe with Edna McCauley is Morell. The Paris party given in his honor by Count Boni de Castellane was described by Richard O'Connor in *Gould's Millions* (1962) and in Morell. Jim's challenge by a customs inspector upon his return to New York was reported in newspapers and summarized by Morell.

12. "This Is Where I Live"

My depiction of New York City and Diamond Jim's house on Eighty-sixth Street was drawn from numerous contemporary sources and histories. For the story of Weber and Fields I consulted several histories of vaudeville, but especially Robert W. Snyder's compact but fact-filled *The Voice of the City.* An important reference for the music of the era was Charles Hamm's *Yesterdays: Popular Song in America* (1983). Descriptions of Diamond Jim's jewelry collection may be found in the appendix of Morell's biography, in Beebe's *The Big Spenders,* and in the *Fortune* article, which noted that in his lifetime he accumulated about 20,000 with an estimated value of $2 million. However, when Parker Morell examined the appraisal of the collection by a jeweler after Jim's death, Morell was shocked to find the gems valued at only $500,000. An explanation for this gross undervaluation was offered to Morell by another gem expert, John R. Keim, who was familiar with the Brady collection. Keim pointed out that selling the diamonds meant there had to be two profits added to the appraisal value, the wholesaler's and the retailer's. "Naturally," said Kleim, "the appraisal could not be too high."

13. "Have You Got the Sauce?"

How Diamond Jim Brady was able to feast on sole with *sauce Marguery* was revealed by Charles Rector in a memoir, *The Girl from Rector's* (1927). This is the recipe for the dish contained in *The Rector Cookbook,* published by Rector in 1928:

FILLET OF SOLE, MARGUERY
Have 8 fillets removed from 2 flounders. Place bones, skin and heads in a stewpan. Add 1 pound of cut up fish (flounder, red snapper or cod), 1/2 cup sliced carrots, 1/2 leek, 2 sprigs of parsley, 10 peppercorns, 1/2 bay leaf and 1 quart of cold water. Bring to boiling point and simmer till fish stock is reduced to 1 pint. Strain, pour fish stock over fillets which have been seasoned with salt and few grains of cayenne and arranged in a

buttered baking pan. Cover fillets with buttered paper and place in a moderate oven to poach for 15 or 20 minutes. Carefully lift fillets out of pan and arrange them on a hot platter (do not overlap or put one fillet on top of another). Strain fish stock into a small saucepan and reduce it by boiling to 1 cup, remove from fire and add 4 tablespoons of dry white wine. Thicken sauce with 3 egg yolks which have been slightly beaten, and add bit by bit, 1/4 pound of fresh butter, stirring constantly until the sauce is perfectly smooth. Then add 1 teaspoon finely chopped parsley. Pour sauce over fillets which have been garnished with 1 dozen small steamed oysters and 1 dozen small boiled shrimps. Place platter under moderate flame until lightly browned.

Descriptions of Death Valley Scotty, "Pearl Jim" Murray, champagne salesmen George Kessler and Mannie Chapelle, and Charles Gates (son of a Bet-a-Million Gates) were found in Crockett's *Peacocks on Parade*. A concise account of the introduction of the "cafeteria" by the Childs brothers and Horn and Hardart is told by the Batterberrys. The building of the Plaza is told by Crockett and described in Kate Simon's *Fifth Avenue: A Very Social History* (1978).

Bet-a-Million Gates's coup at the expense of J. P. Morgan was recorded by Crockett and discussed in the *Fortune* article.

14. Farmer Jim

My primary resource regarding Diamond Jim's farm in New Jersey was Parker Morell. The stories of Café Martin, Bustanoby's restaurant, and other lobster palaces was in contemporary press accounts of New York's world of dining, augmented by Irwin Cobb's observation of Diamond Jim eating at Martin's. Details of Lillian Russell's get-away at Far Rockaway were found primarily in Morell. Florenz Ziegfeld's discovery of Anna Held in Paris and Held's taking New York by storm will be found in numerous Broadway histories and Ziegfeld biographies. New York's fabulous gaming houses are described by Crockett.

15. Off to the Races

The splendors of the Saratoga season are detailed by George Waller, in Hugh Bradley's *Such Was Saratoga* (1940), and by Morell, along with the story of Diamond Jim's experiences as the owner of a racing stable. "King of the Gamblers" Richard Canfield's successes and troubles with the law were widely reported by the newspapers and recounted by Waller, Bradley, Morell, and Crockett, along with Jesse Lewisohn's futile battle to avoid testifying against Canfield.

16. Peacocks Parade

The events of 1905 in New York, the nation, and the lives of Diamond Jim and Lillian Russell were available in the press, the Morell biographies, Crockett, and several histories of Times Square. Diamond Jim's "killing" in the stock of the Central Railroad of Georgia is found in Morell. Bet-a-Million Gates's plan to "buy Seventh Avenue" is in Crockett. An outstanding history of Penn Station is *The Late, Great Pennsylvania Station* by Lorraine B. Diehl (1985).

17. "Oh, My Poor Jim"

The fatal shooting of Stanford White by Harry Thaw at the grand opening the Madison Square Garden rooftop restaurant was given sensational coverage by newspapers nationwide and became the subject of several books. The one on which I relied is Gerald Langford's *The Murder of Stanford White*. Edna McCauley and Jesse Lewisohn jilting Diamond Jim and Lillian Russell is found in Morell's biographies.

18. "Why Ruin a Beautiful Friendship?"

Details of the lives of Diamond Jim and Lillian Russell before and after the Panic of 1907 are related in Morell and in Lillian's "Reminiscences" in *Cosmopolitan*. Portraits of Diamond Jim at dinner and attending the theater came from the memoirs of Charles Rector and Florenz Ziegfeld. Lillian's views on the vote for women and female equality with the male were widely publicized, as was her retort to the Texas clergyman's criticism of actresses. Her fling with Wilson Mizner is noted in Morell and in *The Legendary Mizners* by Alva Johnston (1952). Jim's wedding proposal was reported by Lillian's daughter and memorialized by Morell.

19. "Big, Genial Diamond Jim Brady"

Diamond Jim's illness, surgery, temporary recovery, and relapse were described in detail by Dr. Hugh Young in his autobiography, along with Jim's financing of Young's trip to England and gifts of money to establish Young's urological institute. The dance craze that set Diamond Jim whirling was recounted in Irene Castle's memoir, *Castles in the Air* (1958), and by Crockett. His final months were described by Parker Morell. The funeral and burial received enormous coverage in newspapers. Following Jim's death and United States entry into World War I, Lillian Russell enlisted in the war effort by appearing at a Liberty Bond Rally in New York on October 19, 1917. In 1922 she campaigned on behalf of Warren G. Harding and was rewarded with an appointment as a "special" immigration commissioner. After mentioning during a visit to New York City that she felt an "indisposition," she returned to her home in Pittsburgh and on June 6, 1922, died from "a complication of diseases." She was buried in the Allegheny Cemetery in Pittsburgh with full military honors ordered by President Harding. For four decades she had dominated "the stage." At the height of her career she'd both reflected and set styles. She had embodied for the nation elegance and beauty and, with Diamond Jim Brady at her side, had symbolized the gilded Eighties, Gay Nineties, and Naughty Naughts. Memorial services were held in American cities and towns whose residents probably had never seen her in the flesh, but they knew that with her passing the other half of a uniquely American phenomenon had gone.

Bibliography

❧❧❧

Amory, Cleveland. *The Last Resorts.* New York: Harper & Bros., 1952.

Asbury, Herbert. *The Gangs of New York: An Informal History of the Underworld.* Garden City, N.Y.: Garden City Publishing Co., 1927.

Barnes, Djuna. *Interviews.* Washington, D.C.: Sun & Moon Press, 1985.

Batterberry, Michael and Ariane. *On the Town in New York: From 1776 to the Present.* New York: Charles Scribner's Sons, 1973.

Beebe, Lucius. *The Big Spenders.* New York: Doubleday, 1961.

Birmingham, Stephen. *Life at the Dakota: New York's Most Unusual Address.* New York: Random House, 1979.

Boardman, Gerald. *American Musical Theater: A Chronicle.* New York: Oxford University Press, 1978.

Bradley, Hugh. *Such Was Saratoga.* New York: Doubleday, Doran & Co., 1940.

Burke, John. *Duet in Diamonds: The Flamboyant Saga of Lillian Russell and Diamond Jim Brady in America's Gilded Age.* New York: G. P. Putnam's Sons, 1972.

Castle, Irene. *Castles in the Air.* Garden City, N.Y.: Doubleday, 1958.

Chaplin, Charles. *My Autobiography.* New York: Simon and Schuster, 1964.

Churchill, Allen. *The Great White Way.* New York: Dutton, 1962.

Cobb, Irvin. *Exit Laughing.* Garden City, N.Y.: Garden City Books, 1942.

335

Crockett, Albert Stevens. *Peacocks on Parade: A Narrative of a Unique Period in American Social History and Its Most Colorful Figures.* New York: Sears Publishing, 1931.

Diehl, Lorraine B. *The Late, Great Pennsylvania Station.* Lexington, Mass.: The Stephen Green Press, 1985.

Dressler, Marie, with Harrington, Mildred. *My Own Story.* Boston: Little, Brown & Co., 1934.

Ellis, Edward Robb. *The Epic of New York: A Narrative History.* New York: Old Town Books, 1966.

Goodwin, Nat C. *Nat Goodwin's Book.* Boston: Richard C. Badger, 1914.

Hamm, Charles. *Yesterdays: Popular Song in America.* New York: W. W. Norton, 1983.

Holbrook, Stewart. *The Story of American Railroads.* New York: Crown Publishers, 1947.

———. *Dreamers of the American Dream.* New York: Doubleday, 1957.

Hopper, De Wolf. *Reminiscences.* Garden City, N.Y.: Garden City Books, 1927.

Jeffers, H. Paul. *Commissioner Roosevelt: The Story of Theodore Roosevelt and the New York City Police, 1895–1897.* New York: John Wiley & Sons, 1994.

———. *An Honest President: The Life and Presidencies of Grover Cleveland.* New York: John Wiley & Sons, 2000.

Jones, Howard Mumford. *The Age of Energy: Varieties of the American Experience, 1865-1915.* New York: The Viking Press, 1976.

Klein, Alexander, ed. *The Empire City.* New York: Rinehart & Company, 1955.

Langford, Gerald. *The Murder of Stanford White.* New York: Bobbs-Merrill, 1962.

Lord, Walter. *The Good Years.* New York: Harper & Row, 1960.

Marks, Edward. *They All Had Glamour.* New York: Globe Publishing, 1944.

Middleton, William D. *Grand Central: The World's Greatest Railway Terminal*. San Marino, Calif.: Gold West Books, 1977.

Morehouse, Ward. *Matinee Tomorrow*. New York: Whittlesey House, 1949.

Morrell, Parker. *Diamond Jim: The Life and Times of James Buchanan Brady*. Garden City, N.Y.: Garden City Publishing Company, 1934.

――――. *Lillian Russell: The Era of Plush*. New York: Random House, 1940.

Morris, Lloyd. *Incredible New York*. New York: Random House, 1951.

Rector, George. *The Girl from Rector's*. Garden City, N.Y.: Doubleday, Page, 1927

――――. *The Rector Cookbook*. Chicago: Rector Publishing Co., 1928.

Simon, Kate. *Fifth Avenue: A Very Social History*. New York: Harcourt Brace Jovanovich, 1978.

Smith, Harry B. *First Nights and First Editions*. Boston: Little, Brown & Co., 1931.

Snyder, Robert W. *The Voice of the City: Vaudeville and Popular Culture in New York*. New York: Oxford University Press, 1989.

Stone, Jill. *Times Square: A Pictorial History*. New York: Collier Books, 1982.

Valentine, Alan. *1913: America Between Two World Wars*. New York: Macmillan, 1962.

Van Every, Ed. *Sins of New York*. New York: 1891.

Waller, George. *Saratoga: Saga of an Impious Era*. Englewood Cliffs, N.J.: Prentice-Hall, 1966.

Warshow, Robert L. *Bet-a-Million Gates*. Garden City, N.Y.: Garden City Publishing Co., 1932.

Wechsburg, Joseph. *Red Plush and Black Velvet*. Boston: Little, Brown & Co., 1961.

Weller, John L. *The New Haven Railroad: Its Rise and Fall*. New York: Hastings House, 1969.

Young, Hugh. *A Surgeon's Autobiography*. New York: Harcourt, Brace and Company, 1940.

Ziff, Larzer. *The American 1890s*. New York: The Viking Press, 1966.

Index